# WHERE TO WATCH
# BIRDS IN
# SCANDINAVIA

## Dedication

To the spirit of international conservation work for birds and their habitats.

HAMLYN BIRDWATCHING GUIDES

# WHERE TO WATCH BIRDS IN SCANDINAVIA

## GUSTAF AULÉN

CONTRIBUTORS
DENMARK: KLAUS MALLING OLSEN

FINLAND: TAPANI VEISTOLA, MAURI LEIVO

ICELAND: ÆVAR PETERSEN, ÁRNI WAAG HJALMARSSON,
JOHANN ÓLI HILMARSSON, ÓLAFUR EINARSSON
ÓLAFUR KARL NIELSEN

NORWAY: INGAR JOSTEIN ØIEN, ASBJØRN FOLVIK

## ILLUSTRATIONS BY JOHAN M STENLUND

HAMLYN

# CONTENTS

First published in 1996 by Hamlyn,
an imprint of Reed Consumer Books Ltd
Michelin House, 81 Fulham Road,
London SW3 6RB and Auckland, Melbourne,
Singapore and Toronto

Copyright © Reed International Books Limited
1996

Text copyright © Sweden and general text: Gustaf
Aulén 1996; Denmark: Klaus Malling Olsen 1996;
Finland: Tapani Veistola 1996; Iceland: Ævar
Petersen, Árni Waag Hjalmarsson, Jóhann Óli
Hilmarsson, Ólafur Einarsson, Ólafur Karl
Nielsen 1996; Norway: Ingar Jostein Øien,
Asbjørn Folvik 1996.
Artwork copyright © Johann M Stenlund 1996
Maps copyright © Reed International Books
Limited 1996

ISBN 0 600 58459 3

A CIP catalogue record for this book is available
from the British Library

Edited and designed by D & N Publishing,
Ramsbury, Wiltshire
Maps drawn by Hardlines, Charlbury, Oxon

Printed in the UK

# INTRODUCTION

Dear reader, enjoy your birdwatching trip to Scandinavia! In this book the expression 'Scandinavia' is used as a collective name for the five Nordic countries: Denmark, Finland, Iceland, Norway and Sweden. There are several similarities between these countries but also so many differences in their wildlife and culture that it is well worth visiting them all.

The 200 sites for birdwatching shown in this book, are chosen in order to give you a broad spectrum of different habitats and their most interesting bird species. Many of the sites are listed in the book *Important Bird Areas in Europe* published 1989 by the International Council for Bird Preservation – BirdLife International. We have tried to point out areas with birds that could be of special interest to a foreign visitor. But as the Scandinavian landscape as a whole is pristine by comparison with continental Europe, birdwatching here can be carried out almost anywhere. The choice of sites is primarily made in order to offer you places that are not too difficult to find and where the birds can be studied without disturbance. At some sites you can watch from the car, but at other sites you must explore on foot, so read the text carefully.

The habitats you will find are very varied. Iceland has treeless tundra, expanses of coastal wetlands and rocky islands, while Norway offers a vast Atlantic coastline with numerous sheer-sided, deep fjords. This country, along with Sweden, has huge mountain regions (*fjelds*), the latter, together with Finland, having vast taiga forests and a mosaic of lakes and wetlands, fringed by the Baltic Sea with its archipelagos. Both Sweden and Denmark offer agricultural land with deciduous forests and stretches of sandy coastline.

Which birds do I want to see? This is a question I often ask myself when I travel abroad. Of course I want to see birds that I have not seen before but, equally, I want to see birds typical of the country and habitat that I visit. Fortunately, the two objectives are not necessarily mutually exclusive. Find an area with good wildlife and it will invariably be good for birds.

What type of birdwatcher are you? A twitcher, a Sunday birder, a scientist, a conservationist, a person who feeds birds in the garden, or a wildlife enthusiast? Most likely you will be a mixture of some or all of these categories. If you get in touch with Scandinavian birdwatchers you will find a broad spectrum of ornithological interest too. In general, Scandinavians are used to being outdoors and care about the birdlife. Our ornithological societies deal with all levels of bird interest, always with deference to conservation. It is, therefore, a pleasure that this book has been produced in cooperation with BirdLife International. Because of their mobility, birds are excellent and appropriate symbols for the global approach necessary for worldwide conservation. But birdwatching is also one of the most exciting hobbies you can ever pursue. I wish you lots of fun and wonderful encounters with Scandinavian birds and wildlife in general.

## CODE OF CONDUCT FOR BIRDWATCHERS

Well-behaved birdwatchers do not cause disturbance to birds and show that they respect private property; they are important lobbyists for bird interests and nature conservation as a whole.

Gustaf Aulén, Uppsala, January 1996

# HOW TO USE THIS GUIDE

Each country is introduced with a map which shows the location of all the sites described. Around a quarter of the sites also have a more detailed map to help with orientation.

It would have been desirable to have detailed maps for every given place but it has not been possible due to the limited number of pages available; this would have meant a decrease in the number of sites included. Remember that, although accurate, all maps here are sketches. In order to get as much as possible out of your trip you are strongly recommended to purchase more detailed topographic maps for each country.

For every country there is an introductory section which includes some basic information about the country, its importance for birds, getting there, conservation, habitats and seasons.

For each site, general information is given as an introduction followed by a 'Timing' section detailing seasonal birdwatching. A section called 'Species' informs you of what you are likely to see, sub-divided according to whether birds are *Resident*, present only in the *Breeding season* or in *Winter*, or encountered on *Passage*. The function of the 'Access' section is self explanatory.

As the size of each site can vary from a small lake of some hectares, up to several square kilometres of wilderness in some of the National Parks, it is wise to read the site introduction before a visit. It could be a painful surprise if you plan a one-hour visit to an area where a week would be more advantageous. In the contents you will find a list of birdwatching sites within each country and a page reference.

## ACKNOWLEDGEMENTS

This guide would have been impossible to produce without text contributions from all my colleagues mentioned as co-authors on page 3. They are all experts in their respective countries. Also special thanks to Stein Byrkjeland for providing a first draft to several Norwegian sites.

Many people have also contributed with data and comments on certain sites. Thanks go to: Roger Ahlman, Åke Andersson, Mikael Averland, Mats Axbrink, Per-Göran Bentz, Göran Bergengren, Thomas Birkö, Donald Blomquist, Ola Bondesson, Mads Jensen Bunch, Hå-Ge Carlsson, Leif Carlsson, Lennart Carlsson, Göran Cederwall, Rolf Christensen, Hans Cronert, Börje Dahlén, Björn Ehrenroth, Seppo Ekelund, Mats Eriksson, Ulla Falkdalen, Peder Fält, Börje Flygar, Mats Forslund, Richard Fredriksson, Stellan Hedgren, Claes Hermansson, Per Hjalmarsson, Stig Holmstedt, Svante Joelsson, Staffan Karlsson, Stefan Lagerblad, Thomas Landgren, Tor Lundberg, Hans Odenholm, Lars Olausson, Christer Olsson, Åke Pettersson, Jan Pettersson, Lennart Risberg, Kalle Löfberg Rolflöfgren, Mats Rosenberg, Jörgen Sjöström, Øystein R. Størkersen, Martin Tjernberg, Jussi Tranesjö, Magnus Ullman, Henrik Waldenström, Bengt Warensjö, Anders Wirdheim.

Tommy Tyrberg and Magnus Ullman have been very helpful with the proof-checking work. Finally I am very happy that Johan Stenlund contributed his excellent artistic ability by producing all the wonderful illustrations of Scandinavian birds.

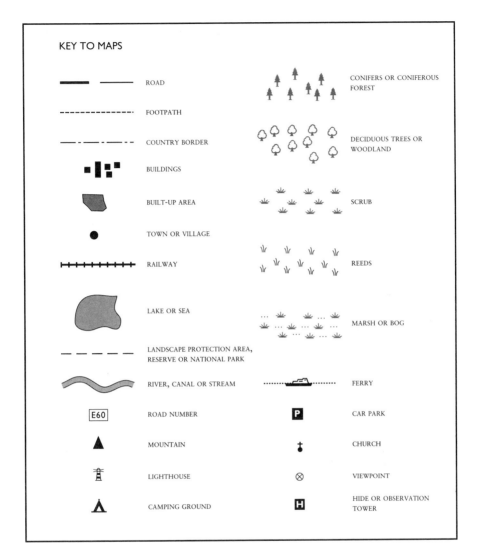

KEY TO MAPS

| | | | |
|---|---|---|---|
| ROAD | | CONIFERS OR CONIFEROUS FOREST | |
| FOOTPATH | | DECIDUOUS TREES OR WOODLAND | |
| COUNTRY BORDER | | SCRUB | |
| BUILDINGS | | REEDS | |
| BUILT-UP AREA | | MARSH OR BOG | |
| TOWN OR VILLAGE | | FERRY | |
| RAILWAY | | CAR PARK | |
| LAKE OR SEA | | CHURCH | |
| LANDSCAPE PROTECTION AREA, RESERVE OR NATIONAL PARK | | VIEWPOINT | |
| RIVER, CANAL OR STREAM | | HIDE OR OBSERVATION TOWER | |
| E60 ROAD NUMBER | | | |
| MOUNTAIN | | | |
| LIGHTHOUSE | | | |
| CAMPING GROUND | | | |

# A NOTE ON PRONUNCIATION AND SPECIAL CHARACTERS

All Scandinavian languages use special characters for three extra vowels in addition to the standard Latin alphabet: å, ä and ö. These approximate the vowels in English in *call*, *pair* and *sir*, and are pronounced more-or-less the same in all the languages but are written differently: Å, å, Ä, ä, Ö, ö in Swedish and Finnish; Å, å, Æ, æ, Ø, ø in Danish and Norwegian; Á, á, Æ, æ, Ö, ö in Icelandic. Å is not used in Finnish but occurs in place names in the Swedish-speaking parts of Finland. Icelandic has several further characters: Ð/ð and Þ/þ are used for voiced and unvoiced *th* sounds similar to those in the English *this* and *the* respectively, and accents are used to indicate long vowels (é, í, ó, ú, ý).

# BIRDLIFE INTERNATIONAL

BirdLife International is a worldwide partnership of organizations working for the diversity of all life through the conservation of birds and their habitats.

The partners in BirdLife International are like-minded national conservation organizations, which represent BirdLife in a country or specific territory. Where there is no partner, an organization or individual may become a BirdLife representative. BirdLife is represented in over 100 countries worldwide.

Birds are the entry point for BirdLife, providing it with a focus for all elements of its strategy. However, the organization recognizes broader environmental objectives. It adopts the rationale of shared responsibility for the global environment and the sustainability of the use of the world's natural resources.

BirdLife International pursues a programme of:

SCIENTIFIC RESEARCH AND ANALYSIS to identify the most threatened bird species and the most critical sites for the conservation of avian diversity, for setting global priorities for bird conservation.

FIELD ACTION to address these priorities, ranging from community-based integrated land-use and management projects to species' recovery programmes, all benefiting wildlife and humans.

ADVOCACY AND POLICY DEVELOPMENT to promote sustainability in the use of all natural resources and the conservation of biodiversity, by targeting intergovernmental agencies, decision-makers, community leaders, non-government organizations and individuals.

NETWORK BUILDING to expand the global partnership of conservation organizations (especially in developing countries and Central/ Eastern Europe) and promote worldwide interest in, and concern for, the conservation of birds and, through that, for wider environmental issues.

An example of BirdLife's work is the Important Bird Areas (IBA) programme. Sites of importance for birds throughout the world are being identified on strict, standardized criteria; IBAs in Europe and the Middle East have already been identified, programmes are under way in Africa, and currently being developed for Asia and the Americas. BirdLife's goal is to identify the world's Important Bird Areas by the year 2000. BirdLife also takes action for the priorities identified, as demonstrated by the successful programmes for the protection of Important Bird Areas in 31 countries in Europe.

BirdLife International has its headquarters in Cambridge (UK), and regional offices in Brussels (Belgium), Washington DC (USA), Quito (Ecuador), and Bogor (Indonesia).

# DENMARK

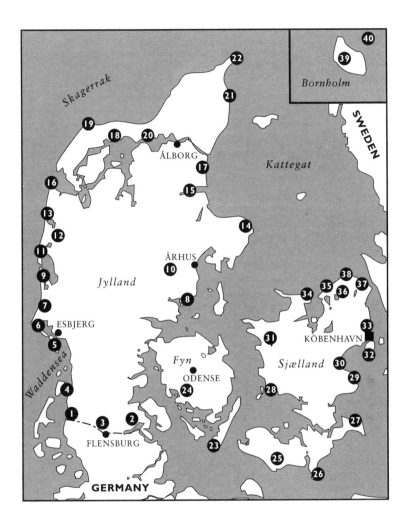

1 Töndermarsken & Vidåen, 2 Gråsten Slotspark, 3 Frøslev Mose,
4 Rømødæmningen/Ballum Enge, 5 Fanø, 6 Blåvandshuk & Skallingen,
7 Fiil Sø, 8 Alrø, 9 Ringkøbing Fjord & Tipperne, 10 Mossø, 11 Vest
Stadil Fjord, 12 Vind Hede/Vosborg Plantage, 13 Nissum Fjord &
Bøvling Klit, 14 Djursland, 15 Mariager Fjord, 16 Agger & Harboøre
Tanger, 17 Lille Vildmose, 18 Vejlerne Area, 19 Hanstholm,
20 Ulvedybet, 21 Hirsholmene and Deget, 22 Skagen, 23 Southern part
of Langeland, 24 Brændegård Sø & Nørre Sø, 25 Hyllekrog/
Maribosøerne, 26 Gedser, 27 Møn, 28 Stigsnæs/Glænø, 29 Stevns,
30 Ølsemagle Revle/Køge Havn, 31 Tissø, 32 Amager, 33 Utterslev
Mose, 34 Rørvig/Hovvig, 35 Tisvilde Hegn, 36 Alsønderup Enge/Nejede
Vesterskov, 37 Hellebæk, 38 Gilleleje, 39 Bornholm, 40 Christiansø.

Denmark is the smallest Scandinavian country, covering 43,000 km², and the most densely populated with about 5,000,000 inhabitants. In most parts of Denmark, the land is flat with a mixture of small woods, farmland and lakes. A long coastline adds alternative interest and is dominated by inlets, small islets – and lots of waterbirds. The coastline with its huge dunes is beloved by holiday makers and in summer almost every beach is packed; large numbers of German tourists visit Denmark.

The climate is rather mild: temperatures being about +17°C in summer and around 0°C in mid-winter. The Danish climate is variable: long, hot periods of high pressure when easterly winds prevail; some springs and summers are hot and dry, but are the exception; winters are mostly quite cold, although snow can occur.

The most commonly spoken foreign language is English; German is also widely understood. The availability of hotels in all price brackets, hostels, camp-sites and bed-and-breakfast accommodation, makes Denmark an easy country to visit. In certain areas, especially in parts of Western Jutland (Jylland), birdwatchers should beware of a certain hostility due to conflicts with hunting interests. Note, too, that private properties *are* private. Always keep on tracks, and respect signs telling you *'adgang forbudt'* (no access). The rule is: **never** trespass. Never hesitate to ask other birdwatchers about the local situation and possible 'stake-outs'. Denmark has many first-rate birders who are normally helpful. The large numbers of migrating birds seen here have resulted in a high degree of identification skill among migration fanatics. The level of hunting pressure in the country has, however, made birders acutely aware of environmental issues with most birders being committed to nature conservation.

## HABITATS

As the most densely populated and most southerly Scandinavian country, Danish habitats have more in common with parts of central Europe than the rest of Scandinavia. Unique, however, is the long coastline with shallow bays and estuaries, marshland and numerous inlets. Do expect to find a rather friendly, rolling landscape. When driving through the countryside, small woods are dotted among agricultural areas, reed-fringed lakes and meadows. Large wetlands occur in the western part of Jutland, many having excellent populations of breeding species.

## IMPORTANCE FOR BIRDS

For birds, Denmark's main importance is as a migration route and wintering place; wildfowl and waders are especially significant. Areas of shallow water support between 1,000,000 and 3,000,000 wintering waterbirds including 500,000 Common Scoters, 125,000 Velvet Scoters, up to 1,000,000 Eiders and 395,000 Razorbills. For 26 species of seabirds and ducks, Denmark is listed as being of international importance. The Western part of Jutland hosts almost the whole Western Palearctic population of Pink-footed and pale-bellied Brent Geese during migration (and sometimes winter).

Few other countries have such large concentrations of dabbling ducks and waders (which has led to a number of Ramsar Sites), especially impressive on the western side of Jutland during migration times. Of special importance to waterbirds are the linked inlets in Northern and Western Jutland, leading south to the Waddensea region where up to 1,000,000 waders may gather at one time, both at spring and autumn migration times. Thankfully, large areas are protected but intensive hunting takes place in many areas.

Situated between the main body of Europe and Scandinavia, spring and autumn sees an impressive migration of landbirds through Denmark. At well known (and described) migration spots such as Skagen, Gilleleje and Stevns, raptor and passerine migration may be just as spectacular as in the more famous spots of Falsterbo and Ottenby.

Denmark has high populations of breeding waterbirds. A good example is the Cormorant which has its greatest European population in this country. Many places have good numbers of breeding coastal species such as Mute Swan, Avocet, Common and Arctic Terns, and gulls. The most impressive numbers are found in the large reserves in Northern and Western Jutland, including the Waddensea Area.

Typical woodland birds are moderately represented in Denmark, which lacks extensive forests. Some species are at their northern European breeding limit in Denmark; these include White Stork, Kentish Plover, Gull-billed Tern, Turtle Dove, Barn and Little Owls, and Serin. All these species are found mainly in the south-western part of the country. Recent settlers are mainly from the east, including Penduline Tit and Common Rosefinch.

# SEASONS

### SPRING

Spring is a very good time to visit and migration can be exceptional. If your main interest is raptor migration, choose eastern Denmark in April or Skagen in May. The most varied migration in eastern Denmark occurs in mid-April; a visit to a site like Gilleleje on a spring day with a hot southerly wind may result in a bird experience of a lifetime. Within 50 km of Copenhagen, several first-class migration sites can be found.

Arguably the most exciting Danish experience is a visit to Skagen in May, with trips to the large wetlands in northern and western part of Jutland. This might start with a couple of days of massive (but unpredictable) migration of divers and raptors at Skagen, and end with huge numbers of wetland species at Vejlerne: the experience will never be forgotten and is among the best bird experiences in the whole of Western Palearctic.

In general, Denmark is not a country to visit to see breeding birds (except for wetland species). Having said this, however, the density of songbirds in many areas is high.

### SUMMER

Good numbers of the commoner waterbirds and passerines breed. In the east, Thrush Nightingales are common, enlivening hot summer evenings with their songs. The well-known tame Greylag Geese at Utterslev Mose (as famous to birdwatchers as *The Little Mermaid* to tourists!) offer an interesting experience together with large numbers of common waterbirds which breed at this urban spot.

In July, numbers of waders start to build up; large flocks of coastal species also gather in the Waddensea. The southern part of the west coast of Jutland holds countless terns and gulls and the tip of Skagen attracts large numbers of the same species; their feeding activities also attract skuas.

AUTUMN

Numbers of wetland birds in western Jutland to the Waddensea area are staggering. A stay can be combined with visits to west coast hot-spots such as Hanstholm and Blåvandshuk, these latter sites being impressive during westerly storms where large numbers of pelagics come close to the shore. Equally impressive are the numbers of birds that settle along west Jutland inlets down to the Waddensea; in October, flocks of dabbling ducks, Pink-footed Geese and Bewick's Swans are encountered.

The eastern part of the country is dominated by masses of migrating birds: raptors, pigeons, corvids and passerines. On certain days, thousands of raptors pass through spots such as Stevns and Stigsnæs. Along the Baltic Coast, a mixed migration of water birds occurs, on some days comprising an endless stream of ducks and geese.

WINTER

The winter climate is relatively mild, and severe snow and ice are rare. Consequently, larger numbers of wintering birds remain in Denmark than in other Scandinavian countries. In the coastal areas, huge flocks of seaducks, such as Eider and scoters gather. Urban lakes and lakelands in the eastern part of the country hold thousands of dabbling ducks, especially Tufted Duck. The west of the country also holds good numbers of wildfowl: in mild winters, most of the Pink-footed Geese remain through the winter. Northern species occur irregularly, Nutcracker and Crossbill occurring most often. Certain long-staying rarities of northerly origin turn up every winter.

## CONSERVATION

Denmark has a good number of reserves and protected areas. A high number of wetlands are protected and this is vital since hunting is extensive in many areas. Generally, conservation is good, although several important areas have no conservation status whatsoever.

## GETTING THERE AND GETTING AROUND

Denmark is easily reached via ferries from Great Britain, Germany and several Baltic countries. Copenhagen has an International Airport (Kastrup) with daily connections to European large cities, USA and the Far East. From Kastrup, a number of towns are served by SAS/Danair domestic flights.

Visitors to Copenhagen will find many localities within a few hours' drive of the city. The capital is even close to Falsterbo and the lakelands in Sweden. Visitors are recommended to hire a car (all major international car hire firms are represented), although getting around by public services is fairly easy.

Please note that Denmark does not have the same public rights of access to the countryside as Sweden (*Allemands-retten*) and many areas are in private hands. In many wetland areas, birdwatchers are not very popular following years of conflicts between hunters and the Danish birdwatching community. Although visitors are generally well received, do not enter any areas which seem to be closed to the public.

As Denmark is a small country with a dense population you will have no problem finding places to stay overnight close to most birdwatching sites. Rooms (in Danish '*vaerelser*') are found in all parts of the county.

# DANISH ORNITHOLOGICAL SOCIETY (DOF)

DOF was founded in 1906. It works to provide information about, and protection of, birds in Denmark. The organization is the country's link between conservation, research and birdwatching and is the Danish partner of BirdLife International. DOF has successfully organized several large projects and is widely heard in discussions concerning environmental questions.

DOF conducts a number of member activities, including an intensive programme of meetings and excursions, ranging from half day walks in the outskirts of Copenhagen to bird tours to all parts of the world. It also publishes three journals: the popular, down to earth *FUGLE*, the more field orientated *'DOF-nyt'* and the more scientific, quarterly journal *DOFT* (*Dansk Ornitologisk Forenings Tidsskrift*). Ornis Consult is a consultancy, founded by DOF. Within DOF many local divisions publish their own journals or make their own arrangements such as local protection activities or travel arrangements.

The private Fugleværnsfonden owns several reserves, some of which are parts of larger, important bird areas. A total of about 8500 members makes DOF one of the largest 'green societies' in Denmark. The address for DOF and its sister organizations, including the bookshop and library, is given in Useful Addresses. Birders are welcome during office hours (11am–4pm most days).

The national birdline is updated daily in Danish (Tel. 90232400), but the number cannot be reached from several parts of the country. If you want to report sightings, Tel. 33255300.

# BIRDWATCHING SITES

## TØNDERMARSKEN AND VIDÅEN

54°58N 8°42E

The river Vidåen in the marshland of Jutland is fringed by dense reedbeds. Margrethekog is an artificial saline lagoon alongside 3200 ha of marshland (Frederikskog). Margrethekogen and parts of Tøndermarsken comprise a state reserve (total area 2500 ha).

TIMING

From March to June, breeding species are at their most active; migratory birds, especially waders can also be seen. During July and August the highlight is undoubtedly the harriers, which spend the night at Vidåen, the crowds of starlings and the shorebirds. Between September and November; masses of geese, ducks and waders are present. Many stay for the winter, attracting 1–2 Peregrines.

SPECIES

◆ *Resident* Bittern, Raven.
◆ *Breeding season* White Stork, Marsh and Montagu's Harriers, waders (e.g. Black-tailed Godwit), Black Tern, Savi's and Grasshopper Warblers, geese, ducks.

◆ *Passage* Raptors, waders (including Kentish Plover), Starling (500,000 or so present in March and late summer).
◆ *Winter* Geese, Peregrine.
ACCESS
To reach Magisterkogen, take the road between Rudbøl and Tønder. 6 km from Tønder, a small dirt road heads south (Gammel Digevej) and leads to a parking spot 100 m or so from the northern dyke, where reedbed species are best seen.

Margrethekog is reached at Højer Sluse. Look for signs showing Højer Sluse in Rudbøl, and continue to the west until the road ends. There is a restaurant and an information map. The birds in the lagoon are often far away, so bring a telescope. Easier access is from the German part of the area, where a dirt road leads through the area.

## GRÅSTEN SLOTSPARK
54°55N 09°35E
Gråsten Slotspark is state owned. Part of the area is protected and comprises old, mixed woodland, several small lakes and the Castle of Gråsten.

TIMING
Spring is the best season to visit. In March and April, woodland species will start singing (e.g. both treecreeper species), but it is not until May that migrant birds arrive in force; time your visit accordingly.
SPECIES
◆ *Resident* Tawny Owl, Treecreeper, Short-toed Treecreeper.
◆ *Breeding season* Great Crested and Little Grebes, Long-eared Owl, Wryneck, Stock Dove, Golden Oriole, Grey Wagtail.
ACCESS
From Åbenrå, drive along Felstedvej to Gråsten. Just before reaching Gråsten there are several parking spots, leading to an extensive system of tracks in the wood. Admittance to the royal castle itself is prohibited.

## FRØSLEV MOSE
54°49N 09°21E
This forested area comprises 1445 ha of mature conifer plantation with plenty of clearings. Added interest is provided, to the south-west, by wet meadows covering 306 ha. Frøslev Plantage is state forest and the meadows are protected.

TIMING
In common with most woodland areas, Frøslev is best in the spring, especially May. The summer months are quiet but, in winter, Crossbills may occur.
SPECIES
◆ *Resident* Buzzard, Goshawk, Willow Tit, Crossbill.
◆ *Breeding season* Wood Sandpiper (rare), Curlew, Honey Buzzard, Nightjar, Wryneck, Turtle Dove, Grasshopper Warbler, Firecrest (occasional), Great Grey Shrike.
ACCESS
Access to the woods is easy. To reach the wet meadows bordering Germany, take the road from Padborg leading west. In Kristiansminde, follow the road leading west to a parking spot bordering the meadows. Do not walk in the meadows in the breeding season to avoid disturbance.

# RØMØDÆMNINGEN/BALLUM ENGE

55°8N 08°29E

The 8.5 km-long Rømø Dam (*dæmning*) runs between the sandy island of Rømø and the Jutland mainland. Associated with the dam are fields and meadows at Ballum, and the reed-fringed Lakolk Lake (on Rømø) surrounded by heathland. At the southern tip of Rømø are coastal meadows bordering the Waddensea. 1700 ha of Rømø south of the main road and Lakolk Lake with surroundings (750 ha) are protected. Stormengene (32 ha), at the extreme south tip of Rømø, is a private reserve (under Fugleværnsfonden). The Waddensea area is a Ramsar Site and the whole Danish Waddensea area (950 km²) has nature reserve status.

TIMING

March to June are best for Lake Lakolk's breeding birds (including Gull-billed Tern from nearby breeding sites), although a fair amount of time is needed to see most of the reedbed species. Huge numbers of waders begin to gather in the Waddensea and along the coast in July/August, their numbers building up during September. As autumn turns into winter, most waders have migrated south although considerable numbers still remain: geese, ducks and raptors make up for their loss, however. Particularly impressive are the thousands, sometimes tens of thousands, of Brent, Barnacle and Pink-footed Geese that pass through or remain around the Danish coast from October to March.

SPECIES

◆ *Resident* Little Grebe, Bittern, Water Rail, Little Owl, Willow and Bearded Tits, Raven.

◆ *Breeding season* Red-necked Grebe, ducks, Marsh and Montagu's Harriers, Spotted Crake, all shorebirds, Kentish Plover, Common, Little, Sandwich and Gull-billed Terns, Grasshopper and Reed Warblers, Firecrest, Redpoll, Penduline Tit.

◆ *Passage* Brent, Barnacle and Pink-footed Geese, ducks, all shorebirds, Merlin, Peregrine.

◆ *Winter* Rough-legged Buzzard, Hen Harrier, Peregrine, Brent, Pink-footed and Barnacle Geese, Twite, Shore Lark, Snow and Lapland Buntings.

ACCESS

Take road A11 (German border to Esbjerg). 1 km north of Skærbæk, turn west to Rømø to reach Lakolk Lake, drive further west to Lakolk, then turn south along the tourist village border, and continue some hundred metres east. Bird life can be observed from a small canal crossing the road. Overlook the lake or walk 2 km to the south for Gull-billed Tern and Kentish Plover. Drive a few more kilometres and you are back on the road leading to Skærbæk. Ballum Enge, the main wintering site for Pink-footed Geese, is reached by a road leading south to Ballum immediately after arriving at the mainland. Take small roads to the east before reaching the geese. Further to the south-west of Skast/Kogsbøl is good for passerines. In Bådsbøl, turn east, and after 1 km turn south in Husum towards Højer (Duborgvej). After 5 km, the wood is passed. Park the car and enter the wood to the east. Willow Tits are found in the willow scrubs south-east of the wood.

# FANØ

55°25N 08°25E

This low, 56 km² island has wet meadows, sand dunes and conifer plantations. 1400 ha of dunes on the southern part of the island are protected; the

Waddensea area is a Ramsar Site. Wetland birds breed here and wildfowl use it both as a migration staging post and for wintering. For most birdwatchers, however, its significance lies in the sometimes phenomenal numbers of migrant landbirds that pass through each autumn: 25,000–50,000 Meadow Pipits and 100,000 thrushes per day are not unusual on good days between late September and early November!

TIMING

Although Fanø has good numbers of breeding coastal and wetland birds, it is perhaps most rewarding from late summer onwards; numbers of waders and ducks begin to build up from mid-July and pass through in greatest numbers from August to September  along with often sizeable flocks of geese and ducks later in autumn; good numbers of birds may remain in winter. September to October sees a large migration of landbirds.

SPECIES

- ◆ *Breeding season* Little Tern, shorebirds.
- ◆ *Passage* Brent and Barnacle Geese, ducks, small raptors, Merlin, Peregrine, waders, Woodpigeon, Meadow Pipit, Richard's and Red-throated Pipits (both scarce but regular), Shore Lark, thrushes including Ring Ouzel, Chaffinch, Brambling, Ortolan and Lapland Buntings.

ACCESS

Ferries run every hour from Esbjerg but need to be booked in advance in summer. If you pay a winter visit, check the fishing port at Esbjerg for gulls and waders, especially the northern harbour limit.

## BLÅVANDSHUK AND SKALLINGEN

55°33N 08°4E

This is the westernmost tip of Jutland, a sandy tip of land (continuing as Horns Rev in the North Sea), with broad, flat beaches and coastal sand dunes. The site includes Kallesmærsk Heath (flat heathland). Blåvandshuk itself is one of the main migration spots in Denmark, especially in autumn; to the south-east are the meadows of Skallingen, the eastern part grading to wet meadows which border the Waddensea. The Skallingen peninsula (2285 ha) is protected as a state-owned reserve. The Waddensea area is a Ramsar Site.

TIMING

Although interesting throughout the year, each season has particular highlights. In spring, (mid-March to early June), some days see thousands of geese, ducks and waders pass through. Passerines are also well represented in spring.

The summer months see huge gatherings of non-breeding gulls resting on the wide, sandy beach, joined by thousands of terns. By late summer, the migration of waders is well under way, the numbers and species composition of the flocks varying on a daily basis; mixed in easterlies and a mass migration of Oystercatchers in westerlies.

Autumn migration comprises two main areas of interest to the birdwatcher: seabird passage and the migration of landbirds. Generally speaking,

*Meadow Pipit*

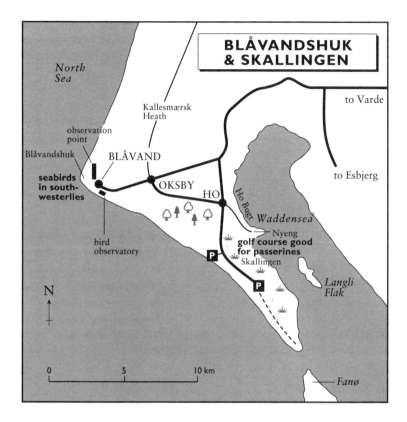

**BLÅVANDSHUK & SKALLINGEN**

*North Sea*

to Varde

Kallesmærsk Heath

observation point

Blåvandshuk

BLÅVAND

seabirds in south-westerlies

OKSBY

HO

to Esbjerg

Ho Bugt

*Waddensea*

Nyeng

**golf course good for passerines**

Skallingen

bird observatory

N

*Langli Flak*

0   5   10 km

*Fanø*

seawatching is best in strong south-westerly or westerly winds, easterly winds bring in the greatest numbers and diversity of common passerines, some raptors and the best chance for Siberian vagrants.

December to February sees large numbers of gulls and seaducks gather here, always with a few unusual ones among them; Sanderlings winter.

SPECIES

◆ *Breeding season* Dabbling ducks, waders, Yellow Wagtail (at Skallingen), Red-backed Shrike, Stonechat, Common Rosefinch.

◆ *Passage* Divers, Gannet, Fulmar, ducks, pelagics and skuas of all kinds, storm-petrels of both species are regular, Oystercatcher, shorebirds, Kittiwake, Common, Arctic, Sandwich and Little Terns, auks, all passerines, Meadow Pipit, thrushes, rarities.

◆ *Winter* Eider, Rough-legged Buzzard, Hen Harrier, Merlin, Peregrine, White-tailed Eagle (rare), Dunlin, Oystercatcher, Curlew.

ACCESS

Blåvandshuk is reached from Varde, where a 26-km road leads directly to the site. Skallingen is reached from Blåvand/Oksbøl–Varde road. 21 km from Varde (5 km from Blåvandshuk) go south towards Ho, and continue to the south, until a parking place is reached. Walk from here (4 km) to the point. Another good spot is east of Ho Klitplantage (Nyeng), where a dirt road leads to a small parking place at the northern edge of Skallingen. Large flocks of waders are seen along Ho Bugt, although rather distant, extensive hunting makes them shy (they feed in the Waddensea area during the day, and visit the meadows at night). The golf course at Nyeng often holds night migrating passerines. There is a bird observatory at Blåvand, organizing ringing and migration counts; it has a small birdwatchers' shop. Use the lighthouse parking, and walk to the beach. In westerly gales, old German bunkers on the beach offer good shelter (needed on account of the regular sand-storms!). Do *not* stray north into the military area when this is closed for shooting!

# Fiil Sø

55°38N 08°16E
Situated some 18 km north-west of Varde, this 100-ha site contains the remains of a formerly large lake which is surrounded by huge fields, moorland and patches of plantation woodland. The lake and its surroundings are protected.

TIMING
Best time to visit is late September to November. Large flocks of geese, notably Pink-footed Goose, frequent the fields; numbers of this species sometimes reach 25,000 in October.
SPECIES
◆ *Resident* Bittern, Crested Tit, Redpoll, geese (in mild winters).
◆ *Breeding season* Garganey, Shoveler, Marsh Harrier, Water Rail, Spotted
  Crake, Red-backed Shrike, Grasshopper Warbler, Penduline Tit.
◆ *Passage* Raptors (including Osprey, Merlin and Peregrine), Pink-footed,
  Bean and Barnacle Geese, rare geese, Pintail, Caspian Tern (rare, autumn).
ACCESS
There is no admittance to the lake-edge, but the area can be viewed from surrounding roads. The best site is the hill of Kløvbakken, at a parking place north of the lake. From here it is possible to observe the evening flights of geese. It is possible to drive on dirt roads around the lake, but ask local farmers at Fiil Sø Avlsgård first. There is free admittance to the western part of the lake. Park south of Kirkeby and walk south-east.

# Alrø

55°52N 10°5E
The island of Alrø is mainly cultivated but has marshes and an interesting coastline. Most of the area lacks protection but Alrø Poller is a reserve (no admittance between 1 April and 15 July). Nearby, Vorsø (57 ha) is a state reserve and 2120 ha of the surrounding land is protected. The whole area is a Ramsar Site. The area is important both for breeding coastal birds and waders: at Alrø Polder, for example, up to 3000 Bar-tailed Godwits, 8000 Dunlin and 5000 Golden Plovers have been counted in spring. Autumn numbers are poorer.

TIMING
Good numbers of waders and terns breed; the thousands of pairs of Cormorants from the colony at Vorsø feed here also. Spring migration of waders lasts from March until early June. Return migration of waders begins again in July and continues to October. The winter months hold plenty of seaducks.
SPECIES
◆ *Breeding season* Cormorant, Eider, waders, Arctic and Sandwich Terns.
◆ *Passage* Ducks, waders (notably Bar-tailed Godwit in spring).
◆ *Winter* Seaduck (notably Eider, Scaup).

ACCESS
Alrø is reached from the Odder-Horsens road 14 km east of Horsens. Pass the dyke and park immediately after reaching Alrø. Waders are best seen where the road turns west.

# RINGKØBING FJORD AND TIPPERNE
55°59N 8°7E

This is the largest inlet in Western Jutland (300 km²). In the east and south are some of the most extensive areas of coastal meadows in Denmark, offering some of the best birdwatching in the country. Best known is the Tipperne Reserve, a large wetland with marshes and small pools. The drier meadows on the west side of the fjord may be good for geese and flocks of passerines, such as Shore Lark, Twite and buntings. The fishing harbour of Hvide Sande has gulls and sometimes resting seabirds. Tipperne is a State Reserve of 800 ha. Værnengene, with its extensive reedbeds, and Bjålum Klit are protected (3000 ha). Breeding wetland birds, in particular waders and ducks, are a speciality, but migrant and overwintering geese, ducks and waders may be present in excellent numbers.

TIMING
For breeding wetland birds, the best time is April to early June. By July, the first signs of return wader migration are seen. Numbers build up throughout the weeks of late July and August and peak in early September; but swans, geese and ducks are plentiful in October and early November. Many birds move south, but in mild winters large numbers remain. Wader and duck numbers build up to a spring peak in April to May.

SPECIES
◆ *Breeding season* Bittern, Greylag Goose, all shorebirds and dabbling ducks, Marsh Harrier, Sandwich Tern.
◆ *Passage* Geese, Wigeon, Teal, raptors (e.g. Merlin and Peregrine), waders, Dotterel (up to 190 have been recorded in fields near Skjern between 10–20 May), all shorebirds, passerines, Lapland Bunting.
◆ *Winter* Pink-footed, Brent and Barnacle Geese, Wigeon, Teal, White-tailed Eagle (scarce but regular), Buzzard, Rough-legged Buzzard, Hen Harrier, Peregrine, Glaucous Gull and sometimes Iceland Gull (Hvide Sande), Short-eared Owl, Shore Lark, Twite, Snow Bunting.

ACCESS
Tipperne is closed (except on Sundays), but good views over the wetlands at Værnengene are possible from the dirt road leading to the reserve. Take road 181 between Nr. Nebel and Hvide Sande. 500 m east of Nymindegab, turn north and drive for a few km. From 3, 5 and 7 km birds are easily seen.

At the reserve entrance there is an information hut, and an observation tower at Værnsande; good views can be had from a large farm building. Most species are seen at close range even from here. Bitterns often boom from the extensive reedbeds at Værnsande in the bottom of the inlet. Tipperne is open on Sunday mornings (1 April–31 August: 5–10am; 1 September–31 March: 10am–noon). The bird observatory and the farm building have bird exhibitions.

# MOSSØ
56°5N 94°5E

Mossø is the largest lake in Jutland (1668 ha) and is surrounded by meadows, reedbeds and mixed woodland. 1457 ha around the lake are protected. Emborg

Odde is prohibited to visitors between 1 April and 30 June. The lake is important for its breeding water birds and in particular its Black-necked Grebes; with 200–250 pairs, this is the most important Danish site for this species.

TIMING
The lake is best in spring/early summer, and in winter. A visit between April and June will be productive for nesting reedbed species and the Black-necked Grebes, as well as woodland birds. From November to March, Mossø is host to large numbers of diving ducks.

SPECIES
◆ *Breeding season* Black-necked and Great Crested Grebes, Black-headed Gull, Green Woodpecker, Wryneck, Kingfisher, Mistle Thrush, woodland birds.
◆ *Winter* Tufted Duck, Pochard, Goosander, White-tailed Eagle (scarce but regular), Buzzard, Goshawk.

ACCESS
The colony of Black-necked Grebes is situated at Emborg Odde, which is reached from a track immediately east of Emborg, leading south to the reserve border.

# VEST STADIL FJORD
56°5N 8°15E

This brackish lake is surrounded by reedbeds and agricultural land; there is no admittance to the area itself, apart from a few roads. The area consisted formerly of large reedbeds and wetlands, but was drained in the 1950s for agricultural use. 1465 ha, including the inlet, parts of the agricultural land and sand dunes, are protected. Vest Stadil Fjord is one of the main resting areas in Denmark for migrating Pink-footed Geese; 15,000–20,000 can be seen in October, with similar numbers again in spring. Other goose species, as well as ducks, are also well represented. The area is a Ramsar Site.

*Black-tailed Godwit,
juvenile*

TIMING

Vest Stadil Fjord is best in late autumn (October and November) where thousands of geese arrive on the surrounding fields. Their departure south-wards depends on when and if snow and ice appear; in mild winters, several thousand overwinter. Numbers of geese and ducks build up again in March and April before the birds depart northward on their spring migration.

SPECIES

◆ *Passage* Pink-footed and Barnacle Geese, Pintail, Wigeon.

◆ *Winter* Pink-footed and Barnacle Geese, (depends on weather), Buzzard, Rough-legged Buzzard, Hen Harrier, Merlin, Peregrine, Glaucous Gull (Thorsminde Havn), Shore Lark, Snow Bunting.

ACCESS

Take road 181 north from Hvide Sande to Thorsminde. The geese are best observed along the road – do not leave the car when they are at close range.

# VIND HEDE/VOSBORG PLANTAGE

56°16N 8°20E

Situated some 15 km south-west of Holstebro, this site of 450 ha comprises gently undulating hills with heathland plains, agricultural land and conifer plantations. Vind Hede is a Bird Reserve, created for the last surviving Black Grouse in Denmark, whose numbers are very low indeed (and may well disappear in a few years).

TIMING

The best time is early spring. From late February to early May, Black Grouse males display at a traditional lek site. Spring too, is best for the woodland and heathland species.

SPECIES

◆ *Resident* Black Grouse, Buzzard, Goshawk, Green Woodpecker, Crested Tit.

◆ *Breeding season* Curlew, Long-eared Owl, Nightjar, Grey Wagtail.

ACCESS

Take the A11 from Holstebro to Skjern. About 10 km south of Holstebro, turn west to Vind. At Vind church, take the small road leading north-west. At the point where heather grows on both sides of the road, the Black Grouse lek can be seen on the north side of the road (where fields border the heath). Be there at dawn; please stay in your car.

# NISSUM FJORD AND BØVLING KLIT

56°20N 8°11E

This 8000-ha stretch of coastal meadows and sand dunes separates the North Sea from the inlet of Nissum Fjord (Bøvling Klit). In the south-eastern corner of the inlet there are dense reedbeds at Felsted Kog . Fjandø and parts of Bøvling Fiord (370 ha) are protected, being a Ramsar Site because of its importance to migrating geese and wildfowl. Part of the area of wet meadows is a private reserve (Fugleværnsfonden); Bøvling Fjord and Felsted Kog are game reserves.

TIMING

The area is best known for its wildfowl. During mild winters, thousands of geese, and large numbers of ducks, can be found here. The largest numbers, however, occur in spring. In March and April, numbers can be phenomenal and includes European wintering species, waders and ducks (both breeders and migrants). Numbers of waders are highest from late July to early September, with wildfowl flocks building up until November; in mild winters, thousands of birds stay.

SPECIES
◆ *Breeding season* Marsh Harrier, waders, gulls, Sandwich Tern.
◆ *Passage* Whooper and Bewick's Swans (up to 2500 of the latter), Pink-footed, Barnacle and Brent Geese, rare geese, dabbling ducks, waders (especially Bar-tailed Godwit and Dunlin).
◆ *Winter* Geese, ducks, Glaucous and sometimes Iceland Gulls (Thormsminde fishing harbour).

ACCESS
View the area from the coastal road 181 between Lemvig and Thorsminde. The best areas for geese and ducks are Bøvling Klit north of Thorsminde. To the south, Fjandø can be viewed from the parking spot north of Nr. Fjand (reached by small road leading north). Felsted Kog may be viewed from surrounding roads, especially those leading west from the villages of Vemb and Ulfborg Kirkeby; observation sites are at Kytterup, and to the south of Gørding.

## DJURSLAND
56°25N 10°53E

Birdwatchers will find several interesting locations at the eastern tip of Djursland. There is agricultural land and the Ramten-Dystrup Lakes which are well-vegetated, shallow lakes surrounded by reedbeds. 76 ha of coastal scrub at Fjellerup Strand and Gjerrild are protected as are the Ramten-Dystrup Lakes and surrounding land (190 ha in all). Djursland is best known as a spot for observing the spring migration of raptors and other landbirds. In late autumn, seabirds, especially auks, occur. More than 100,000 Razorbills have been counted in a few hours some mornings in early December.

TIMING
Spring movements of passerines can be good from March to May, especially in Gjerrild. Buzzards, as well as other raptors, and Woodpigeons are most in evidence during westerly winds. Spring is the time for the breeding waterbirds at Ramten-Dystrup lakes. In the west, Fornæs may be good in late autumn and winter, when thousands of auks can be seen.

SPECIES
◆ *Breeding season* Grebes, Greylag Goose, Teal, Yellow Wagtail, Marsh and Reed Warblers, Penduline Tit, Common Rosefinch.
◆ *Passage* Raptors (spring), auks (especially Razorbills; late autumn), Woodpigeon, passerines.
◆ *Winter* Auks, Rock Pipit.

ACCESS
Gjerrild (reached from roads from Grenå). It is situated 13 km north of Grenå. In Gjerrild, turn north to Gjerrild Nordstrand. Fornæs (situated at the lighthouse) 6 km to the north east of Grenå is the main spot for auks.

## MARIAGER FJORD
56°42N 10°19E

This 35 km² area comprises a shallow inlet surrounded by fields and mixed woodland. It was once of international importance for waders but has been heavily drained in the last 100 years. The small islands of Treskelbakkeholm

*Barnacle Geese*

and Lemos Pold are reserves with no admittance from 1 April to 15 July. The site is significant due to its wintering wildfowl, especially pale-bellied Brent Geese who find refuge here before flying to Agerø and north-west Jutland in mid-winter.

TIMING

Between November and March the eastern part of the inlet holds several thousand Brent Geese (pale-bellied race). Other species of wildfowl are also present in good numbers. Large wader flocks may be found in August and September.

SPECIES

◆ *Passage* Ducks, Golden Plover, Dunlin.
◆ *Winter* Whooper and Mute Swans, Brent Goose, Shelduck.

ACCESS

From Randers, take the road between Mariager and Ålborg and turn to Hadsund. In Hadsund, take the road leading north-west to Visborg (3–4 km outside Hadsund), then turn south to Havnsø and on. From the road, geese and other waterbirds are seen well, especially south of the woodland.

# AGGER AND HARBOØRE TANGER

56°38N 8°10E

Agger and Harboøre Tanger are narrow tongues of land, with sand dunes on their western sides, and sheltered bays, lagoons and marshes to the east. Although two distinct areas (by Limfjorden), they are treated here as a whole. 2400 ha of Agger and Harboøre Tanger as well as coastal stretches at Krik Vig are protected. Huge numbers of wetland birds gather during migration and many stay in mild winters. It is one of the best places in Denmark for waders in spring. The area is a Ramsar Site.

TIMING

Spring migration is excellent from late March to late May. The large flocks of wildfowl are an impressive sight, including several thousand Pink-footed Geese peaking early May, at which time good numbers of waders are also present, most notably up to 3800 Bar-tailed Godwits and 14,000 Dunlin at Agger Tange. The meadows and wetlands hold fair numbers of breeding waders. In July migrant waders start arriving, their numbers building up until September. As the autumn progresses, thousands of migrant swans, geese and

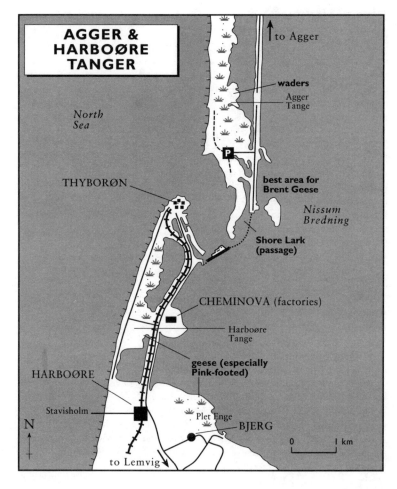

ducks start to arrive with passerines in evidence also. Flocks of geese, which remain for the winter in most years, should be searched for the occasional rare species (Red-breasted, Snow and Lesser White-fronted Geese have occurred in past years).

SPECIES

◆ *Breeding season* Black-necked Grebe (Harbøøre/Veserne), waders.
◆ *Passage* Bewick's Swan, Brent and Pink-footed Geese, waders, passerines (e.g. Shore Lark and Lapland Bunting).
◆ *Winter* Brent Goose (mainly southern Agger Tange), Pink-footed Goose (mainly at Harbøøre Tange), Glaucous and sometimes Iceland Gulls (Thyborøn fishing port).

ACCESS

The area is situated at the western mouth of Limfjorden, and is easily reached by car. Ferries between Harbøøre and Agger Tange take 10 minutes. At busy times, ferries cross continuously, but outside the tourist season, they depart twenty minutes past every hour. More birds are seen from the public roads, especially the dirt roads which border the sand dunes and the North Sea.

# LILLE VILDMOSE

56°50N 10°7E

Lille Vildmose is an area of mature, mixed woodland with agricultural land and open meadows. Tofte Sø is an artificial 100-ha lake. The whole area is a private nature reserve with no admittance. The observation tower at Tofte Sø does, however, allow visitors to get a good view of the entire area. The observation tower is best visited in the afternoon, when light conditions are most favourable.

TIMING

In spring and early summer, Lille Vildmose is good for breeding waterbirds, including grebes and ducks, as well as for raptors. Migrant waders begin to gather from late July onwards and numbers of these, together with dabbling ducks, build up through August to October. Numbers depend much on water level, but may be good. Raptors appear in late autumn and, during the winter, these are joined by up to 1000 Bean Geese.

SPECIES

◆ *Breeding season* Red-necked, Great Crested, Little and Black-necked Grebes, Cormorant (colony at Tofte Sø), Greylag Goose, Gadwall, Garganey, Buzzard, Honey Buzzard, Goshawk, Sparrowhawk, Marsh Harrier, Common Crane (has bred in recent years), Curlew.

◆ *Passage* Wildfowl, waders (dependent on water level).

◆ *Winter* Bean Goose, Golden and White-tailed Eagles (both scarce and occasional), Buzzard, Rough-legged Buzzard, Hen Harrier, Short-eared Owl, Great Grey Shrike, Twite.

ACCESS

Tofte Sø lies around 20-km south-east of Ålborg, and 15-km north of Hadsund. From the road between Hadsund and Ålborg, turn right to Kongerslev (around 15 km from Ålborg), and from here the road leading west to Dokkedal. An alternative road is the coast road between Hals and Als. Follow road signs to Kongerslev around 10-km south of Hals. About 5 km from both Dokkedal and Kongerslev, a small dirt road leads about 1-km south to the observation tower.

# VEJLERNE AREA

57°5N 9°15E

Vejlerne is a 6000-ha area of lowland marsh. Within the overall site, there are several excellent brackish lakes, inlets, wetland meadows and reedbeds. A number of unsuccessful drainage projects during the 1880s have helped create a unique mixture of wet and dry habitats for birds. Vejlerne originally comprised two distinct inlets on the peninsula of Hannæs. The area was drained in 1880 thereby creating the large wet meadows at Bygholms Vejle. Today, a network of old channels and overgrown ditches criss-cross the site. This is the largest Danish reserve and it is protected both privately and by the State. Most of the area is a Ramsar Site. Within the overall location, 600 ha of land is a wildlife reserve with no public access.

Wetland birds are superb throughout the year. An impressive range of species breed and huge numbers of waterbirds gather at Vejlerne during migration times. Maximum numbers include 3000 Bewick's Swans in autumn, and spring counts of 1000 Bean Geese, 1000 Pink-footed Geese, 2000 Greylag Geese, 2000 Wigeon, 12,000 Gadwall and 26,000 Dunlin!

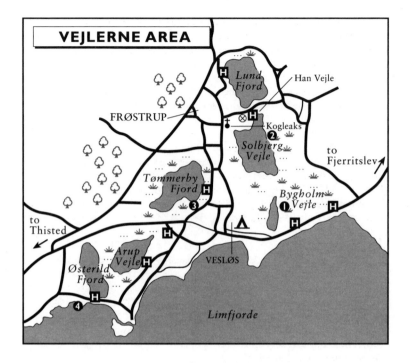

TIMING

From late March until June, the area is full of breeding birds and a visit at this time of year will be a thoroughly rewarding experience. Until late May numbers are augmented by huge flocks of migrating waders which stop off briefly to rest and feed. Many return by mid-July and are soon followed by the numerous raptors, ducks and passerines. Late autumn brings large flocks of migrating swans and geese, and increasing numbers of ducks and waders. These reach a peak in September–October and many stay during mild winters.

SPECIES

◆ *Breeding season* Red-necked Grebe, Bittern, White Stork (Vesløs village), Greylag Goose, Gadwall, Marsh Harrier, Water Rail, Spotted Crake, waders, terns (e.g. Black Tern), Savi's Warbler, Bearded Tit.

◆ *Passage* Bewick's Swan, ducks, waders, geese, rarities.

◆ *Winter* Whooper and Bewick's Swans, Bean Geese, ducks, White-tailed Eagle (scarce but regular), Buzzard, Rough-legged Buzzard, Hen Harrier, Peregrine, Rock Pipit, Shore Lark, Twite, Snow Bunting.

ACCESS

Vejlerne is c. 60 km west of Ålborg. It is easily reached by road A11 between Ålborg and Thisted. Coming from the south (Viborg), you can 'cut off' Ålborg, and turn NW from A13 shortly before Års. For individual areas, see the map. It is easy to watch birds from the surrounding roads. The area is large and some areas are protected, making access difficult. You need a detailed map which can be obtained at Vejlerne Ecological Field Station (Lyngevej 15, at Frøstrup), where a small museum is sited. Two or three full-time observers operate from this field station. The most rewarding and accessible places within the Vejlerne area are: **1. Bygholm Vejle.** From road A11 between Ålborg and Thisted, several parking places offer excellent views (and information maps) over the huge, wet meadows. It is excellent for migrants, and holds thousands of swans, geese, ducks and waders. Breeding wetland species are impressive. **2. Kærup Holme/Han Vejle**. The best site for reedbed species and Black Tern. The area can be viewed from the gate at the pumping station (excellent new observation tower) and from the northern road (disused railroad) along Lund Fjord. **3. Østerild Fjord/Arup Vejle**. Another good breeding site, holding Greylag Geese and large numbers of other wetland species. In winter, the fields around Arup Church hold hundreds of geese. **4. Hovsør Røn**. Good numbers of waders during migration and interesting wintering species. Take the dyke from Arup to Hovsør. Hovsør Røn is situated on the southern side of the dyke. The inlet north of the dyke holds flocks of swans in autumn. Regularly wintering Peregrine and Shore Lark. **5. Bulbjerg**. Although slightly out of the area, this place is worth visiting for its breeding colonies of Kittiwakes; 350 pairs in recent years. Fulmars are also regular. They fly just below the cliff edge.

## HANSTHOLM

57°7N 8°36E

The Hansted Reserve is a huge area covering 3400 ha of heath with small lakes and plantations. It is one of the few places in Denmark to have a true 'wilderness' feeling although bird life is poor. Fortunately, nearby is the great fishing port of Hanstholm which is both a first-rate site for gulls and excellent for autumn seabird migration in north-westerly to westerly winds. To the south, Ørhage (in Klitmøller) is better for seabird movements in south-westerly to westerly winds.

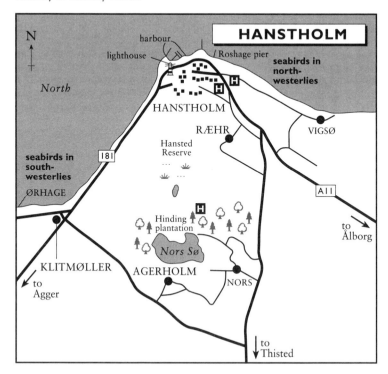

TIMING

There is little of interest here during spring and early summer except for the few pairs of Common Cranes breeding in the heathland. By mid-summer, however, a good number of seabirds can be found loafing along the coastline; these include gulls, terns and skuas. The best seawatching is from September to November, when, depending on the wind direction and speed, phenomenal numbers of seabirds can be seen. Their numbers include common species as well as many more unusual ones. Unlike many Scandinavian sites, winter is almost as reward-ing as autumn, with huge numbers of gulls providing the main interest; during severe gales, there is potential for seawatching even at this time of the year.

SPECIES

◆ *Breeding season* Common Crane, Common Rosefinch (gardens at Hanst-holm Fyr lighthouse).

◆ *Passage* Gannet, pelagic seabirds (rarities regular), Grey Phalarope, Little Auk (late autumn), thrushes and warblers (includes pelagics and Siberian vagrants) (gardens at Hanstholm Fyr lighthouse), rarities.

◆ *Winter* Red-throated Diver, Slavonian Grebe (Nors), Shag (occasional), Whooper and Mute Swans, Bean Geese, Common Scoter, gulls (including Glaucous and usually Iceland), Purple Sandpiper, Kittiwake (especially after severe gales), Snow Bunting.

ACCESS

Hanstholm is reached from Ålborg or Thisted (road A11). At Østerild (c. 10-km north-east of Thisted) a T-junction leads north-west to Hanstholm. To approach Nors Sø, take the road between Thisted and Klitmøller. 10 km from Thisted, turn right to Agerholm. 1.1 km along this road turn right to a dirt road. Follow this road for 800 m, then turn right to a parking place overlooking the lake. There is an observation tower at the south-western end of Nors Sø. Another possibility – especially for a closer approach to the reserve – is to take the road Thisted–Hanstholm. In Nors (7 km from Thisted), turn left to Hinding. After 4 km, the road ends at a car park in a pine plantation. Walk from here along the lake or north-west to the sand dunes overlooking the reserve.

Ørhage (c. 12-km south-west of Hanstholm) is situated at the village of Klitmøller. Take road 181 between Hanstholm and Agger, and turn west to Klitmøller. At the beach, park the car at Ørhage Naturcenter. In south-westerly to westerly winds, seabird migration is good, and the Nature Centre walls offer perfect shelter from the harsh winds.

The fishing port is the largest in Denmark, but rather easily overlooked. Take care in strong winds when waves regularly break over even the inner harbour walls, making piers and roads slippery. Note also that the harbour is a working area – respect local fishermen. It is advisable to park the car at the office area (or at the café) and walk from there. An alternative area is the dumping site just south of the harbour, which often holds passerines and large gulls on days when fewer gulls are in the harbour. The Hansted Reserve is overlooked from the lighthouse garden at Hanstholm, and from the road between Hanstholm and Klitmøller.

At Hanstholm harbour, seabird migration may be excellent in gale force autumn north-westerlies. Migrating birds pass closest a short distance from Roshage, 1 km east of the harbour itself, to which there is no admittance in high winds. They can be observed from the dunes – but preferably from the shelter of the windmill or your car. Especially following several days of storms, exhausted seabirds may pass very close to land!

# ULVEDYBET

57°4N 9°42E

Ulvedybet is a former bay in Limfjorden, cut off from the sea today by an embankment protecting agricultural land from flooding. The site is dominated by wet meadows and is a very good wetland area like a small scale version of Vejlerne. The area is a Ramsar Site and 775 ha is a Game Reserve. Like its larger sister reserve, Ulvedybet is excellent for waterbirds. Large numbers of geese, swans, ducks and waders, are present on migration. Numbers are impressive with autumn counts of 20,000 Wigeon, 6000 Teal, 10,000 Coot and 2000 Pochard being just some of the statistics for the reserve. Winter birding may be rewarding as well.

TIMING

Spring sees excellent numbers of migrant ducks and waders on the reserve from late March until early June; of particular note are the Temminck's Stints, up to 100 having been recorded in the middle of May. A reasonable number of waterbirds breed in the area in July and August, post-breeding Mute Swans and Great Crested Grebes moult in Ulvedybet. They are joined by increasing numbers of waders and ducks in autumn. By December, many of the birds will have departed the area but there are still plenty of swans, ducks and raptors to make a mouth-watering birding spectacle.

SPECIES

◆ *Breeding season* Pintail, Marsh Harrier, Water Rail, waders, Reed and Sedge Warblers, Bearded Tit.
◆ *Passage* Great Crested Grebe (summer moult), Mute Swan, Wigeon, Teal, Mallard, Pochard, Goldeneye, Osprey, Coot, waders (especially Temminck's Stint in spring).
◆ *Winter* Mute and Whooper Swans, Tufted Duck, Red-breasted Merganser, Buzzard, Rough-legged Buzzard, Hen Harrier, Peregrine, Shore Lark, Twite, Snow Bunting.

ACCESS

The lagoon is 20-km west of north-west of Ålborg; a car is needed. Take road A11 between Ålborg and Thisted. At Halvrimmen (31 km from Ålborg, 66 km from Thisted), turn south to Øland. Drive through the broad-leaved wood (Oksholm Skov), and, in the wood, turn left to Østerby to the dyke, where there is an observation tower.

# HIRSHOLMENE AND DEGET

57°30N 10°36E

Hirsholmene are a group of stony islands, situated in Kattegat 6-km north-east of Frederikshavn. The islands, and the waters which surround them, were protected in 1929, as one of the first reserves in Denmark. In 1981, the protection was enlarged and a total of 2000 ha of sea and all the islands (including Deget to the south) are now a National Reserve.

TIMING

In spring and summer, the islands are host to large breeding colonies of gulls and terns. Migrant spring birds, include many passerines (regular Bluethroat and Lapland Bunting). There is still plenty of interest in the winter with divers, seaducks and auks in the waters around the islands.

SPECIES

◆ *Breeding season* Black-headed Gull (10,000 pairs), Herring Gull, Great Black-backed Gull, Lesser Black-backed Gull, Kittiwake (Nordre Rønner), Sandwich Tern (1500–3000 pairs), Black Guillemot (500 pairs), Rock Pipit (45 pairs).

◆ *Passage* Wryneck, passerines (e.g. Bluethroat and Lapland Bunting).

◆ *Winter* Red-throated Diver, Eider, Common Scoter, Razorbill.

ACCESS

Access is by fishing boat from Frederikshavn (access described under Skagen). A regular boat service leaves in the morning.

# SKAGEN
57°43N 10°35E

Skagen is the northernmost tip of Jutland. The city is beautifully positioned in lowland sand dunes with pine plantations; to the north and east of the town, boggy heathland is found. In summer Skagen's picturesque buildings, painted mainly yellow and red, are an important tourist attraction; visited by thousands of tourists, who come also to see the meeting of the two seas, Skagerrak and Kattegat. Shagen is, however, never crowded in the birding seasons. 350 ha of moorland between Batterivej and Grenen are protected, as is the 10-ha town park and 62 ha of sand dunes and agricultural land south-west of Skagen (close to Flagbakken and Den Tilsandede Kirke).

Skagen is an excellent spring migration point, visited by growing numbers of birdwatchers. Up to the spring of 1994, a total of 332 species had been recorded here (the highest number at a single location in Denmark), of which, in the last 20 years, 7 have been new national records.

TIMING

Spring migration starts early here with the passage of seabirds beginning in March; divers and raptors (especially northern breeding species) numbers build

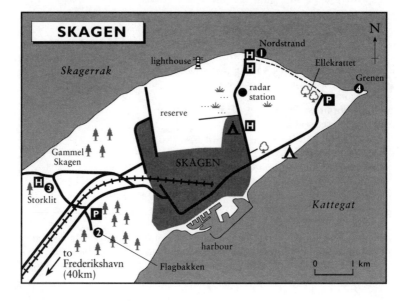

up towards late April and early May. This is also when passerine migration can be at its most impressive, Hooded Crow (up to 10,000 in one day). Day counts have included 2500 divers, 600 Rough-legged Buzzards, 135 Hen Harriers and several hundred falcons! The migration is especially rewarding in winds from the east. There is always an excellent chance of finding rarities in spring; the later in the season, the more likely a vagrant is to turn up.

In late summer plenty of terns are around. In autumn skuas are regular, often including concentrations; juvenile Long-tailed Skuas may be observed at close range. As autumn approaches, the birdwatching improves with huge numbers of seabirds particularly during strong north-westerly winds. Passerine migrants also pass through from September to early November. From December to March, the gull flocks may harbour rare species; including regular Glaucous and Iceland Gulls.

SPECIES

◆ *Breeding season* Avocet (Jerrup Strand), Arctic and Sandwich Terns, Nightjar, Tawny Pipit, Woodlark, Crested Lark, Crested Tit, Redpoll, Common Rosefinch.

◆ *Passage* Red-throated Diver, Great Northern and White-billed Divers (both regular early May and late autumn), Gannet, pelagics, Rough-legged Buzzard, Marsh and Hen Harriers, Sparrowhawk, Osprey, Hobby, Peregrine, Merlin, Kestrel, skuas (all species regular in autumn), auks, Wryneck, Red-throated Pipit, Great Grey Shrike, Bluethroat, Red-breasted Flycatcher, Lapland Bunting, rarities.

◆ *Winter* Seaducks, Herring, Glaucous and Iceland Gulls, Parrot Crossbill, Arctic Redpoll (both frequent during influxes).

ACCESS

Skagen is 40-km north-east of Frederikshavn, and is easily reached by car (take the A10 until it ends!). There are several trains and buses from Frederikshavn. Frederikshavn is a travel crossroads, with ferry services to Gothenburg and Norway, and several daily trains to Copenhagen (and the rest of Denmark).

Spring migration is best observed from Nordstrand (1), actually the northernmost tip of Denmark (not Grenen!). If the wind is southerly or south-easterly, Nordstrand is the best place to watch the migration throughout the day. Nordstrand itself, as well as small bunkers and dunes at the northern part of Batterivej, are good observation spots. The Storklit/Pælebakke Klit (3) is an alternative observation site.

In other winds, most raptors are seen from Flagbakken (2) and from the middle of Batterivej. Ellekrattet and inner part of Batterivej are especially good spots for passerines. Grenen (4) may be good in westerly winds, and on certain mornings, passerine migration is better here than at Nordstrand. It is the place to see seabirds in autumn.

Skagen can be surprisingly devoid of birds, so a few other areas between Skagen and Frederikshavn are worth a mention. Although not primarily birding areas, they may offer a nice break or a pleasant way to spend a westerly wind dominated day. Råbjerg Mile (take road 40, leading west 8-km north of Ålbæk from A10) consists of large, inland sand dunes (the largest in Northern Europe), wet heathland and pine plantations, (for 'hard-core' birders, only to be recommended on days with westerly winds!).

Jerup Strand (at A10/road 40, 13-km north-east of Frederikshavn, just north of Jerup, take a small dirt road to an abandoned hut at the coastline) holds breeding waders and terns and has migrant waders, especially in late summer and autumn.

*Hooded Crow*

# SOUTHERN PART OF LANGELAND

54°45N 10°40E

The southernmost tip of the island Langeland, Dovns Klint, is a good autumn migration spot. Breeding birds are present at the nearby Gulstav Mose (8 ha) and Tryggelev Nor (85 ha). These are reed-fringed, lowland lakes, both with observation towers. The Dovns Klint area is protected. Tryggelev Nor is a private reserve (Fugleværnsfonden).

TIMING

Interest in spring is mainly confined to breeding wetland birds and the nesting season lasts from late March until June. In the summer months, wader numbers start to build up, the birds having returned on migration from their breeding grounds further north in Europe. As the autumn progresses, raptors pass through in good numbers and seaduck, geese and passerines also appear in good numbers. There is still some birdwatching interest during the winter months with seaduck present in sizeable flocks.

SPECIES

◆ *Breeding season* Great Crested, Little and Red-necked Grebes, Bittern, Gadwall, Marsh Harrier, Water Rail, Marsh and Savi's Warblers (Sædballe Fredsmose), Golden Oriole, Bearded Tit, Common Rosefinch.

◆ *Passage* Brent and Barnacle Geese, Eider, Osprey, Honey Buzzard, Sparrowhawk, Marsh and Hen Harriers, Red Kite, rare raptors, waders (e.g. Curlew and Wood Sandpipers and Temminck's Stint), Woodpigeon, passerines.

◆ *Winter* Scaup, Eider.

ACCESS

Dovns Klint is the southernmost tip of the island of Langeland. From the road between Rudkøbing and Bagenkop (2 km from Bagenkop) turn to Gulstav. At the end of the road, a parking spot is situated at the foot of the 16-m high cliff. The more westerly Gulstav Klint may be used in westerly winds.

Tryggelev Nor is situated c. 8-km north of Dovns Klint. This private reserve (owned by Fugleværnsfonden) is reached from the same road described above in the village of Nordenbro, following signs towards Vestereng. After 3 km turn north at a T-junction towards Stenbæk. After a few hundred metres, the southern part (Salme Nor) is visible. There is a parking spot, with signs to the observation tower and an information hut. Several signs make it easy to find the place.

# BRÆNDEGÅRD SØ AND NØRRE SØ

56°15N 14°4E

These two lakes nestle in a wooded setting similar to Southern Scania. Nørre Sø covers 73 ha, Brændegårds Sø 117 ha. The two lakes and their surrounding woodland (in total 532 ha) are protected as a Nature Reserve.

TIMING

From March to June, the attractions of this site are the colonies of breeding waterbirds. The woods harbour good numbers of breeding raptors and some songbirds. For sheer numbers, autumn and winter are the seasons to visit: larger flocks of diving ducks appear and raptors are also well represented.

SPECIES

◆ *Breeding season* Great Crested Grebe, Cormorant (4000 pairs), Grey Heron, Greylag Goose, common raptors, Woodcock, Icterine Warbler, Thrush Nightingale, Raven, Short-toed Treecreeper.

◆ *Passage* Ducks, raptors (including Osprey).

◆ *Winter* Diving ducks, White-tailed Eagle and Peregrine (both regular).

ACCESS

The area is reached by road between Nyborg and Fåborg. 1-km east of Brahetrolleborg, turn south towards Brændegård. After a few hundred metres, there is a parking spot at Nørre Sø, with tracks into the wood. The more bird-rich Brændegård Sø is reached by driving further 2 km. At Brændegård, there is a parking spot, overlooking the lake and the colony of Cormorants.

# HYLLEKROG/MARIBOSØERNE

54°42N 11°27E

The Maribo lakes and the wooded surroundings comprise an area of roughly 1300 ha of lakes, partly overgrown with reedbeds. There are several lakes within the boundaries of the site: Maribo Søndersø, Hejrede Sø and Røgbølle Sø. Lungholm Inddæmning is a lowland, agricultural area (100 ha) to the east including the Hyllekrog peninsula, the name used by birdwatchers for the whole area east of the ferry-harbour of Rødby. 1100 ha of Maribo lakes and the surrounding woodland are protected. Small islets (Tjørneholm and Hylleholm) are reserves with access prohibited from 1 March to 15 July. The shallow water area at Rødsand, to the east of Hyllekrog, is a reserve for seals. Access is prohibited 1 March to 30 September. The Hyllekrog area is a Ramsar Site.

TIMING

From March to June, the breeding wetland birds of the area are the main birdwatching attraction. It is not until September that significant numbers of ducks arrive, their numbers building up to a peak in December. The duck flocks attract the occasional White-tailed Eagle.

SPECIES

◆ *Breeding season* Great Crested and Red-necked Grebes, Bittern, Greylag Goose, Gadwall, Marsh Harrier, Honey Buzzard, Goshawk, Black-tailed Godwit (Hyllekrog), Golden Oriole, Red-backed Shrike, Great Reed Warbler (occasional), Thrush Nightingale.

◆ *Passage* Greylag Goose (up to 5000 in autumn), Ducks (Gadwalls up to 150), raptor migration and waders (Hyllekrog), passerines (often impressive migration of Swallows at Hyllekrog).

◆ *Winter* Bean and Canada Geese, Tufted Duck (up to 35,000), Pochard (up to 3000), White-tailed Eagle.

ACCESS

The surroundings of Maribo Lakes are private, but access is possible from several small tracks leading to the lakeside. Hyllekrog is reached from the road leading south from the Rødby to Errindlev road. 5.5 km from Rødby, take the road to Bunddrag, where parking is possible right on the coast; this is the best observation site for migration.

# GEDSER

54°33N 11°57E

Gedser Odde is the southern tip of the island of Falster. It consists of agricultural land with scattered, low plantations and holiday villages. Bøtø Nor is a small, lowland lake surrounded by wet meadows, covering 173 ha, with two protected areas. Although some interesting wetland birds breed on the lake, the area is best known as a migration spot. Spring migration is comparatively poor but, in autumn, Gedser Odde can be one the best sites in Europe for movements of seabirds, raptors and passerines.

TIMING

Breeding wetland birds in spring. By late July and early August movements of terns and waders have begun. Other seabird numbers are highest from September to early November with ducks and *Branta* geese; skuas are regular, sometimes in huge numbers; Little Gulls are a speciality late in the season. Easterly winds encourage a stream of ducks and geese while raptor migration is best in northerly winds following a cold period. By mid-November, the migratory movements of birds have dwindled but Long-tailed Ducks are present at sea.

SPECIES

◆ *Breeding season* Gadwall, Greylag Goose, Marsh Harrier, Common Rosefinch.

◆ *Passage* Brent and Barnacle Geese, Eider (up to 50,000 per day), Scaup, Wigeon, White-tailed Eagle (scarce but regular), Honey Buzzard, Buzzard, Rough-legged Buzzard (200–400 per day not unusual), Sparrowhawk, skuas (in influx years many juvenile Pomarines in late October), Little Gull (up to 1000 per day), passerines, rarities.

◆ *Winter* Bean and Canada Geese, Long-tailed Duck, some raptors.

ACCESS

From the town of Gedser, take small dirt roads leading to the southern tip. Park at the military station. Bøtø Nor is situated 8 km north of Gedser. From the road between Gedser and Nykøbing, turn east at Marrebæk, and at a T-junction in Bøtø, turn south for 3 km. There is parking at Lævej, close to the two observation towers/platforms.

# MØN

54°58N 12°15E

Møn is a flat island, rising to the east, where large sea-cliffs at Høje Møn, are covered by broad-leaved woodland. To the north-west, the island of Nyord and the peninsula of Ulvshale harbour extensive wet meadows. 2085 ha of the eastern part (Høje Møn), are protected as is most of the peninsula of Ulvshale (1110 ha). Part of the meadows at Nyord (400 ha) is a private reserve (owned by Fugleværnsfonden).

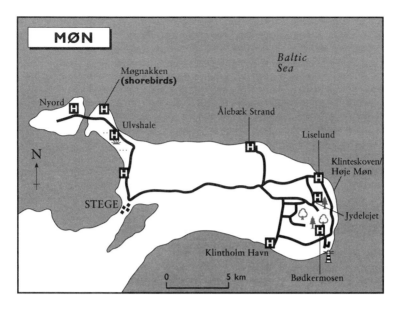

Høje Møn woodlands are very good for passerines, both breeding species and resting migrants. In Bødkermosen, Mandemarke Bakker and Jydelejet hundreds of warblers, flycatchers and chats may be present in May. The area is also noted for migrating raptors and its rarities (e.g. Denmark's first Rüppell's Warbler) and several records of rare eagles and Pallid Harrier.

TIMING
During the breeding season, wetland birds are the speciality of the region. Woodland species are also present (a few singing Red-breasted Flycatchers and Greenish Warblers from late May). In July and August, waders gather at Ulvshale but from September to November, geese flocks are the main attraction; Check Klintholm Havn for Yellow-legged Gulls in early autumn.

SPECIES
◆ *Breeding season* Garganey, Pintail, Shoveler, waders (e.g. Ruff and Black-tailed Godwit), Tawny Owl, Wryneck, Golden Oriole, Greenish Warbler, Red-breasted Flycatcher, Common Rosefinch.
◆ *Passage* Stork species (both regular), Barnacle and Brent Geese (autumn), Hobby, Red-footed Falcon, waders, gulls, terns, Ring Ouzel, Ortolan Bunting, rarities.
◆ *Winter* Mute Swan, Canada Goose, raptors.

ACCESS
Møn is reached from the E4 between Rødby and Copenhagen. At Vording-borg, take the road to Stege/Møn. In Stege (the main city of Møn), continue eastwards (for Klinteskoven), or turn north to Ulvshale. In Ulvshale, turn east to Nyord, which is reached from a bridge – often good for ducks. Then continue for 500 m until the observation tower (situated in small plantation) is reached. Good views over the meadows are available, and an information exhibition is present. Bring a telescope – or stay in the car if you observe the birds from the road. Alternatively, drive to a small churchyard at Nyord. The small woods and scrub are often good for migrants.

For resting waders, park at camping site in Ulvshale, and walk north-east along the beach to reach the northern tip.

Klinteskoven is reached by driving eastwards from Stege. After 20 km, the road passes a camping site. Here, turn north for 100 m to a parking place at a farm. From here, walk eastward in a beautifully surrounded valley (Jydelejet) to the sea. Jydelejet and more open areas to the south are often even better for migrants. Bødkermosen is reached by turning south in village of Borre towards Klintholm. 3 km south of Borre, turn east towards Busene. After 2 km, Mandemarke Bakker rises to the north. Further to the east, Bødkermosen is situated. When the road turns north, there is a track leading east along a plantation. Walk for about 1 km.

# STIGSNÆS/GLÆNØ

55°12N 11°26E

The south-western tip of Zealand, Stigsnæs is regarded as the 'Falsterbo of Eastern Denmark': in the autumn, the migration of geese, ducks, raptors and passerines can be spectacular. Yearly averages of certain species include 20,000 Buzzards, 2300 Honey Buzzards, 4200 Sparrowhawks, 50 Ospreys, 160 Marsh Harriers, 150 Hen Harriers and 50 Red Kites; many hundreds of thousands of Chaffinches and Bramblings pass through each September and October.

There are sheltered bays, areas of mature woodlands, wetlands and agricultural land. The wooded island of Glænø has coastal meadows. Shallow coastal waters (Holsteinsborg and Basnæs Nor) divide the island from the mainland, to which Glænø is connected by a dam. Borreby Mose is protected and is a Ramsar Site. 276 ha at the northern part of Holsteinsborg Nor, and 980 ha of Basnæs Nor are a game reserve; Glænø Vesterfed is a game reserve with hunting prohibited. There is no access to Glænø Veste and Østerfed (wet meadows) between 1 March and 30 June.

### TIMING

During the spring, breeding wetland birds are the main attraction, the colony of Cormorants at Ormø being notable as well as a good number of waterbirds at Borreby Mose north of Stignæs. Honey Buzzard, Osprey and Marsh Harrier migration starts in August and by the beginning of September migration of other species is really under way. Raptors, geese, doves and passerines migrate in largest numbers in south-westerly or sometimes southerly winds; visible migration effectively ceases during periods of northerly winds. In winter, the area, especially Glænø, is best for flocks of swans and geese as well as raptors.

### SPECIES

- *Breeding season* Red-necked Grebe, Cormorant (4000 pairs at Ormø), dabbling ducks, Marsh Harrier, Water Rail, shorebirds, Marsh and Reed Warblers, Bearded Tit, Black Redstart.
- *Passage* Greylag Goose, ducks, Buzzard, Honey Buzzard, Marsh and Hen Harriers, Red Kite, Osprey, Sparrowhawk, Red-throated Pipit, Grey Wagtail, all common passerines, Ortolan Bunting.
- *Winter* Mute and Whooper Swans, Bean and Canada Geese, dabbling ducks, Tufted Duck, Goldeneye, Goosander, Red-breasted Merganser, White-tailed Eagle, Buzzard, Rough-legged Buzzard, Hen Harrier, Goshawk, Coot.

ACCESS

Stigsnæs is reached from Skælskør by a road leading south towards Borreby and Stigsnæs. Borreby Mose is passed after 2–3 km. The best observation site is your own car. Stigsnæs itself is reached by continuing a few kilometres, then turn west to Stigsnæs. You will drive through a wood, where the road suddenly ends in a small harbour (with small ferries leading to Agersø and Omø – itself worth a visit for birds). At the parking place, walk north along dyke, from where migration may be observed. The wood here is now rather overgrown, and this, together with the late morning lighting, makes the harbour itself a better choice, or walking a few hundred metres along the dyke.

Glænø is reached by a small road leading east at Magleby. Drive to Ørslev, and from here south-east to Glænø via a dyke. To reach Vesterfed, continue to the first farm, and park the car, then take the track leading to this protected area; note that there is no access during breeding season. Ormø is best overlooked from Glænø Skov. Continue along the only road about 1.5 km from the dyke, and turn north on to a dirt track leading to the wood. Park at the end of the track, and walk eastwards for a few hundred metres.

# STEVNS

55°17N 12°28E

Stevns is an area of agricultural land with small, mixed woodland. The seacliffs of Stevns are not as large as at Møen, but worth visiting for migrating raptors in autumn.

Autumn migration numbers are often impressive, equalling or sometimes surpassing, Falsterbo counts. It is best observed in light westerlies and on such days, thousands of Buzzards pass by along with hundreds of many other raptor species. Stevns' main advantage is that migration in from the sea is low level, but movements may take place over a 10–15 km broad front. In the morning, most migrating birds are seen from the southern part of Stevns, whereas the afternoon migration is more to the north. Best observation sites are Højerup Church in the mornings and Bøgeskoven in the afternoons.

Spring migration, which is usually good in westerlies and includes not only raptors but also pigeons and passerines, is best observed from Bøgeskoven.

TIMING

Stevns is interesting mainly as a migration watching site, especially in autumn. From March to May, the migration of raptors and passerines is best observed in north-westerly winds; autumn migration lasts from mid-August until November. There is little of birdwatching interest during the winter months.

SPECIES

◆ *Passage* Buzzard, Honey Buzzard, Hen and Marsh Harriers, Red Kite, Sparrowhawk, other raptors (including eagles), doves, passerines.

ACCESS

Højerup is reached by taking small roads from Køge and Store Heddinge. Park at the parking place just by the church and walk a short distance to the coast. Storedal (at Tommestrup) is another good site, as well as Mandehoved (especially in light winds) and both are reached from the village of Sigerslev. Further to the north, Bøgeskoven is a good site (at Gjorslev); in spring this is the best place.

# ØLSEMAGLE REVLE/KØGE HAVN

55°27N 12°11E

Ølsemagle Revle consists of low sand dunes and a sheltered, shallow shore; there are small reedbeds, wet meadows and bays. Access to the north and south tips are prohibited from 1 April to 15 July to protect breeding birds.

### TIMING

There is birdwatching interest here for much of the year. Breeding terns and other coastal birds are present in good numbers from April to June, and in July and August waders and terns provide the interest. As autumn approaches, flocks of geese arrive and, from September to November, the movements of seabirds are sometimes notable (best from Køge Havn). Many of the waders and ducks remain in the area for winter and raptors and passerines add interest on land.

### SPECIES

◆ *Breeding season* Waders, Arctic and Little Terns, Yellow Wagtail.
◆ *Passage* Brent and Barnacle Geese, Eider, waders (both Broad-billed Sandpiper, and Red-necked Phalarope), skuas, Little Gull, terns (including Caspian and Black Terns).
◆ *Winter* Eider, Rough-legged Buzzard, Hen Harrier, Dunlin, Short-eared Owl, Twite, Snow Bunting.

### ACCESS

Køge Havn is reached immediately east of the railway station of Køge; the southern pier is best. Ølsemagle Revle is located 5 km to the north, just east of the village of Ølsemagle. Take the dirt road to the east (at the reningsverk station), park the car and walk to the dam. The best spots for shorebirds are the dam itself and the points, which are closed in the breeding season. There are several buses between Copenhagen (Valby Station) and Køge.

# TISSØ

55°35N 11°18E

Tissø comprises 1330 ha of lake, surrounded by agricultural land, and fringed on the eastern side by reedbeds; 75 ha on the south-eastern shore are protected.

### TIMING

Good numbers of wetland breeding birds can be found here, and many ducks and waders (especially Ruff in May) stop during migration. Numbers of migrant waders and ducks start to build up again from mid-July onwards and geese and swans start arriving from October until mid-November. Winter is the time for swans, ducks and geese in large flocks as well as for raptors.

### SPECIES

◆ *Breeding season* Marsh Harrier, ducks, waders, Marsh, Reed and Grasshopper Warblers.
◆ *Passage* Great Crested Grebe, Bewick's Swan (October and November), Greylag Goose, Caspian Tern (summer), waders.
◆ *Winter* Whooper and Mute Swans, Canada Geese, ducks, Golden and White-tailed Eagles (both regular), Buzzard, Peregrine, Kingfisher, Dipper (the two latter at Strido Mølle north of Tissø).

### ACCESS

The best observation spots are at the south-east corner (at Sæby Church) and the north-east lake shore. Both places are easily reached and viewed by car but there is no access to the lake shore itself.

# AMAGER

55°37N 12°35E

This island lies on the eastern edge of Copenhagen. It is mostly built up, but the south-western part has several large open areas with mixed birch, scrub and wetlands. The southern part of the reclaimed area, Vestamager, is protected (1652 ha, of which 400 ha is a bird reserve). Bird life was richer once; some of the wetland areas are now overgrown. Wetlands between Konge-lunden and Dragør are protected. Aflandshage is a game reserve and military area with prohibited access.

TIMING

Despite the proximity to urban areas, many wetland and open country birds breed here in good numbers. The return wader migration starts in mid-July and builds up through August. It is followed, from September to November, by movements of raptors and passerines. In winter, waterbirds are present especially in Kalveboderne west of Vestamager.

SPECIES

◆ *Breeding season* Red-necked Grebe, Garganey, Marsh Harrier, waders, Grasshopper Warblers, Thrush Nightingale, Penduline Tit.

◆ *Passage* Raptors, waders (including Broad-billed Sandpiper and Red-necked Phalarope), Common, Arctic and Caspian Terns, passerines (including Red-throated Pipits in September).

◆ *Winter* Little Grebe, Tufted Duck, Pochard, Goldeneye, Goosander, Smew, Rough-legged Buzzard, Hen Harrier, Kestrel, Coot, Short-eared Owl, Great Grey Shrike, Nutcracker (occasional), Twite.

ACCESS

Amager Fælled is north of the main road between Kastrup Airport and the main road south of Copenhagen. At the crossing at Englandvej, turn north to Grønjordskollegiet, where parking is possible. Walk a few hundred metres south-west until the lake is reached (grebes, sometimes Black-necked included).

*Avocet*

Vestamager is crossed by the main road between Copenhagen and Rødby. It is, however, not possible to drive, and you may enter the area only on foot (take at least half a day) or by bike. Sydvestpynten/ Kongelunden is reached by 36 bus from Kastrup Airport.

# UTTERSLEV MOSE

55°41N 12°34E

The site comprises three lakes with reedbeds in an urban setting; it offers genuine good birding as well as easy access from the Danish capital of Copenhagen, the whole area covering 80 ha. It is best known for its breeding birds, many of which are very tame, and is good for migrating ducks and raptors, especially in autumn.

TIMING
During the months of March to June, the breeding colonies of waterbirds, notably Greylag Geese and Black-headed Gulls, are the main attraction of Utterslev Mose. Geese and ducks are here in large numbers in August and, from September to November, raptors and passerines pass through. The small wintering group of Long-eared Owls (at Holmevej) is of interest in the winter.
SPECIES
◆ *Resident* Greylag Goose, Bearded Tit.
◆ *Breeding season* Great Crested Grebe, Greylag Goose (50–100 pairs), Tufted Duck, Pochard, Reed, Marsh and Icterine Warblers, Thrush Nightingale.
◆ *Passage* Buzzard (up to 1000 per day in westerly winds), Osprey (mainly April), Common Crane (mainly in easterly winds), passerines.
◆ *Winter* Bittern, ducks, Long-eared Owl, Waxwing, Fieldfare.
ACCESS
Very easy to reach from Copenhagen with several bus lines (e.g. 5, 7, 8, 16, 19, 63, 68 and 330). There is an extensive system of paths around the lakes. Utterslev Mose is very good for photographing and observing commoner wetland species as the breeding species are tame.

# Rørvig/Hovvig

55°58N 11°52E
The Rørvig peninsula consists of a tourist area and a fine sandy coastline. Migration (including seawatching in autumn) is best observed from Korshage. On good days, hundreds of Buzzards can be seen along with excellent numbers of most migrants typical of the region; e.g. 100,000 Chaffinches on single days in April. The inland lake and reedbeds of Hovvig hold migrating waterbirds as well as breeding wetland species. There is an observation tower at the eastern side of Hovvig. Several smaller areas near the tip (Korshage), Dybesø and Hovvig are protected. Hundested Harbour is good for gulls in winter.

TIMING
In the spring, migrating birds can be seen in the area from March until the end of May; landbird migration is best in easterly to south-easterly winds. At the same time, Hovvig has a good range of breeding wetland birds. From late July, wader migration begins along the coast with many of the birds stopping to rest at Hovvig. As the first gales of autumn hit the coast, seabird migration can be seen offshore in north-westerly winds. Winter is the time to see seaducks in the area with thousands of Eiders being the main attraction.
SPECIES
◆ *Resident* Black Woodpecker.
◆ *Breeding season* Red-necked and Black-necked Grebes, ducks, Marsh Harrier, Lapwing, Redshank, Redpoll, Common Rosefinch.
◆ *Passage* Seabirds (autumn), White and Black Storks (rare), raptors (spring), waders, Kittiwake, skuas, Wryneck, Woodpigeon, pipits, warblers, flycatchers, Bluethroat.

◆ *Winter* Divers, Velvet and Common Scoters, Eider, King Eider (rare), auks.

ACCESS

Korshage is reached from a road in Rørvig, where signs show the way to Korshage. Hovvig is reached from Nakke (south-west of Rørvig, on the road between Rørvig and Nykøbing). From Nakke, turn south for about 1.5 km to a crossing, where a sign points west to Hovvig. After a further 500 m of driving, a parking-place is reached. Walk from here 100 m or so west before reaching the dam and the observation tower, overlooking the wetlands.

# TISVILDE HEGN
56°4N 12°5E

Tisvilde Hegn comprises 2000 ha of mixed plantations (mainly conifer) on the north Zealand coastline; the coastal area is dominated by sand dunes. 145 ha of heathland at Melby Overdrev are protected (but are still used for military training) as are several small parts of the forest. The rest of the woodland is state forest. Birdwatchers should be warned that, in summer, the area attracts bathers, including nudists. Fortunately, wader migration usually takes place on colder, more windy days, when removing clothing is the last thing a visitor would want to do!

TIMING

In the spring, a good range of woodland species can be found breeding in the area and the migration of raptors and passerines adds extra interest. Waders begin their return migration in late July, their numbers building up as autumn approaches; westerly winds are best for these birds. Main migration is in spring, when landbirds migrate in easterlies and south-easterlies (see Gilleleje). Autumn months of September to November are unpredictable but north-westerlies bring seabirds close to shore.

SPECIES

◆ *Resident* Goshawk, Black Woodpecker, Crossbill.
◆ *Breeding season* Nightjar, Woodlark, Mistle Thrush, Tawny Pipit (rare; has probably disappeared), Redpoll.
◆ *Passage* Divers, raptors (spring), Bar-tailed Godwit (up to 1000 in late July), Sanderling, Whimbrel, Kittiwake, passerines.
◆ *Winter* Divers, Eider, Scoter, Velvet Scoter, auks, Crossbill, Nutcracker, Parrot Crossbill and Two-barred Crossbill (in irruption years).

ACCESS

From the village of Tisvildeleje you can walk in the woods and along the shoreline. Those preferring a more peaceful site will find Asserbo Strand and Melby Overdrev best. Both are reached by car from the road between Helsinge and Melby. At Sandkroen, turn west at a T-junction (signs leading to Liseleje 5), after c. 2 km, a (well hidden) sign showing Kattegat 2, leading to a dirt road to the beach. Black Woodpecker occurs anywhere in the wood. At the parking place at Stængehus, walk 100 m until the beach is reached. Migration is best observed from the sand dunes.

# ALSØNDERUP ENGE/NEJEDE VESTERSKOV
55°56N 12°19E

The artificial lake of Alsønderup is a bird reserve of 300 ha; bordered by old, mixed woodland at Nejede, and was created in 1987; nearby Solbjerg Enge was created in 1993.

TIMING

Spring is the time to visit these lakes for breeding grebes, Greylag Geese and ducks, the months of April–June being best. The return migration of waders begins in late July; summer–early autumn also sees Osprey fishing regularly. Geese, ducks and raptors pass through from September to November and, during the winter, flocks of geese and swans provide interest, as well as regular White-tailed Eagle.

SPECIES

◆ *Breeding season* Red-necked and Little Grebes, Black-necked Grebe, Greylag Goose, Garganey, Gadwall, Buzzard, Goshawk, Redshank, Wood Warbler, Chiffchaff, Treecreeper, Penduline Tit (occasional).

◆ *Passage* Geese, ducks, Osprey, Marsh Harrier, Ruff, Little Ringed Plover, Greenshank, Redshank, Wood Sandpiper, Curlew Sandpiper.

◆ *Winter* Whooper Swan, Canada Goose, dabbling ducks, Smew, White-tailed Eagle, Dipper (Solbjerg Engsø), Raven.

ACCESS

The observation tower is reached from Nejede. Use the parking stop in Nejede Vesterskov, reached by the small road between Nejede and Alsønderup (a small wooden sign may easily be overlooked), and walk for about 1 km through the woods to reach the observation tower (follow yellow spots on large trees). Birds may be distant, so bring a telescope.

# HELLEBÆK

56°4N 12°32E

This is an area of mixed woodland, reed-fringed lakes and agricultural land; parts of the site are military areas. Hellebæk Gods is state-owned and 350 ha of woodland and the lakes of Bøgeholm Sø, Bondedammen and Kobberdam are protected. The main birdwatching interest comes from the area's observation opportunities for migrating raptors which are most varied in spring. Yearly autumn totals of Buzzard regularly surpass those of Falsterbo, often reaching 10,000–17,000 individuals per season.

TIMING

Spring highlights in the area include migrating raptors, most varied in April, and breeding wetland and woodland birds. Raptors are again good in autumn as they return south. The winter months are not very productive.

SPECIES

◆ *Resident* Goshawk, Black Woodpecker.

◆ *Breeding season* Greylag Goose, Green Sandpiper.

◆ *Passage* Divers (autumn), White-tailed and Golden Eagles (annual), Osprey (up to 95 have been recorded in one day in April), Buzzards (more than 1000 per day in March), other raptors, Common Crane, Short-eared Owl, Great Grey Shrike.

ACCESS

The area is easily reached by bus or road from Helsingør. By car from Copenhagen, take the road to Helsingør; just west of Helsingør, turn west through Græsted. After c. 7 km, at a crossing, turn north to Nygård, and from here to Hellebæk. By rail, take the train for Gilleleje, and get off at Hellebæk. From here (or if you arrive by coastal road 237 between Helsingør and Hornbæk) take the south road at Bøssemagerstræde; by foot, walk south-west until an open hilly area is reached. By car, continue c. 2 km after crossing the railway until the large farm building at the parking spot is reached. The best observation site is the hilly countryside between the villages of Hellebæk and Nygård. The area is regularly used for military training.

# GILLELEJE

56°8N 12°19E

The northernmost tip of Zealand, Gilleleje, is a picturesque fishing village. A short distance to the west of the village, Gilbjerghoved rises about 40 m above sea level and overlooks agricultural land; there are also small pockets of woodland and gardens. 48-ha west of Gilleleje (at Gilbjerghoved) and 50 ha east of Gilleleje are protected, primarily for recreational use.

The best time to visit is mid-April, where North Zealand migration is most varied. It is, however, extremely weather dependent and so you should check the weather forecast. Migration is often as good as at Skagen later in the season; Danish observers regard migration at Gilleleje as being the spring counterpart to Falsterbo!

## TIMING

Spectacular spring migration from March to mid-May; southerly to south-easterly winds are best, especially associated with warm weather from the south. On such days, an endless stream of raptors, Woodpigeons and passerines passes at close range, with numbers of passerines, for example, regularly exceeding 100,000 birds per day. In fact, migration for some species such as Jackdaw starts as early as February but it is from mid-March onwards that the greatest variety is seen, the peak being in mid- to late April. Daily counts for selected species include 3000 Barnacle Geese, 1000 Buzzards, 500 Rough-legged Buzzards, 85 Ospreys, 1000 Common Cranes, 10,000 Fieldfares, 26,000 Meadow Pipits and 200,000 Chaffinches and Bramblings. Ring Ouzels are regular in the last half of April.

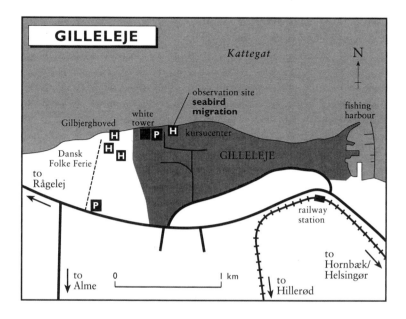

Summer months are generally quiet but in strong north-westerlies, July and August can produce migrating waders and pelagic seabirds. Seabird migration begins in earnest in autumn, strong north-westerlies again producing the best results; daily counts include 400 Fulmars, 36 Manx Shearwaters, 30 Long-tailed Skuas and 10,000 Kittiwakes.

The fishing harbour regularly holds gulls, especially following storms; wintering gulls occasionally include interesting species.

SPECIES
- ◆ *Passage* Divers, pelagic seabirds (autumn), Eider, King Eider (rare), scoters, raptors, skuas (autumn), Kittiwake, Little Auk, passerines (including day migration of warblers and flycatchers in May).
- ◆ *Winter* Eider, gulls (regular Glaucous Gull (especially January to April)).

ACCESS
Gilbjerghoved is situated 2-km east of Gilleleje. There are trains every hour from Helsingør and Hillerød (connections several times an hour to Copenhagen). A regular bus service passes close to Gilbjerghoved. It takes roughly one hour to drive from Copenhagen. To Gilbjerghoved, go east from Gilleleje to Rågeleje. On the outskirts of Gilleleje, a large open area can be found. Park the car at a parking place at Gilbjerghoved, and walk a few hundred metres north. Migration is best overlooked from the hills and from Gilbjerghoved itself. Seabird migration is observed from several sheltered places between the harbour and Gilbjerghoved. In lighter easterly winds, migrants pass too far to the south to be observed from Gilbjerghoved, and are then better viewed from hills immediately to the south of Nakkehoved Fyr (Hesbjerg).

# BORNHOLM
50°46N 7°44E

Although small in area, this island in the Baltic contains most habitats typical of Denmark. Several small areas are protected. A selection of Danish woodland birds breeds here but Bornholm is better known as a migration spot.

TIMING
A few interesting birds breed on the island in spring and reasonable numbers of migrants pass through, interest being confined mainly to Common Cranes and raptors. In late July and August, returning migrant waders begin to arrive. Caspian Terns are regular but it is not until September that autumn migration really begins: huge numbers of geese and Common Cranes, as well as impressive numbers of Rough-legged Buzzards, pass through. Autumn migration lasts until November and, thereafter, wintering ducks and grebes provide the interest.

SPECIES
- ◆ *Breeding season* Common Crane (scarce), Black Woodpecker, Tengmalm's Owl (rare), Dipper (rare), Greenish Warbler (occasional), Common Rosefinch.
- ◆ *Passage* White-fronted, Barnacle and Brent Geese, ducks, Goshawk (mainly spring), Rough-legged Buzzard, other raptors, Common Crane, waders, Caspian Tern, passerines.
- ◆ *Winter* Slavonian Grebe, Eider, Long-tailed Duck.

ACCESS
Migration is generally best at Dueodde. Spring migration of raptors is best at the northern tip, Hammeren, where autumn movements of geese and ducks

can be seen well in north-westerly winds. Waders are restricted to the south-eastern part of the island (between Nexo and Snogebæk).

# CHRISTIANSØ

55°19N 15°11E

Christiansø is the largest of Ertholmene, a small group of rocky islands in the Baltics roughly 20-km east of Bornholm. The two main islands – Christiansø and Frederiksø – are inhabited, and there is a ringing station. The uninhabited islands are just small rocky outcrops with no public access. The whole area is protected, and Græsholm, an inhabited 11-ha island, is a bird reserve.

Large colonies of seabirds are a feature of the island, these comprising mainly 6000–8000 pairs of Herring Gulls and 2500 pairs Eiders. Græsholm has the only Danish breeding colonies of Guillemot (2500) and Razorbill (400); several other seabirds breed here in smaller numbers.

As a migration spot, especially for passerines, Christiansø is outstanding, both in spring and autumn, hosting thousands of migrants. Especially large numbers occur in foggy weather, whereas in clear weather many move to Bornholm during the day. In April, the main species are Goldcrest, Dunnock, Robin and thrushes while in May, warblers predominate: 1500 Lesser Whitethroats, 200 Icterine Warblers, 1200 Garden Warblers and 5000 Willow Warblers have occurred. Needless to say, unusual species are regular at migration times and this is the best Danish site for passerine rarities.

TIMING

Spring is the best season to visit this site: from April to late June, there are breeding colonies of Eider, gulls and auks to be seen. At this time of year, of course, migration is taking place and there is always a chance of something unusual turning up; south-easterly winds in May are best. Return passerine migration starts again from late July and continues through until November. From December to February, flocks of seaducks, notably Long-tailed Ducks, occur around the coast and Purple Sandpipers feed on the rocky shores.

SPECIES

◆ *Breeding season* Eider, Red-breasted Merganser, Herring, Common, Lesser Black-backed and Great Black-backed Gulls, Guillemot, Razorbill, Greenish Warbler, Common Rosefinch.

◆ *Passage* White-fronted and Barnacle Geese, Common Crane, Long-eared and Short-eared Owls, Lesser Whitethroat, Garden, Icterine, Wood, Greenish and Willow Warblers, Goldcrest, Pied, Spotted and Red-breasted Flycatchers, Dunnock, Robin, Bluethroat, thrushes, Ortolan Bunting, rarities (including regular Subalpine, Blyth's Reed, Radde's and Dusky Warblers), Pallas's and Yellow-browed Warblers in autumn, Little and Rustic Buntings (both almost yearly).

◆ *Winter* Eider, King and Steller's Eiders (both rare), Long-tailed Duck, Purple Sandpiper.

ACCESS

Daily rail service from Svaneke (departing in the morning, returning in the middle of the afternoon), and in summer months even from Gudhjem. If you arrive by ferry from Copenhagen, there are good bus connections from the harbour of Rønne to the ports.

# FINLAND

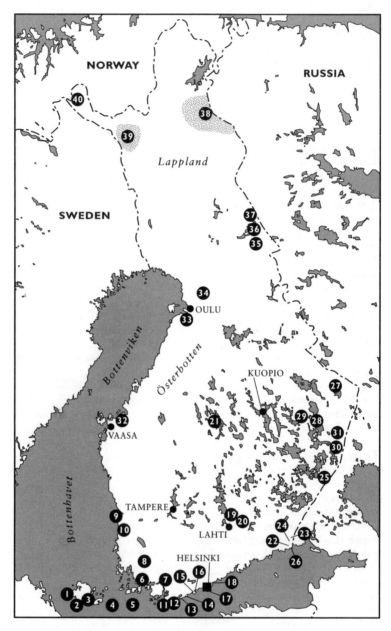

1 Signildskär, 2 Lågskär, 3 Herröskatan, 4 Kökar, 5 Korppoo Jurmo,
6 Turku Ruissalo (Runsala), 7 Salo Halikonlahti, 8 Kurjenrahka,
9 Pori Yyteri, 10 Pori Previikinlahti, 11 Hanko Täktom & Täktbukten,
12 Hanko Svanvik & Högholmen, 13 Kirkkonummi Porkkala,

14 PORKKALA TOWER, 15 ESPOON SUOMENOJA, 16 ESPOO LAAJALAHTI,
17 SUOMENLINNA (SVEABORG), 18 VIIKKI (VANHAKAUPUNGINLAHTI),
19 ASIKKALAN PULKKILANHARJU, 20 HEINOLA, 21 SAARIJÄRVI PYHÄ-HÄKKI,
22 VIROLAHTI VILKKILÄNTURA, 23 YLÄMAA SAMMALINEN, 24 LAKE VÄKEVÄNJÄRVI,
25 PARIKKALA SIIKALAHTI, 26 VIROLAHTI HURPPU, 27 PATVINSUO NATIONAL PARK,
28 HÖYTIÄINEN CANAL ESTUARY, 29 LAKE SYSMÄJÄRVI, 30 BAY PÄÄTYENLAHTI,
31 LAKE SÄÄPERI, 32 MUSTASAARI VASSORFJÄRDEN, 33 LIMINGANLAHTI,
34 HIRVISUO BOG, 35 KUUSAMO TORANKI, 36 KUUSAMO VALTAVAARA,
37 OULANKA NATIONAL PARK, 38 URHO KEKKONEN NATIONAL PARK,
39 PALLASTUNTURI – OUNASTUNTURI, 40 KILPISJÄRVI SAANA.

Finland stands between West and East. After the Ice Age most Finns came from the south, but their language is an eastern one which is not related to Indoeuropean languages of their neighbours. Finland was part of Sweden for some 700 years, and today some 4 per cent of the people still speak Swedish as their mother language. After the Swedish era Finland was part of Russia in the nineteenth century and 6 per cent of Finns belong to the Orthodox church (90 per cent to the western Lutheran church). Finland fought for her independence in 1918 and defended it successfully in the Second World War between 1939–1945. Nowadays Finland is a post-industrial society, which leads Scandinavian social welfare policy. Most young people can speak English.

Finland has over 5,000,000 inhabitants. It has one autonomous region, the Åland islands, which has its own flag and stamps. Many thousands of Lapps use their native language in local matters. The economy depends on its forests, but ships and cellular phones are important products too. Agriculture is in decline. The most important fishing industry is salmon farming.

## HABITATS

Finland is world famous for its thousands of lakes, taiga forests and bogs. In the south there is the unique Baltic archipelago and in the north, in Lapland, there is flat land with mountains and bogs.

## IMPORTANCE FOR BIRDS

In summer, Finland has 50,000,000 pairs of breeding birds, but 80–90 per cent of them leave in the autumn and migrate to the south. There are over 240 breeding species, 330 species are seen annually and 420 species have been recorded.

Finland has only three globally endangered breeding birds: White-fronted Goose (15–20 pairs), Spotted Eagle (0–2 pairs) and Corncrake (500–1000 pairs). However, Finland has the main responsibility for the protection of many eastern and northern European specialities. Terek Sandpiper, Red-flanked Bluetail and Yellow-breasted Bunting are the most famous eastern specialities of Finland. On the mountains, Rough-legged Buzzard, Dotterel, Ptarmigan and Snow Bunting are typical. In bog pools there are interesting waders: Spotted Redshank, Greenshank, Green and Broad-billed Sandpipers, Jack Snipe, Bar-tailed Godwit and Red-necked Phalarope among them. Long-tailed Skua, Red-throated Pipit, Bluethroat, Ring Ouzel and Lapland Bunting are typical for Lapland. In taiga and northern and broad-leaf forests you can find, for example, Little and Rustic Buntings, Redpoll, Siberian Tit, Siberian Jay, Pine

*Terek Sandpiper*

Grosbeak and Waxwing. Highly typical of Finnish forests are the gamebirds, including Capercaillie, Willow Ptarmigan, Hazel Hen, and the owls, including Eagle, Hawk, Pygmy, Tengmalm's, Ural and Great Grey; the abundance and distribution of owls varies from year to year. In old-growth forests there are many woodpeckers, the most sought-after being Black and Three-toed Woodpeckers; White-backed is unfortunately doomed to extinction in due course. Raptors: Golden Eagle, Peregrine and Gyrfalcon are rare and secretive but Hobby, Goshawk, Sparrowhawk, Buzzard and Osprey are easier to see.

The most common birds in Finland are Willow Warbler and Chaffinch. Species with more than 1,000,000 pairs are Robin, Song Thrush, Redwing, Tree Pipit, White Wagtail, Garden Warbler, Spotted and Pied Flycatchers, Willow and Great Tits, Brambling and Yellowhammer. Cuckoo, Whooper Swan, Common Crane and Black Grouse can be seen in most areas.

Thousands of lakes and the Baltic coast make Finland an important country for many waterbirds including Red- and Black-throated Divers, Red-necked and Slavonian Grebes, Pintail, Goldeneye, Smew, Red-breasted Merganser and Goosander. In addition, half the European population of the nominate race of Lesser Black-backed Gull and Black Guillemot breed in Finland. May and June sees the arrival of several eastern songsters like Golden Oriole, Thrush Nightingale and River, Blyth's Reed and Reed Warblers.

## SEASONS

### SPRING
The spring migration begins in February on the southern coast (waterfowl and auks), increases in March (fair-weather migrants like Skylark, Snow Bunting and Lapwing), is good in April (swans and Bean Goose, Common Crane, raptors, etc.) and is at its best in May despite half the country possibly still being under snow. In late May, migration can be one of the most spectacular events in European birding: millions of Arctic ducks and geese fly over Finland to Siberia with up to 1,000,000 birds passing a single location in a day!

### SUMMER
The best time to visit Finland for birds is the end of May and early June: nights are short and do not get truly dark, and there are many singing birds. However, the season is very short in the north: when Arctic Warbler and Red-flanked Bluetail are just arriving, the first waders are already leaving Finland! Summer is a very intensive breeding season, and after Midsummer the concert of the forest is over. In July, birds are feeding their young and at the same time acquiring new plumage. The autumn shooting of ducks begins on 20 August, and previously bird-rich lakes are not worth visiting after this.

AUTUMN

In September, most birds will have migrated south. Many species are accompanied by their young and so numbers are larger and the migration period longer than in the spring. The best places are the southern peninsulas like Hankoniemi. The migration of Arctic ducks and geese is most impressive near the Russian border, but sometimes these Siberian birds can be seen all over the country. In October easterly winds bring Siberian warblers, pipits, buntings and other rarities. The first snow comes to the south in October or November.

WINTER

In the Lapland winter, it is possible to go birding all day and not see a single bird: birds are scarce and the days are short. In Finland however, over 220 species have been recorded from December to February. February is the coldest time of the year, but owls begin calling and crossbills breeding!

# CONSERVATION

Ornithologists have always been at the forefront of the Finnish conservation movement. The most famous species project has been Whooper Swan, the national bird: after the Second World War there were 30–40 pairs in southernmost Lapland. After protection the population has grown to over 1000 pairs and it now breeds all over the country. Finland has rather good site protection programmes, but the state does not have the money to fulfil its obligations: in Finland you must pay in full – even the speculative building value of the land – to the landowner. Finland's national disgrace is its extensive hunting of waterfowl. It is against principles of sustainable development and international treaties. BirdLife Finland is now trying to adjust patterns of agriculture, forestry and building to a greener way.

# GETTING THERE AND GETTING AROUND

Finland is easy to reach by car, ferry, train, boat or plane from most of Northern Europe and Russia. Nearly all sites described in this book can be reached by public transport, but a car makes it easier to see more places because of the long distances involved. Most international car hire firms are represented in the biggest cities of Finland.

The easiest way to go birding is to hire a guide who has a car. Many species are extremely local and very difficult to find. Notably, the owls, which only call for a brief period and are, as a consequence, virtually impossible to find without a guide. The sites of most endangered species are of course secret.

# BIRDLIFE FINLAND

Guides, telephone numbers of bird station officers, maps, books and recordings can be obtained from BirdLife Finland, the national organization for birdwatching research and conservation. It has 29 local bird clubs and over 7300 members. The organization employs five full-time officers and it has its own book and binocular shop (Lintuvaruste Oy.), and two magazines (with English summaries): *Linnut* (popular) and *Tiira (*member magazine). If you are interested in membership of any Finnish bird club or want to submit your records, contact the headquarters in Heinola (*see* Useful Addresses).

# BIRDWATCHING SITES

## SIGNILDSKÄR

**60°12N 19°25E**

Signildskär is an island between Åland and Sweden. Within its 3 km² area can be found cliffs, a few small areas of woodland, scrub, meadows and coastal features. Several old buildings remain but there are no permanent inhabitants. The whole island can easily be studied in one day. Signildskär is the oldest Finnish bird observatory (established in the 1920s) and is a base for large studies of West Åland seabirds. Breeding birds, and spring and autumn migration can be interesting.

**TIMING**

November to March are cold with very few birds being present. During April and May, migratory species such as ducks, raptors, waders, doves, gulls and passerines can be seen. The breeding season is from June to August with Arctic waders returning in July. From September to November, autumn migration is good.

**SPECIES**

- ◆ *Breeding season* Eider, Velvet Scoter, Oystercatcher, gulls, Arctic and Caspian Terns, Arctic Skua, Black Guillemot, Razorbill, Eider, Water Pipit.
- ◆ *Passage* Wildfowl, waders, passerines.
- ◆ *Winter* White-tailed Eagle.

*Arctic Tern*

*Raven*

ACCESS
By boat from Eckerö. Because of limited accommodation and transport, contact the bird observatory warden before your visit.

## LÅGSKÄR

59°50N 19°55E

This solitary bird observatory island, 3 km² in area, lies south of Åland's mainland and has a lighthouse, a couple of houses, cliffs, scrub, reedbeds, woods and beaches. It is one of the more likely spots for rarities.

TIMING

From November to March, wintering ducks favour the area; it is the best place in Finland for wintering Steller's Eiders. Migration during April and May with ducks, raptors, waders, gulls and passerines in good numbers. Breeding birds are present from June to August and the return migration of Arctic waders begins in mid-summer. September to November is the autumn migration period, which can produce good numbers of Siberian passerines.

SPECIES

◆ *Breeding season* Eider, Velvet Scoter, Oystercatcher, gulls, Arctic and
   Sandwich Terns, Arctic Skua, Guillemot.
◆ *Passage* Passerines (including regular Richard's Pipit and Yellow-browed,
   Pallas' and Dusky Warblers).
◆ *Winter* Seaducks (notably Steller's Eider), Guillemot.

ACCESS

Information concerning transport to the island should be obtained from BirdLife Finland in advance of your visit.

## HERRÖSKATAN

59°59N 20°10E

This 3 km² area is the southernmost headland of Åland. In addition to the cliffs there are areas of scrub and woodland, old ruins and, of course, the sea.

TIMING

Wintering ducks can be seen at sea from November to March with White-tailed Eagles, gulls and Ravens. April and May are the best months for spring migration. Breeding birds can be seen from June to August; September and October are the most intensive months for autumn migration.

SPECIES

♦ *Breeding season* Oystercatcher, Eider, Velvet Scoter, gulls, terns, auks, Barred Warbler.
♦ *Passage* Wildfowl, pipits, warblers.
♦ *Winter* Seaducks, White-tailed Eagle, Raven.

ACCESS

Herröskatan is reached from Mariehamn, the capital of the county Åland. Take road 3 from Mariehamn to the east and drive 23 km, then turn to right and drive 10 km to the village of Flaka and then right again, driving to the end of the road (some 6 km). At the parking area is an information board. There is a path to an observation tower which offers a superb view.

# KÖKAR

59°55N 22°58E

This beautiful 75-km² island in the Åland archipelago has cliffs, small fields, meadows and forests. Cottages are dotted across the landscape, and this is a popular area for tourism in summertime. Seawatching, from the cliffs just south of the coastguard station in the west of the island, is a favoured morning pursuit (keep out of the fenced area).

TIMING

Winter from November to March can be good for passerines and ducks. The breeding season is under way from June to August and the rather extended autumn migration lasts from September to early November. Black Grouse are a speciality of the island.

SPECIES

♦ *Resident* Black Grouse.
♦ *Breeding season* Eider, Velvet Scoter, Osprey, Oystercatcher, gulls, Arctic and Caspian Terns, skuas, Water Pipit, Nutcracker.
♦ *Passage* Wildfowl, waders, passerines.
♦ *Winter* Seaducks, White-tailed Eagle.

ACCESS

Kökar can be reached by ferries either from Åland mainland or from Finland (Korppoo Galtby). It is wise to book in advance.

# KORPPOO JURMO

59°50N 21°32E

Jurmo Island, 'The pearl of the Finnish Archipelago'. 6 km² in area, it is part of the Saaristomeri National Park and comprises mainly clifftop moorland with juniper scrub and heather, sandy and muddy shores which are suitable for waders.

Jurmo Bird Observatory, founded in 1962, can be visited by prior arrangement. If visiting as a tourist, the strict walking restrictions must be obeyed; consequently, you will miss some of the best places. However, the cliffs to the west of the harbour and the walk along the path to the village can be rewarding. Jurmo is one of the best birding sites in Finland.

TIMING

During January and February, there are resident Black Grouse and tits to look for. March brings the first migrants: ducks (especially Eiders), gulls, raptors, passerines, and in April and May the main migration gets under way. The breeding season is from June to August and the first waders return from Lapland. September and October are the best autumn migration months and during November and December you can still find interesting birds.

SPECIES

◆ *Resident* Black Grouse.
◆ *Breeding season* Mute Swan, Greylag Goose, Mallard, Eider, Common Scoter, Goosander, Ringed Plover, Turnstone, Oystercatcher, Redshank, Arctic Skua, Wryneck, Water Pipit, Red-backed Shrike. Little Tern, Dunlin.
◆ *Passage* Waders, warblers, Goldcrest, Robin, finches.
◆ *Winter* White-tailed Eagle, Purple Sandpiper.

ACCESS

By boat from Nauvo Pärnainen, some 80 km from Turku to south-west by road 180. There are just two ferries and you may have to queue if there is heavy traffic. The bird observatory can accommodate only five observers so please contact the warden in advance.

# TURKU RUISSALO (RUNSALA)

60°26N 22°10E

'A piece of Central Europe in Finland', this 800-ha island has more oak trees than in the whole of Finland outside Ruissalo. Deciduous forest dominates the eastern half of the island and there are meadows and fields in the middle of the island. There is also one small shallow bay in the south which is good for waders and ducks.

The best forests are protected today, but many private building projects have caused environmental conflicts.

Around 250 species have been recorded in Ruissalo and nearly 100 species breed. Woodpecker species are particularly well represented with Black Woodpeckers favouring coniferous forest close to the hotel; the Honkapirtti-café is the best place in Finland to see Grey-headed Woodpecker.

TIMING

Ruissalo is the best year-round birding site near Turku. From February to April, woodpeckers, owls, tits and other residents are at their most active and easiest to see, while May and June are months when bird song is most apparent. Spring migration consists mainly of waders, gulls and passerines. July and August are the main breeding period. The best autumn migration occurring from September to November; look for raptors, ducks, waders, gulls and passerines. There are wintering ducks and resident species in winter time.

SPECIES

◆ *Resident* Canada Goose, Black, Grey-headed, Great Spotted and Lesser Spotted Woodpeckers, Tawny Owl, Blue Tit.
◆ *Breeding season* Barnacle Goose (feral population), Eider, gulls, terns, Blackcap, Thrush Nightingale, Common Rosefinch.
◆ *Passage* Wildfowl (including Barnacle Goose), waders, terns, passerines.
◆ *Winter* Seaduck.

ACCESS

The island is located 7-km west from the centre of Turku. Ruissalo cannot cope with too many cars so please take the bus no 8 from Turku Kauppatori. Walk the 7-km nature trail that crosses the whole island. Waterbirds can best be observed from the westernmost tip of the island, Saarronniemi. The best places for woodpeckers and warblers are in the middle of the island. Most birders also walk the shore path between the harbour and the park for waders and ducks. The two observation towers on Ruissalo are more useful for landscape scanning than for birding.

## SALO HALIKONLAHTI

60°20N 23°05E

This 2-km$^2$ wetland area contains the delta of The Salonjoki River and muddy ponds associated with the waterworks; the wetland is fringed by large fields. Despite its comparatively small size, nearly 250 species have been recorded.

TIMING

From November to February, ice usually covers the water, but flocks of Redpolls and associated birds can be found in woodland and scrub. March to May and September to November are migration seasons for Common Cranes, ducks, geese, gulls, raptors, waders, doves and passerines; the return migration for Grey Heron and Arctic waders may start as early as July.

SPECIES

◆ *Breeding season* Great Crested and Slavonian Grebes, Mute Swan, Canada Goose, Mallard, Osprey, Hobby, Black-headed Gull, Sand Martin, Sedge, Marsh and River Warblers, Thrush Nightingale, Bearded Tit, Common Rosefinch.

◆ *Passage* Waders (including Wood and Green Sandpipers), Ruff, Great and Jack Snipe.

ACCESS

From the city of Salo, follow the camping signposts. Drive over the railway and after 1 km you see the sea on your left and a bird tower to the right. Park by the crossroads next to the bird tower; here you will find an information board and map. There is a path to the observation tower, from which there is a good view of the whole area. The muddy ponds, which make Halikonlahti the best wader location in south-west Finland, can be checked from the path – if you can stand the smell that is! There is a logbook in a mailbox in the middle of the pond area.

## KURJENRAHKA

60°14N 22°28E

Covering an area of 10 km$^2$, this is the best bog near Turku: it comprises a mosaic of marshes, ponds, Lake Savojärvi and coniferous forest and has National Park status. As well as wetland

*Osprey*

species, gamebirds, woodpeckers and owls are well represented in Kurjenrahka, and elk live here too.

TIMING

From November to March, snow and ice cover the landscape and only resident birds can be found; these include grouse, woodpeckers and crossbills. The best time to visit Kurjenrahka is from March to May, when the breeding birds are most active. Visitors should listen for calling Willow Ptarmigan, displaying Black Grouse and drumming woodpeckers; Tengmalm's, Pygmy and Ural Owls also breed in a good year for voles. Migrants arrive at this time of year and, from June to August, the breeding birds have their young. Autumn migration is not pronounced at Kurjenrahka, but the colours of the forest and bog make up for the lack of birds.

SPECIES

◆ *Resident* Black Grouse, Willow Ptarmigan, Capercaillie, Hazel Hen, Black Woodpecker, Grey-headed Woodpecker, Crested Tit, Parrot Crossbill.
◆ *Breeding season* Black-throated and Red-throated Divers, Common Crane, Sparrowhawk, Goshawk, Buzzard, Honey Buzzard, Hobby, Osprey, Golden Plover, Lapwing, Wood and Green Sandpipers, Snipe, Curlew, Wryneck, Willow Warbler, Jay, Rustic Bunting, Chaffinch, Brambling.

ACCESS

From Turku take road 9 some 20 km to the north. In Lieto, turn left on to road 204 and drive for 20 km or so until you see a parking place for Kurjenrahka on the left. From the parking place walk to Lake Savojärvi and join the network of natural and woody paths. Please do not stray from the paths.

# PORI YYTERI

61°35N 21°30E

Despite its popularity as a tourist spot, Yyteri is the best wader site in Finland. The 5-km² area comprises muddy shores in the south and sandy beaches in the north as well as meadows and small patches of woodland.

TIMING

November to February is an icy period with virtually no birds. In March to April migrants, mainly ducks, gulls and passerines arrive. The main migration period is May. By late July and early August, the return migration of adult waders has already started.

October sees the last waders and other migrant species passing.

SPECIES

◆ *Breeding season* Caspian Tern.
◆ *Passage* Hobby, Osprey, Ruff, Dunlin, Wood, Green and Curlew Sandpipers, Broad-billed Sandpiper, Knot, Little and Temminck's Stints, Sanderling, Redshank, Spotted Redshank, Red-necked Phalarope, Great and Jack Snipe (autumn only).

ACCESS

From the city of Pori, follow signs to Meri-Pori. Turn left at the signpost to Huhtala and drive slowly until you reach the parking place. Take the path to the shore. You can walk several kilometres north to the Hotel, watching birds along the shoreline as you go; the amount of shore exposed depends both on tide and wind. There is also a bird watching tower in the south. Please do not walk in the meadows!

## PORI PREVIIKINLAHTI

61°34N 21°30E

Within the confines of this 5-km² area is a bay called Previikinlahti and in the distance are the famous wader sands of Yyteri. Meadows, reedbeds and woodland add to the area's ornithological interest.

TIMING

Between November and February virtually no birds are present. The first migrants arrive in March, these being ducks, gulls, passerines; a second and more significant influx of arrivals coming in April with swans, geese, Rough-legged Buzzards and waders. May is good for passerines. The adult waders return from their breeding grounds in July and August followed, in September, by the main migration of juvenile sandpipers.

SPECIES

◆ *Breeding season* Bittern, Mute Swan, Eider, Goosander, Marsh Harrier, Water Rail, Caspian Tern, Bearded Tit.
◆ *Passage* Wildfowl, waders (typically Ruff, Dunlin, Wood and Green Sandpipers), gulls, terns.

ACCESS

From Pori, take road 265 signposted to Meri-Pori. After some 8 km turn left, signposted to Preiviiki where there are two bird towers. For the first, called Kaarluoto, drive 2 km from the Preiviiki signpost and turn right to Kaarluoto Lintutorni (= bird tower). After 0.5 km there is a parking place at the start of a board-walk to the tower. The other tower, called Preiviiki, is in the harbour, to the west from the Kaarluoto tower; the distance is some 2 km and you can either drive or walk.

## HANKO TÄKTOM AND TÄKTBUKTEN

59°51N 23°04E

Täktom is a famous raptor spot, located at Hanko airport. Täktbukten is a wetland 2-km south of the airport car park and worth visiting at the same time; it has a bay, a meadow and a modest cliff face. Täktbukten is partly a nature protection area, and the rest of it is in a bird wetland programme.

Most Finnish migratory bird species can be seen in the area. Migrants are often concentrated here, especially irruptive species from Siberia such as Three-toed and Great Spotted Woodpeckers, Siberian, Great, Blue, Willow and Long-tailed Tits, Nutcracker, Nuthatch, Jay, Tengmalm's Owl and Pine Grosbeak.

TIMING

From November to February, ice and snow in most years mean that few birds remain here. The best migration periods are from March to May and August to November. Cranes, ducks, geese, raptors, waders, gulls, doves and passerines can all be numerous; the best raptor migration occurs around noon in April and October, when hundreds of birds can be seen. From July onwards, the return migration of waders and Grey Heron begins in Täktbukten.

SPECIES

◆ *Breeding season* Mute Swan, Mallard, Shelduck (scarce in Finland), Eider, Goosander, Redshank, Lapwing, Dunlin (subspecies *schinzii*), Black Woodpecker, Wryneck, Meadow Pipit, Yellow Wagtail, Sedge, Marsh and Barred Warblers, Red-backed Shrike, Thrush Nightingale, Reed and Ortolan Buntings.

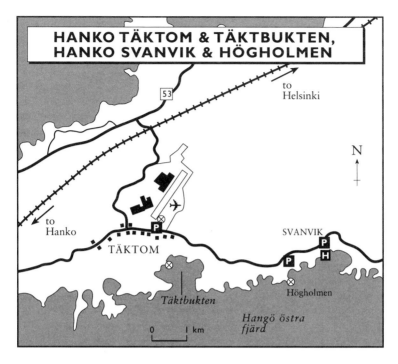

**HANKO TÄKTOM & TÄKTBUKTEN, HANKO SVANVIK & HÖGHOLMEN**

◆ *Passage* Grey Heron, Common Crane, Great and Jack Snipe (September and October only), Golden Eagle (mainly early October), Buzzard, Honey and Rough-legged Buzzards, Hen Harrier, Goshawk, Hobby, Richard's Pipit (September-October).

ACCESS

From Helsinki, drive 94 km on road 51; after the city of Ekenäs begins take road 53 on the left. Drive 9 km and turn left on to the beach road. After 11 km, turn right in the village of Täktom at the signpost to Lentokenttä/ Flygstation. Leave your car in the airport car park. Hanko can also be reached by bus or train. In this case, you should walk, cycle or take a taxi along the beach road 7 km from Hanko centre. Migrating birds can be seen from the car park but don't even think of walking on the runway! If there is no visible migration at the airport, you can walk 2 km to the south to Täktbukten. There you can watch birds either from the road or from the clifftop. Do not walk in the meadow during the breeding season (March to August) for obvious reasons.

# HANKO SVANVIK AND HÖGHOLMEN

59°50N 23°05E

This 2-km² wetland comprises two bays side-by-side, the first is Svanvik, which means 'Swan Bay' in English. Part of the area is a nature protection area, the rest being in a bird wetland programme.

TIMING

From November to February few birds are present as ice covers the water. March to May and September to November are the best months for migration of Common Cranes, ducks, geese, raptors, waders and passerines.

SPECIES
- *Breeding season* Hobby, Osprey, Mute and Whooper Swans, Mallard, Eider.
- *Passage* Grey Heron, Whooper and Bewick's Swans, Wigeon, Long-tailed Duck, Eider, Wood and Green Sandpipers, Ruff, Redshank, Great and Jack Snipe (September and October only), passerines.

ACCESS
From Helsinki drive 94 km on road 51, and after the city of Ekenäs take road 53 on the left. Drive 9 km and turn left on the beach road. After 9 km you will see a wooden signpost to Svanvik on the left. After a further 1 km there is a parking place at Högholmen with information posts. Hanko can also be reached by bus or train. In this case, you should walk, cycle or take a taxi along the strand road 9 km from Hanko centre. The birds can be watched from two points. At Svanvik there is a bird tower, and 1 km to the west there is self-guided nature trail to a headland, from which you can see the western part of the area. Do not leave the path to avoid damaging the beach flora.

## KIRKKONUMMI PORKKALA
59°57N 24°27E

Covering an area of 6 km², the headland of the Porkkala peninsula affords the visitor magnificent views to the Baltic Sea. The area is mainly forested.

TIMING
In mild winters you can see ducks, swans and gulls. Spring migration begins in the first warm days of March, with a peak of waterfowl in the middle of May. Porkkala is also good for Comomon Cranes, raptors, waders, doves and passerines. From June to August, breeding seabirds can be seen locally from the cliff. Migration interest returns in September and continues to November, although autumn migration is not as good as in spring.

SPECIES
- *Breeding season* Mute Swan, Mallard, Eider, Goosander, Oystercatcher, Turnstone, Arctic Tern.
- *Passage* Barnacle and Brent Geese, Common and Velvet Scoters, Long-tailed Duck (all five species best in May), Steller's Eider (over 1000 birds sometimes seen in early May), White-tailed Eagle, Honey Buzzard, Red-breasted Flycatcher, Greenish Warbler.

ACCESS
From the city of Helsinki drive road 51 to the west. Before the centre of Kirkkonummi, turn south from the crossroads 'Porkkalanniemi', drive 19 km and then turn right 'Porkkalanniemen virkistysalueet'. Drive 0.7 km and turn right again ('Porkkalanniemen virkistysalueet', etc., signs). Drive some 2 km and you will find two parking places. The last bus stop is some 4 km before the headland. From the second parking place there is a path to the left. Follow this for 2 km and you reach the headland.

## PORKKALA TOWER
59°58N 24°28E

The bird tower is situated in Lähteelä. It stands over the forest and meadows and is one of the best raptor-watching spots in southern Finland. Since this is mainly a mid-day occupation, most birders visit the tower after a morning's seawatching at nearby Porkkalanniemi.

TIMING

December to March is not good. From April, cranes, raptors, doves and passerines can be seen. In May, some waterfowl migration may be seen from the tower, but Porkkalanniemi is better. Birdwatching from June to August is confined to local breeding birds but from September to November migration begins again with raptor watching from the tower being of prime interest.

SPECIES

◆ *Resident* Capercaillie, Parrot Crossbill.

◆ *Breeding season* Barred Warbler, Red-backed Shrike.

◆ *Passage* Common Crane, Golden Eagle, Buzzard, Honey and Rough-legged Buzzards, Sparrowhawk, Kestrel, Hobby, Woodpigeon, passerines.

ACCESS

From Helsinki take road 51 to the west. Before the centre of Kirkkonummi turn south at the crossroads signposted 'Porkkalanniemi', drive 18 km and turn left 'Lähteelän ulkoilualue'. The bird tower can be seen from the crossroads. Porkkalanniemi can be reached by bus too. From the parking place there is a path up to the left to the cliff.

# Espoon Suomenoja

60°07N 24°45E

Set against an industrial landscape, Espoon Suomenoja is a man-made muddy pond with reedbeds 1 km² in area. Although there are two bird towers, birding is easy from the surrounding path. Migrant birds are well represented.

TIMING

December to February are usually ice-bound. March to May and September to November are migration seasons for Common Cranes, ducks, geese, raptors, gulls, waders, doves and passerines; wader maxima are seen in June and August.

SPECIES

◆ *Breeding season* Slavonian Grebe, Little Grebe (occasional), Moorhen, Mallard, Black-headed Gull, Sand Martin, Marsh, Blyth's Reed, Great Reed, River and Sedge Warblers, Thrush Nightingale, Common Rosefinch.

◆ *Passage* Grey Heron, Wood and Green Sandpipers, Ruff.

ACCESS

From the city of Helsinki, take road 51 heading west. Turn right at the crossroads 'Espoon keskus'. Join the signs 'Kaitaa' and turn left at the crossroads 'Suomenojan venesatama'. Go 400 m and turn right to 'Suomenojan venesatama'. After 400 m, the forest ends and you will see huge power station chimneys; turn left to the parking place.

# Espoo Laajalahti

60°10N 25°07E

The best birdwatching lake near Helsinki, with open water, reedbeds and wet meadows. The surrounding land has drier meadows and old forest stands. Nearly half of the 300-ha area has nature protection status. Conservation work is carried out by the local forestry park service which includes cattle grazing and forest management. More than 240 species have been recorded in the area.

TIMING

The area is best visited between spring and autumn. Migration is most noticeable in April and May, and again in August and September, with duck

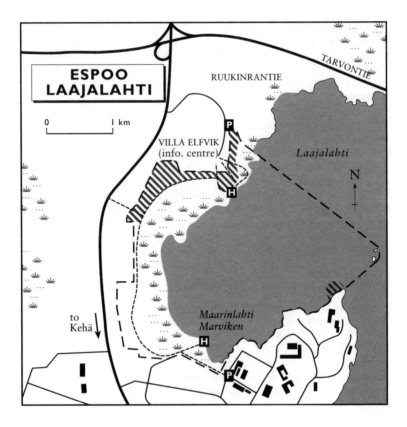

numbers being particularly noteworthy. If water levels are low, waders can be good from May to August but, from November until March, Lake Laajalahti is nearly always under ice. You can, however, still find a few passerines and woodpeckers in the forest in winter.

SPECIES

◆ *Resident* Great Spotted Woodpecker.
◆ *Breeding season* Great Crested Grebe, Mute Swan, Mallard, Gadwall, Hobby, Marsh Harrier, Coot, Water Rail, Spotted Crake, Corncrake, Curlew, Lapwing, Redshank, Red-backed Shrike, Sedge Warbler, Bearded Tit.
◆ *Passage* Ducks, waders.

ACCESS

The site lies some 10-km west of the centre of Helsinki. Buses depart from Helsinki Bus Station (101, 206, 212, 213). From Ruukinrannantie crossroads there is a 500-m walk to Villa Elfvik. If you go by car, take the road to Tarvontie and turn left on the road to Kehä and then again left at the sign 'Gallen-Kallelan museo'. You will see the sign 'Villa Elfvik', which is the information centre, in front of you. The parking place is well marked and there is a walk of 300 m to the first of two observation towers. A boardwalk runs between this and the second tower (2 km). There is also a boardwalk through the reedbeds at Villa Elfvik. Another good observation spot is from the northern shore of the Lake Tarvas.

# Suomenlinna (Sveaborg)

60°10N 24°59E

The easiest way to study seabirds in the Helsinki area is to take a ferry to the island of Suomenlinna. Here are several old forts from the eighteenth century. Some of the land is cultivated and the habitat consists of small cliffs, bushes and gardens. Suomenlinna is a UNESCO World Heritage site and is managed for both tourism and conservation.

TIMING

Spring migration is easily observed on Suomenlinna. Movements of passerines start in earnest as early as March and continue for raptors, geese, ducks, and gulls until early June. The highest concentration of Arctic ducks and geese usually takes place between 20 May and 30 May each year. By July and August birdwatching is confined to local breeding species including ducks, gulls and passerines. Autumn migration lasts from September to November. Thereafter, a few ducks and gulls, notably Glaucous Gull, remain in the area if the sea is not totally frozen.

SPECIES

◆ *Breeding season* Barnacle Goose, Shelduck, Mallard, Eider, Goosander, Oystercatcher, Turnstone, Redshank, Lesser Black-backed Gull (subspecies *fuscus*), Great Black-backed Gull, terns.

◆ *Passage* Raptors, Brent and Barnacle Geese, Long-tailed Duck, gulls, terns.

ACCESS

Boats operate from Kauppatori in Helsinki. The trip takes half an hour. It is worth looking for seabirds from the boat. On Suomenlinna the best seawatching site is Kustaanmiekka, the southernmost tip of the island.

# Viikki (Vanhakaupunginlahti)

60°13N 25°00E

Often described as the best birding site in Helsinki, Viikki is a 1-km² area encompassing a bay where the Vantaanjoki River reaches the Baltic Sea. The wetland with its reedbeds is surrounded by meadows, fields and forests. The main part of the area is a Nature Reserve and Viikki is a Ramsar Site.

TIMING

Viikki is best in spring, from April to May, with many ducks and waders passing through. A few passerine migrants remain to breed and are present from April to August. Autumn migration may start as early as July with movements of Grey Herons and waders. Good numbers of raptors, geese, ducks and passerines pass through until November. From December to February, these are official feeding places for wintering birds, mainly passerines, and close to these spots there is a chance to see Pygmy Owl.

SPECIES

◆ *Breeding season* Mute Swan, Mallard, Marsh Harrier, Osprey, Coot, Redshank, Black-headed Gull, Yellow Wagtail, Sedge Warbler, Bearded Tit, Reed Bunting.

◆ *Passage* Grey Heron (August and September), raptors, geese, ducks, waders, rarities.

ACCESS

The bay is situated some 6-km north-east of the city of Helsinki. The easiest way to get there is to take bus 57, 71V, 74, 76, from the railway station to

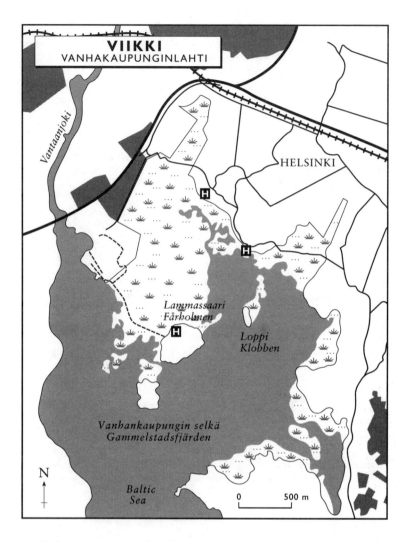

the Technical Museum and walk 500 m to the closest observation tower. You can see the most important parts of the bay and surrounding meadows from the three observation towers (map) and by walking along the path. Do not leave the path.

## ASIKKALAN PULKKILANHARJU
61°17N 25°31E
This site is a bridge on a ridge, with a magnificent view over Lake Päijänne, and passing migrating birds. Part of the ridge is a nature protection area.

### TIMING
Best time is from September to October, when irruptive birds from the taiga can be observed. In other months, birdwatching is poor although the scenery is dramatic.

SPECIES
- *Passage* Great Spotted and Three-toed Woodpeckers, White-backed Woodpecker (very rare), Jay, Nutcracker, Nuthatch, Willow, Great, Blue, Long-tailed and Crested Tits, Siberian Tit (rare but annual), Brambling.

ACCESS
Take road E4 from Lahti to the north to Asikkala, and turn on to road 314 also heading north. Drive 8 km and you will see Lake Päijänne on both sides. Drive 2 km or so and and cross the bridge Karisalmi to a parking place on the right. Birds can be watched from the bridge or from the short nature trail.

# HEINOLA

61°13N 26°02E

Heinola is a an attractive little town between Lahti and Mikkeli. The Kymijoki River is one of the best waterfowl sites in Finland in winter. The office of BirdLife Finland is placed in Heinola Water Tower and nearly all owls and other 'difficult' birds can be seen in Heinola Bird Sanctuary, which holds some 400 injured birds of 100 species as well as donated parrots and other tropical species; entry is free. The town has many gardens and riverside parks.

TIMING
Golden Orioles can be heard in the town. The summer is a quiet time but in October and November the lakes and rivers begin to freeze, and ducks concentrate on the last ice-free places. Dippers can usually be seen by walking under the railway bridge.

SPECIES
- *Breeding season* Owls, Black Woodpecker, Wryneck, Tree Sparrow.
- *Passage* Nutcracker.
- *Winter* Divers, Little Grebe, Mallard, Smew.

ACCESS
Heinola is situated 138-km north-east of Helsinki between Lahti (35 km) and Mikkeli (100 km). Leave the motorway no 5 and drive to the centre of the town. Most long-distance buses from Helsinki to Mikkeli or Savonlinna go to Heinola. Park the car close to the water tower and walk either to the Heinola Bird Sanctuary or the Kymijoki River on the opposite side of the water tower. The BirdLife Finland office is easy to find, because the water tower is seen all

*Dipper*

over the town (the office is open Monday–Friday 9am to 3.30pm). You can get current birding information for the whole region from the organization secretary tel. +358 (9)18 7152579 or fax +358 (9)18 7143682.

# SAARIJÄRVI PYHÄ-HÄKKI
62°44N 25°30E

Covering an area of 12 km², this site harbours ancient taiga forest, the trees being between 250 and 500 years old. Bogs and little ponds add to the wildlife value making it an excellent place to visit. Keen-eyed observers may see a small creature (not a bird) gliding from tree to tree; this is a flying squirrel.

TIMING

Between November and April, harsh winter weather favours only resident birds which include grouse, woodpeckers and crossbills. By May the migratory birds start to return and in June and July Pyhä-Häkki is at its best for birdwatching. The season is short and from August many of the birds begin to depart, the migrants having left by early October.

SPECIES
◆ *Resident* Capercaillie, Black Grouse, Hazel Hen, Great Spotted, Black and Three-toed Woodpeckers, Parrot Crossbill.
◆ *Breeding season* Common Crane, Goshawk, Sparrowhawk, Ural, Tengmalm's and Pygmy Owls, Treecreeper, Willow Warbler, Song Thrush, Robin, Redstart, Collared Flycatcher, Siberian Jay, tits, Chaffinch, Brambling, Rustic Bunting.

ACCESS

From Saarijärvi centre take road 651 to the north-east towards Viitasaari, Pyhä-Häkin Kansallispuisto is well signposted on this road. The distance is some 21 km. In the parking place you can find a map of the area with two nature trails marked (3 km and 6.5 km).

# VIROLAHTI VILKKILÄNTURA
60°31N 27°51E

A famous bird lake in Finland which is at its best when Arctic waterfowl migration is taking place. The area is surrounded by forests, meadows and fields and covers 3 km².

TIMING

The first birds arrive with the start of the thaw, usually in March. In April and May spring migration occurs, with swans, ducks, waders and terns. Migrant songbirds and local breeders are features of June and July and, from August to November, wildfowl and especially swans concentrate on Vilkkiläntura.

SPECIES
◆ *Breeding season* Ducks, Corncrake, waders, Little Gull, terns, Wryneck, Golden Oriole, Icterine, Blyth's Reed and Grasshopper Warblers, Common Rosefinch.
◆ *Passage* Whooper Swan, Bewick's Swan, ducks.

ACCESS

Travelling along to the east from Helsinki and turn to the south to Virojoki (road 351). After 5 km take the crossroads to the left (road 3511) 'Virolahti'. Drive 11 km to the left 'Hurppu 4'. After 2 km there is a signpost 'Vilkkilänturan lintutorni', join it to the left and after 300 m there is a parking place from which a nature trail starts. There is a new tower in the Strand Hotel Lintulahti on the west side of the lake too.

## YLÄMAA SAMMALINEN

60°37N 27°59E

A 1-km² area comprising a high cliff overlooking forest, bog and lake.

TIMING

Most people visit Sammalinen from May to August. Arctic geese pass through in late May and Spotted Eagle is a speciality of Lake Väkevänjärvi in late spring and early summer. During September and October, there is sometimes good autumn migration of raptors, geese and ducks.

SPECIES

◆ *Breeding season* Spotted Eagle.

◆ *Passage* Raptors, ducks.

ACCESS

Drive 20 km from road 7 to the north-east (road 387) and take to the east at the crossroads 'Sammalinen' for 2.5 km. Parking on the right under the cliff.

## LAKE VÄKEVÄNJÄRVI

60°37N 27°59E

Formerly known only as a lake harbouring common waterbirds, Väkevänjärvi became famous when Spotted Eagles began visiting the area. Although this species breeds beyond the Russian border, it visits Väkevänjärvi and the cliff at Sammalinen regularly.

TIMING

Winter lasts from November to April. The area is visited mostly between May and August, migrating Arctic geese passing through in late May. Visitors also come hoping to see Spotted Eagle and other rarities. During September and October, autumn migration is under way but the area is seldom visited.

SPECIES

◆ *Breeding season* Spotted Eagle (Sammalinen Väkevänjärvi is the best place to look for this species in Finland).

◆ *Passage* Ducks, rarities.

ACCESS

Between Virolahti and Lappeenranta on road 387. The crossroads to the east is 'Nurmela'. Drive 4 km to the first bridge and 6 km to the other. You can see best from the two bridges. Beyond the road is the border area – do not explore under any circumstances!

## PARIKKALA SIIKALAHTI

61°40N 29°32E

This is one of the most important of Finnish wetlands after Liminganlahti. The bird lake is mainly covered with reeds and the whole area is surrounded by large fields and forests. Siikalahti has been thoroughly watched for the past 30 years and 40 species regularly breed here.

TIMING

From November to March few birds are present. Migration can best be observed in April and May, and again in September and October. Perhaps the ideal time to visit Siikalahti is from late May to early June: at this time birds are singing and species diversity is greatest. Autumn migration is not as marked at Siikalahti as it is in spring.

SPECIES

◆ *Breeding season* Slavonian Grebe, Bittern (5–8 pairs breed), Whooper Swan, Osprey, Marsh Harrier, Hobby, Corncrake, Water Rail, Spotted Crake, Baillon's Crake (recent new breeding species), Mallard, Black-headed and Little Gulls, Sedge, Grasshopper, River, Blyth's Reed and Reed Warblers, Golden Oriole, Thrush Nightingale, Common Rosefinch.

◆ *Passage* Common Crane, geese, ducks, raptors, waders, gulls, passerines.

ACCESS

Take road 6 near the Russian border and drive some 60-km north from Imatra and you'll arrive at the tiny village of Parikkala. Siikalahti is well signposted to the right. After some 3 km you will reach the parking place from which a nature trail starts; this goes first to the centre and after that to the bird tower. You can also walk from the parking place north to the dam and listen for singing birds there.

# VIROLAHTI HURPPU

60°30N 27°52E

The south-eastern corner of Finland and arguably the most important site for observing the migration of Arctic waterbirds. It comprises a peninsula with pine forests and little villages with beautiful views of the Baltic Sea.

TIMING

The area is mostly ice-bound from December to April. Spring is the best season for birdwatching here, Arctic ducks and geese peaking between 15 May and 25 May in most years. There can be some wader migration at the beginning of June. Thereafter, local breeding birds provide the main interest until August when return migration begins. This continues until early November. In October, hundreds of swans can be seen before the ice forms.

SPECIES

◆ *Breeding season* Mallard, Eider, Goosander, Oystercatcher, gulls, terns, Nightjar, Woodlark, Parrot Crossbill.

◆ *Passage* Divers (including White-billed), Barnacle and Brent Geese, Scoter, Velvet Scoter, Steller's Eider, Long-tailed Duck, Glaucous Gull, Kittiwake, Pomarine Skua.

ACCESS

Drive road 3 to the east from Helsinki and turn south to Virojoki (road 351). After 5 km take the crossroads to the left (road 3511) 'Virolahti'. Drive 11 km to the left 'Hurppu 4'. After 3 km there is a signpost 'Arktisen muuton torni', join it to the right and after 500 m there is a parking place with a bird tower.

# PATVINSUO NATIONAL PARK

63°07N 30°40E

Ten-thousand hectares of the park is moorland. The park protects nearly 4000 ha of forest, almost half of which is truly old forest. The forest is dominated by coniferous species. In some areas the conifers are mixed with old birches and aspen.

Two oligotrophic lakes, Suomunjärvi and Hietajärvi, are within the park's boundary. Together they are 700 ha in extent and boast crystal clear water and sandy beaches. Although poor for birds, the lakes echo to the mournful calls of both Red-throated and Black-throated Divers in the half-light of northern summer nights.

The park is managed by the Finnish Forest and Park Service. Brown Bear, Wolf and Wolverine are regularly seen here although usually at a distance.

TIMING

Winter lasts from November to April. However, many interesting resident birds can be found all year round. The appearance of the first Whooper Swans at the end of March heralds the arrival of spring although there could still be a metre of snow on the ground.

In April sun starts to melt the snow and ice, and by the beginning of May the backbone of winter is finally broken. Numerous wildfowl and waders favour the moors, and a good variety of raptors visit the park regularly. Slushy snow on the boardwalks has normally melted enough to allow people to walk to the observation towers by the start of May. Towards the end of May and the beginning of June, the breeding season reaches its climax: birds are displaying and singing and are often easy to see from the boardwalks and towers.

Spring is also the best time to visit the old forests since most woodland species become more vocal and easier to see. Although still present, the birds become silent and more unobtrusive in summer. In autumn, good numbers of waterfowl and waders rest and feed on the moorland and lakes.

SPECIES

◆ *Resident* Golden Eagle, Capercaillie, Black Grouse, Willow Ptarmigan, Hazel Hen, Three-toed Woodpecker, Siberian Jay, Siberian Tit, Pine Grosbeak, Parrot Crossbill.

◆ *Breeding season* Black-throated and Red-throated Divers, Whooper Swan, Bean Goose, Osprey, Hobby, Merlin, Common Crane, Lapwing, Golden Plover, Whimbrel, Green, Wood and Broad-billed Sandpipers, Spotted Redshank, Jack Snipe, Ural and Tengmalm's Owls, Waxwing, Greenish Warbler, Red-breasted Flycatcher.

◆ *Passage* Geese, ducks, waders (including Red-necked Phalarope).

ACCESS

The site is situated 30-km south-east of Lieksa, 40-km north of Ilomantsi and 80-km north-east of Joensuu. From Joensuu it is reached by car by driving 40 km along the road number 73 towards Lieksa. Then 10 km along the road '516' north-east to Kivilahti, 2 km to the left (north-west) along the road '520', 25 km to the right (north-east) along the road '5202' to Kitsi, and finally, follow the National Park signs for the remaining 8 km to the Information Centre 'Suomu'. By public transport everything is more difficult. The nearest bus service is found in Kivilahti (25 km) or Kitsi (15 km).

There is a high observation tower as well as two lower ones in the park, all sited near the best wetlands; they are easily reached via the wooden nature trails. The Suomu Information Centre is the best place to start and there are good maps of the park available.

# HÖYTIÄINEN CANAL ESTUARY

62°38N 29°36E

This 100 ha area consists of a mixture of small ponds, dense reedbeds, wet meadows and deciduous forest. To the south, Lake Pyhäselkä dominates the scenery; northwards are mainly urban and agricultural areas. The canal

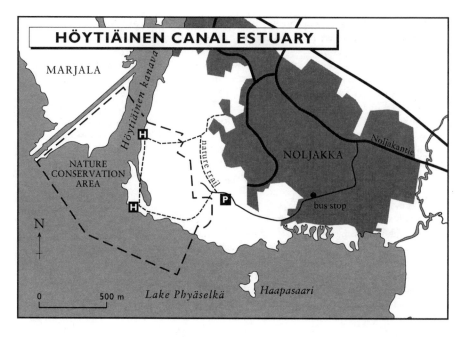

continues 10 km as a narrow river up to Lake Höytiäinen. The area has nature reserve status and hunting and forestry are prohibited; the site is mentioned as a wetland of national importance in the national Wetland Conservation Programme. A scrape has been created for waders close to the observation tower.

TIMING

Winter lasts from November until the first half of April during which time feeding stations are maintained for ringing purposes, attracting woodpeckers and a few passerines. It is not until mid-April that a narrow strip of open water appears at the edges but, by the end of April and the beginning of May, the water is ice-free and duck and raptor migration started.

The best time to visit the site is in the latter half of May and the beginning of June. Then, northbound Arctic bird migration will be in full swing and a good selection of species such as divers, ducks, waders and skuas can be seen. At the same time, passerine migration reaches its peak.

Return wader migration begins in August with the adults, followed by juveniles in September. At this time of year, however, the area is best known for invasions of irruptive birds from Siberia. September is the best time for these, but some appear in August and October is sometimes as good as September.

SPECIES

◆ *Breeding season* Slavonian Grebe, Bittern, Marsh Harrier, Little Gull, Thrush Nightingale.

◆ *Passage* Divers, Common Crane, Golden and White-tailed Eagles, Rough-legged Buzzard, Osprey, Peregrine, ducks (including Steller's Eider), Curlew and Broad-billed Sandpipers, Red-necked Phalarope, Pomarine and Arctic Skuas, Waxwing, Red-throated Pipit, Yellow-browed, Arctic and Greenish Warblers, Arctic Redpoll, Pine Grosbeak, Siberian Tit.

◆ *Winter* Pygmy and Tengmalm's Owls (both very occasional), White-backed Woodpecker, Long-tailed Tit, Parrot Crossbill, Pine Grosbeak.

ACCESS

By car take the main road from Joensuu to Kuopio. After 3 km turn right on the two-level cross where there is a blue-and-white sign 'Noljakka' (with some other signs). Turn to Noljakka and drive along the road 'Noljakantie' 1 km until you come to the road 'Aavarannantie' (suburban road to the right starting from a little shopping centre). Drive along Aavarannantie and continue beyond the point where the tarmac ends. Continue along the sandy road for 300 m until you come to a small hill, then continue to the right. After 150 m, at the next cross turn right. An centrally-placed observation tower is an excellent place for birdwatching. Even the track that leads to the tower is good.

# LAKE SYSMÄJÄRVI

62°41N 29°03E

This 750-ha area includes a shallow eutrophic lake surrounded partly by agricultural land and mixed forest. The area of open water, lake margins and meadows has diminished over the years due to uncontrolled growth of plants. The amount of submerged and floating vegetation is remarkable in autumn, making rowing a boat difficult.

Regrettably, the lake lacks protection and consequently is probably the most popular hunting area in the province in autumn. In the past, springtime

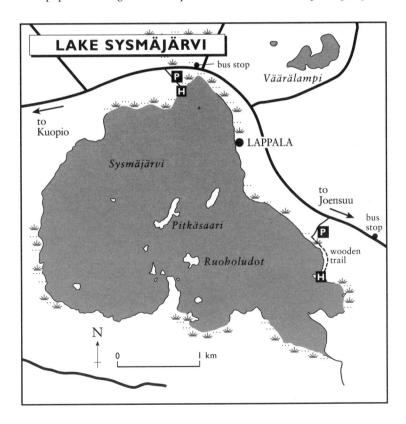

shooting of unprotected birds was a problem; this was outlawed by a local hunting organization in 1992.

Sysmäjärvi is the most important wetland in Karelia and is cited in the National Wetland Conservation Programme (1981) as being of national importance; a 1990 survey indicated its international significance. 70 species regularly breed in the area.

TIMING

The first Whooper Swans and ducks appear in mid-April, concentrated on open stretches of water that appear at river mouths entering the southern and north-eastern corners of the lake. Peak wildfowl migration normally lasts from the end of April to mid-May by which time the lake is free of ice. Active hunting from 20 August drives those few ducks and other birds that are present away, and so autumn is quiet. Winter, from December to February, is long and hard with few birds around.

SPECIES

◆ *Breeding season* Red-necked and Slavonian Grebes, Bittern, Whooper Swan, Wigeon, Teal, Common Crane, Osprey, Honey Buzzard, Marsh and Hen Harriers, Hobby, Merlin, Jack Snipe, Little Gull, Blyth's Reed Warbler, Thrush Nightingale, Yellow-breasted Bunting.

◆ *Passage* Black-throated and Red-throated Divers, Bewick's Swan, White-fronted, Pink-footed and Bean Geese, Scaup, Long-tailed Duck, White-tailed and Golden Eagles, Common Buzzard, Rough-legged Buzzard, Black Kite, Peregrine, waders, Little Gull, rarities.

ACCESS

The lake is situated beside the main road between Joensuu (45 km) and Kuopio (100 km). The bird watching towers are marked with black-and-white signs 'Lintutorni' along the road. A small driveable track to the southern tower starts about 300-m north-west of the border of Liperi and Outokumpu districts (district signs along the road). A track to the northern tower starts about 1-km north-west from the former tower and 300-m north-west of the crossroads to Kaavi (road number 573) and Polvijärvi (504), which are marked with the blue-and-white signs. There are about ten buses daily between Joensuu and Kuopio, and bus stops are found on the border of Liperi and Outokumpu and the cross to Kaavi and Polvijärvi (*see* above).

# Bay Päätyenlahti

62°07N 30°07E

A shallow eutrophic bay bordered partly by agricultural land and partly by thickets of young birches, alders and willows, in all covering 320 ha. About 100 ha of the bay is a nature conservation area but, despite this, hunting is permitted in the whole area in autumn. The breeding bird fauna was surveyed in 1992 with 800 pairs of more than 50 species found in the area. The breeding population of wildfowl consisted of 240 pairs and 15 species. The bay has been considered as the second best bird lake in Karelia.

TIMING

Following ice-bound, bird-less winters, which last from November to March, the first stretches of open water appear in mid-April in front of both towers. By the end of April the area is large enough to hold the first returning swans, geese, ducks and Ospreys. The ice has melted by mid-May and, towards the

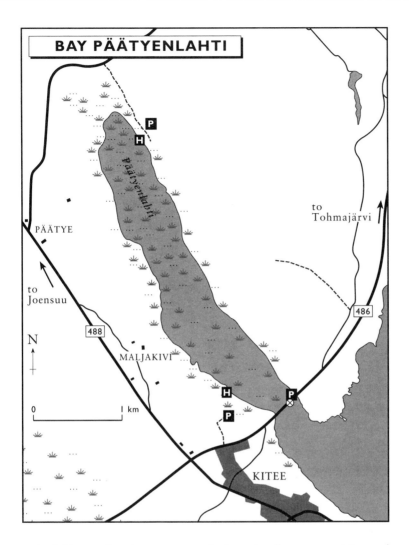

**BAY PÄÄTYENLAHTI**

Päätyenlahti

PÄÄTYE

to Joensuu

to Tohmajärvi

N

488

486

MALJAKIVI

0    1 km

KITEE

end of this month, migrant raptors, ducks and gulls are present in good numbers. The summer months are relatively quiet. At the end of August and the beginning of September, duck hunting violently shatters the peace of the bay, and hardly any birds can be seen.

SPECIES

◆ *Breeding season* Red-necked and Slavonian Grebes, Whooper Swan, ducks, Osprey, Marsh Harrier, Corncrake, Spotted Crake, Little Gull, Lesser Spotted Woodpecker, Blyth's Reed Warbler, Thrush Nightingale.

◆ *Passage* Whooper Swan, Bewick's Swan (occasional), Bean Goose, White-fronted Goose (occasional), ducks, White-tailed and Golden Eagles, Black Kite.

ACCESS

Easily reached from Kitee. The parking place at the southern edge of the bay stands along the Kitee and Tohmajärvi road (road number 486). The road is marked with a blue-and-white sign in the centre of Kitee. The southern tower is reached by taking the first tarmac road to the right about 400 m from the parking place in the direction of the city. On that road take the first road to the right (after about 200 m) and follow 100 m to the easternmost corner of the S-loop of the road. Walk the last 20 m to the tower through forest. The northern tower can be reached by driving 5 km to the north along the road number 488 (to Tolosenmäki or Joensuu – Lappenranta main road). Then the road with the blue-and-white sign 'Haarajärvi' is taken for 2 km. Just after passing the head of the bay take the first just driveable track with the black-and-white sign 'Lintutorni' to the right. The tower is reached after a 300-m drive on the right. Kitee is easily reached by train or by bus.

# LAKE SÄÄPERI

62°13N 30°40E

This shallow, 146 ha lake lies close to the Russian border. Sääperi is surrounded by agricultural land, though there are coniferous forests and moorland especially to the north and east. Although eutrophic in character, there are only reedbeds along the shores.

Since the lake is unprotected, hunting and other activities are permitted here. In the National Wetland Conservation Programme (1981) its national importance as a conservation area is cited; a later survey (1991) recorded 550 pairs of 64 breeding species, among which were 108 pairs of 13 species of waterbirds. Spring migration of wildfowl can be spectacular: in many years, up to 10,000 Barnacle Geese are seen on daytime counts around 20 May; at the same time, thousands of Common Scoters and Long-tailed Ducks can be seen and heard.

TIMING

Following harsh winters (November to March), mid-April sees the start of the thaw on the lake, usually on the southern shores around the mouth of the River Jänisjoki. By the beginning of May, the snow has melted but the greater part of the lake will still be ice-bound; not until mid-May will the lake become free of ice.

In the latter half of April, geese, ducks and waders gather and raptor migration reaches its peak with up to 300 birds seen in a day. Numbers of geese build up until mid-May and for the next few weeks, eastern and southern rarities are a possibility. The first half of June is excellent for the twilight songsters for which Finland is famous. July and August are still good months for breeding birds of the area, but arguably the most exciting time of year for a visiting birdwatcher will be in September and October when the numbers and variety of migrating raptors, geese and ducks are best.

SPECIES

◆ *Resident* Black Grouse.
◆ *Breeding season* Red-necked and Slavonian Grebes, Osprey, Black Kite, Spotted Crake, Corncrake, Marsh Sandpiper, Black-headed and Little Gulls, Sedge, River, Blyth's Reed, Arctic and Greenish Warblers, Thrush Nightingale, Reed, Rustic and Yellow-breasted Buntings.
◆ *Passage* Bean and White-fronted Geese, White-tailed and Golden Eagles, Rough-legged Buzzard, Peregrine, Common Crane, Curlew, Golden Plover, Greenshank, Spotted Redshank, Wood Sandpiper, Ruff, Red-throated Pipit, Arctic Redpoll, Lapland Bunting, rarities (notably raptors).

ACCESS

Lake Sääperi is situated in the middle of Värtsilä district, about 20 km east of Tohmajärvi district. Take the road number 500 from Niirala to Ilomantsi. Drive 4 km passing the minor Värtsilä centre until you reach the black-and-white sign 'Lintutorni' along the main road on the right. A parking place is just beside the road. The walk from the parking place along a trail takes about 20 minutes. There is a daily bus service to Värtsilä from Tohmajärvi. There are many other points around the lake from where to watch birds. On the south-eastern side of the lake there is a field called 'Hopeakallio' which is well placed for migrating raptors and geese; it is very popular among local bird watchers. Ask the locals for directions to other good birdwatching spots nearby.

# MUSTASAARI VASSORFJÄRDEN
63°10N 22°00E

This 5 km² wetland is one of the best waterbird sites in Finland. The muddy bay is one of the most outstanding areas for waders on the coast of Bothnia.

TIMING

During the harsh winter that lasts from November to March, the bay is ice-bound and there are no birds. The months of April and May see the best of spring migration with swans, geese, ducks, waders and gulls appearing in good numbers. Bird numbers are again good during autumn migration which lasts from late August until October.

SPECIES

◆ *Breeding season* Common Crane, swans, ducks, Osprey, Marsh Harrier, Hobby, Lapwing, Black-headed and Little Gulls, Caspian Tern, Common Rosefinch, Reed Bunting.

◆ *Passage* Geese, ducks, raptors, Ruff, Dunlin, Wood and Green Sandpipers.

ACCESS

The area is very easy to check when driving road 8, some 20 km north from Vaasa. Driving from the south, turn to the parking place 500 m after you pass the crossroads to road 725 on the right. The parking place is well signposted. Birds can be studied from the parking place and adjacent land.

# LIMINGANLAHTI
65°50N 24°30E

Liminganlahti (100 km²) is the best coastal wetland for birds in Finland and comprises the bay where the Temmesjoki and Lumijoki Rivers reach the Gulf of Bothnia. It is fringed by large meadows and fields. The area is important for migrant birds but more than 70 species breed here, their numbers including more than 1500 pairs of ducks and 3700 pairs of gulls.

Despite its importance to wildlife, Liminganlahti has no protection yet; as a consequence, hunting pressure in autumn is severe and thereafter it is impossible to count migratory species.

TIMING

Spring migration begins in March with the appearance of the first Goosanders and Snow Buntings. In April, tens of thousands of swans, geese and ducks stop off from migration and rest, along with Arctic waders and passerines in good numbers. In June and July, the breeding season is under way with family groups of birds seen in early August along with the first

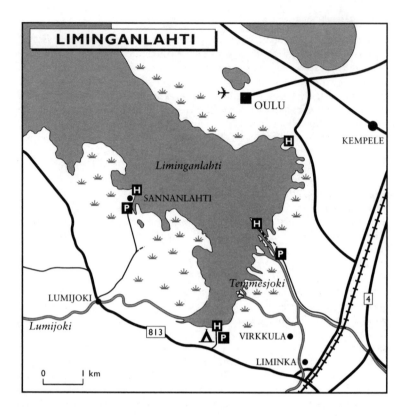

returning migrant waders. After 20 August the hunting season starts and frightens most birds away. From October to February, the area is invariably ice-bound.

SPECIES
- ◆ *Breeding season* Common Crane, Mallard, Wigeon, Montagu's Harrier, Black-tailed Godwit, Black-headed and Little Gulls, Short-eared Owl, Bearded Tit, Common Rosefinch, Ortolan and Yellow-breasted Buntings.
- ◆ *Passage* White-fronted and Lesser White-fronted Geese, Terek and Marsh Sandpipers, Bluethroat, Lapland Bunting.

ACCESS
Take road 4 from the centre of Oulu (Uleåborg) southwards. After 25 km turn to the right at road 813 in the direction of Lumijoki. Drive another 4 km and you will find the WWF guide centre on your right. At the centre you can get detailed information on where to go. From three observation towers you will get excellent views over the bay and the most interesting surroundings. In the early morning, start with the northernmost tower because of the light, and then go to the south tower when the sun moves. At the WWF centre you can also buy coffee, lunch and books, and hire a guide.

# HIRVISUO BOG

65°10N 26°15E

This 12 km² area of bog is situated along road 20 between Oulu and Kuusamo.

TIMING

From November to April, snow and ice cover the land and birdwatching interest is limited to resident birds like grouse, woodpeckers and crossbills. In May the migratory birds start to arrive, some staying to breed, others resting before continuing their journeys. June and July are perhaps the best months for birdwatchers, although from August to October you can experience the thrill of autumn migration.

SPECIES

◆ *Resident* Capercaillie, Willow Ptarmigan, Black Grouse, Black Woodpecker, Parrot Crossbill.

◆ *Breeding season* Whooper Swan, Bean Goose, Golden Eagle, Kestrel, Hobby, Merlin, Osprey, Common Crane, Lapwing, Curlew, Golden Plover, Green Sandpiper, Meadow Pipit, Yellow Wagtail, Brambling, Rustic Bunting.

◆ *Passage* Raptors.

ACCESS

Hirvijärvi is situated in Ylikiiminki commune 30 km east from Oulu along the road 20. From the parking place you can find a map and a nature trail (2.5 km) with a bird tower.

# KUUSAMO TORANKI

65°55N 29°15E

A bird lake surrounded by forests, meadows, parks and gardens covering, in all, an area of 30 km². It is generally considered to be the best bird lake in Kuusamo. It is perhaps best known for its Little and Rustic Buntings which sing from the lakeside bushes.

TIMING

From November to March, ice and snow exclude birds from the area, the first birds returning with the thaw. June, when the birds are singing is the optimum time to visit. July is a relatively quiet month, with numbers and variety of migrant ducks, waders and passerines improving in August and September, before the onset of winter in late October.

SPECIES

◆ *Breeding season* Black-throated Diver, Great Crested and Red-necked Grebes, Whooper Swan, Pochard, Smew, Shoveler, Goldeneye, Goosander, Little Gull, Short-eared Owl, Little and Rustic Buntings.

◆ *Passage* Ducks, waders, Arctic Warbler.

ACCESS

Lake Torankijärvi town can be viewed from many places, but the best is the bird tower. From the crossroads (roads 5 and 20) turn to the Kuusamo centre, and turn right at the first crossroads. Join the street 'Torangintaival' and signpost 'Lintutorni' (bird tower) some 3.5 km. Paths to the bird tower start at the parking place, the main one passing the ruin of an old church. Turn to the right towards the shore to find the bird tower.

# KUUSAMO VALTAVAARA

66°10N 29°10E

This 10 km² area of old taiga is world famous as a site for Red-flanked Bluetail. An excellent range of other species occurs as well, many making good use of the numerous nest holes in the old trees. Part of the area has nature protection status.

TIMING

Harsh winters, lasting from November to April, limit birdwatching interest to resident birds like grouse, woodpeckers and crossbills. May sees the return of migratory birds and June is perhaps the best month for birding; the hour before dawn and early in the morning are particularly rewarding. The breeding season lasts until August.

SPECIES

◆ *Resident* Capercaillie, Black Grouse, Hazel Hen, Great Spotted, Black and Three-toed Woodpeckers, Siberian Jay, tits, Two-barred Crossbill, Pine Grosbeak.

◆ *Breeding season* Collared Flycatcher, Redstart, Red-flanked Bluetail (difficult to see but can be heard singing), Redwing, Arctic and Greenish Warblers.

ACCESS

From Kuusamo centre drive road 5 to the north 30 km and turn to the right to the east (road 8694 'Jyrkänkoski'). The parking place is situated on the hill after 4 km. The road divides the area into two separate forests. The better place is the higher area to the south of the parking place. Do not hurry your birdwatching here – the path is rough and it takes time to hear and see the birds given the vast size of the site.

# OULANKA NATIONAL PARK

66°27N 29°20E

This vast area of old taiga boasts deep valleys, magnificent waterfalls (like Kiutaköngäs), bogs, ponds and meadows; 270 km² are contained within the boundary of this National Park which extends over the border into Russia. In addition to its birdwatching interest, Oulanka has plenty of reindeer and a few Brown Bears.

TIMING

Winter lasts from November to April with snow and ice blanketing the landscape; a few hardy resident birds are present, including species of grouse, woodpeckers and crossbills. May sees the return of the migratory birds and June is the best month for birding, the period just before dawn and early in the evening being the most rewarding times of day. By mid-August, the breeding season has come to an end and migratory species begin to move southwards.

SPECIES

◆ *Resident* Capercaillie, Willow Ptarmigan, Great Grey and Hawk Owls, Black and Three-toed Woodpeckers, Siberian Jay, Crested and Siberian Tits, Pine Grosbeak, Parrot and Two-barred Crossbills.

◆ *Breeding season* Whooper Swan, Bean Goose, Smew, Golden Eagle, Hen Harrier and Rough-legged Buzzard (in vole years), Common Crane, Jack Snipe, Red-necked Phalarope, Green Sandpiper, Ruff, Cuckoo, Dipper, Raven, Waxwing, Arctic and Greenish Warblers, Red-flanked Bluetail, Bluethroat, Little and Rustic Buntings.

ACCESS

From Kuusamo farm, take road 5 northwards for 36 km and then turn right to the east (road 950 'Salla'). Drive 6 km and turn east to road 8693 Liikasenvaara. The guide centre is after 13 km and is well signposted. There are three nature trails. Birders visit mainly Kiutaköngäs.

*Spotted Redshank, summer*

# URHO KEKKONEN NATIONAL PARK

**68°15N 27°30E**

This vast area of wilderness covers 2530 km² and harbours superb areas of old forest, bogs, rivers, meadows and hills. The establishment of Urho Kekkonen National Park (named after the president) in 1983 was one the most important victories of the Finnish nature conservation movement.

### TIMING

Winter lasts from October to May. The best birding is to be had in June and July; by August, the migratory species are feeding up for their return. In September, autumn migration is well under way. The stunning autumn colours of the trees make up for the diminishing numbers of birds at this time of year.

### SPECIES

- *Resident* Capercaillie, Willow Ptarmigan, Three-toed Woodpecker, Siberian Jay, Siberian Tit, Pine Grosbeak.
- *Breeding season* Whooper Swan, Golden Eagle, Rough-legged Buzzard, Common Crane, Red-necked Phalarope, Ruff, Whimbrel, Jack Snipe, Broad-billed and Green Sandpipers, Spotted Redshank, Yellow Wagtail, Red-throated Pipit, Waxwing, Bluethroat, Brambling, Lapland Bunting, Snow Bunting (hills).

### ACCESS

The Tankavaara guide centre is along the road E4, the best place to begin a visit. For a brief visit, there are three short nature trails, 'Redpoll route' (1 km with a little bird tower – with hardly any birds), 'Capercaillie route' (3 km) and 'Siberian Jay route' (6 km, with a bird/view tower on the top of the hill Pieni Tankavaara). If you have time, you can hike tens or hundreds of kilometres, but it is essential to discuss potential routes with the guides: they will know if there is room in some of the 40 free or cheap cottages along the route, or if some areas are too wet. Perhaps the best area for the birds is called Sompio Nature Park in the southern part of the area. There are also information points in the tourist traps Saariselkä and Kiilopää.

## PALLASTUNTURI – OUNASTUNTURI
68°05N 24°05E

This area comprises 500 km² of the best mountain landscape in forested Lapland. There are also beautiful river valleys, ponds, small bogs and meadows. Ounastunturi has National Park status.

TIMING

Winter runs from October to May and a few hardy, resident bird species remain. June and July are the best for birding, the breeding species singing or displaying. The season is short and by August and September migratory birds are leaving.

SPECIES

◆ *Resident* Ptarmigan, Willow Ptarmigan, Siberian Jay, Siberian Tit, Pine Grosbeak.

◆ *Breeding season* Rough-legged Buzzard, Dotterel (mountains), Red-necked Phalarope, Ruff, Whimbrel, Jack Snipe, Broad-billed and Green Sandpipers, Spotted Redshank, Yellow Wagtail, Red-throated Pipit, Ring Ouzel, Bluethroat, Brambling, Lapland and Snow Buntings (mountains).

ACCESS

Ounastunturi guide centre is the main site. Leave road 21 in Muonio and drive to the east on road 79 for 11.5 km. Turn to the north to road 957 and drive 14.4 km. Then choose the left way 9571, and the hotel and guide centre is located where the road ends after 6 km. There are 260 km of routes and nature trails beginning from Ounastunturi guide centre. It is possible to walk for many days, e.g. to another guide centre in Hetta in Enontekiö (55 km) – and take a taxi boat over the lake and go on. Usually birders visit only the top of Taivaskero along the nature trail (some 5 km).

## KILPISJÄRVI SAANA
69°05N 20°45E

From the summit (1029 m) visitors get a great view over Lake Kilpisjärvi and towards other mountains in the distance. There is some woodland on the nature trail within the 10-km² area of this site but the main attractions are the mountain and tundra birds that are found here.

TIMING

Winter lasts from October to May. June and July are the best birding months. By August and September, autumn migration has begun.

SPECIES

◆ *Resident* Ptarmigan.

◆ *Breeding season* Rough-legged Buzzard, Dotterel, Long-tailed Skua, Ring Ouzel, Red-throated Pipit, House Martin, Arctic Warbler, Bluethroat, Siberian Tit, Redpoll, Brambling, Lapland and Snow Buntings.

ACCESS

The nature trail is well signposted in the village of Kilpisjärvi from road E8. The longer route begins from Kilpisjärven matkailuhotelli, another from Kilpisjärven retkeilykeskus. **It is essential to follow the nature trail: some people have died after leaving the path and falling from the mountain.**

# ICELAND

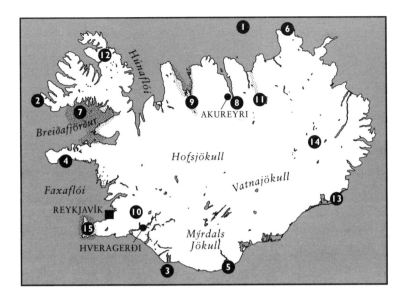

1 GRIMSEY, 2 LATRABJARG, 3 VESTMANNAEYJAR, 4 STAÐARSVEIT-LONDRANGAR AREA, 5 MÝRDALUR, 6 MELRAKKASLÉTTA, 7 BREIÐAFJÖRÐUR, 8 AKUREYRI AND SURROUNDINGS, 9 SKAGAFJÖRÐUR, 10 LAKE ÞINGVALLAVATN AND ITS OUTLET, 11 MÝVATN – LAXA, 12 HORNSTRANDIR, 13 HORNAFJÖRÐUR & LON, 14 JÖKULDALSHEIÐI, 15 REYKJANES PENINSULA.

Iceland is an island of 103,000 km², Europe's second largest. Icelanders (population 265,000) are the descendants of Vikings from Scandinavia, particularly Norway, and Gaelic people, who settled in Iceland eleven centuries ago. The native language is Icelandic, basically the old Norse language which was spoken in Scandinavia during the Viking Age. English and the Scandinavian languages are commonly spoken by the inhabitants, making travelling around for the visitor somewhat easier.

Iceland is geologically a very young country, the oldest rocks being only about 15,000,000 years old. Since Iceland is sited on the middle of the Mid-Atlantic Ridge, the land is constantly expanding by a few centimetres a year. The oceanic climate is surprisingly mild due to the warming influence of the Gulf Stream. Around the coast, summer temperatures normally vary between 10–15°C, and temperatures around zero or a few degrees below are normal in winter. Severe frosts are relatively rare.

Marine products comprise about 75 per cent of the exports, the rest mostly from industry; tourism is an expanding business.

## HABITATS

The greater part of Iceland is covered by moorland vegetation which is Alpine in nature. Large wetland areas are to be found, although considerable drainage has taken place for agricultural purposes, especially in lowland areas. Agricultural land (hayfields, vegetable areas, etc.) is estimated to cover about 1 per cent of the country, but a much larger land area has been modified for grazing purposes or for future agricultural development. These disturbed areas are not evenly spread but concentrated mostly below 200 m. About 10% of the country is covered by ice caps, including Vatnajökull the largest ice shield in Europe. Lava fields cover another 20% of the country. Around 70 per cent of the country is above 400 m, and the interior highlands are totally uninhabited.

## IMPORTANCE FOR BIRDS

Iceland is a land of waterbirds: waders, wildfowl, and seabirds. Passerines constitute a much smaller proportion of the regular species than in most other countries. Regular breeding species number around 70, while some 30 more species have bred on one or more occasion.

Altogether 334 species are found on the Icelandic checklist. Many non-breeding species regularly overwinter or are seen on migration. These species are just as likely to originate from North America and Greenland as from Spitzbergen, Russia and Scandinavia.

Iceland has several North American specialities, namely Great Northern Diver, Barrow's Goldeneye, and Harlequin Duck. Other species which normally rank high on the expectation list of bird enthusiasts, are Gyrfalcon, Puffin, Brünnich's Guillemot, Red-necked and Grey Phalaropes and Golden Plover. This century a number of new species have started breeding and some are common now, such as Shoveler, Garganey, Pochard, Curlew, Wood Sandpiper, Black-headed Gull, Herring Gull, Lesser Black-backed Gull, Short-eared Owl, Blackbird, and House Sparrow. Fortunately, Iceland has only lost a few breeding species. The Great Auk became globally extinct in 1844 and two species are on the brink of extinction as Icelandic breeding species: Little Auk and Water Rail, both of which may be gone by the time this book is published.

Iceland has huge seabird colonies with over 20 breeding species. Some of the most spectacular bird cliffs in the world are found here. Substantial parts of the world population of some breeding species are found in Iceland, including the Puffin, Razorbill, and Great Skua. Iceland is a very important breeding area for some waders, such as Golden Plover, Whimbrel, Dunlin, and Red-necked Phalarope while the Black-tailed Godwit constitutes a special subspecies. Wildfowl are also numerous with an important population of Whooper Swan and the world's largest breeding colony of Pink-footed Geese. Lake Mývatn is renowned the world over for its ducks, while the Eider is Iceland's most common duck species and of economic importance for its highly-insulating down.

## SEASONS

### SPRING

This is a good time of year for birds in Iceland, especially during April and May. Most migrants are beginning arrive, and several migrant species break their northbound journey at this time; these include Brent Goose, Barnacle Goose, White-fronted Goose, Turnstone, Knot, and Sanderling.

SUMMER
Breeding generally starts for most bird species in the second half of May to early June. The seabird cliffs are best visited from June to early July, while the ducks are in their prime plumage in late May and June. Moorland birds are on their territories during these months.

AUTUMN
Wader migrants from the Arctic start returning towards the end of June with highest numbers from late July into August. Most of the migrant breeders move south in August and September, and many of the cliff-nesting seabirds have already left. Arctic geese return in September, staying into October. September and October are prime months to look for vagrant birds, of European or North American origin. In the autumn, winter visitors start showing up, including high-Arctic species like Iceland Gull and Little Auk.

WINTER
Over one hundred species have been sighted (of which about 40 are regular) during annual Christmas counts. Iceland receives large numbers of over-wintering birds from higher latitudes which belong to species that breed here as well; Eider, Long-tailed Duck, Purple Sandpiper, Glaucous Gull, Little Auk, Black Guillemot, and Snow Bunting are among them.

# CONSERVATION

In general, Icelanders are conservation-oriented and have been for a long time. There are long traditions of full protection for many species, especially the moorland birds and passerines, some of which are game birds in other countries. This attitude does not extend, however, to the harvesting of eggs or the taking of young seabirds.

The first actual conservation act took force in 1882 although this did not apply to as many species as later. Surprisingly, White-tailed Eagles have been fully protected since 1913 although naïvely disliked for some for their predatory habits. The present conservation act came into force on 1 July 1994. A totally new way of thinking was introduced so that all bird species are fully protected from gratuitous hunting, although killing for food or pest control is permitted with certain species. A hunting licence is required and hunting statistics have to be compiled. The bird conservation act is under the auspices of the Ministry for the Environment, Vonarstræti 4, 150 Reykjavík, aided by a consultative committee which advises on all matters relating to conservation, protection, and hunting of birds.

Over 70 areas are protected as National Parks, reserves and the like, and many of them have been set aside because of their birdlife. These are under the auspices of the Nature Conservation Council (NCC). The Icelandic Society for the Protection of Birds is the only NGO body in Iceland which has bird conservation and their habitats as its primary goal. The Icelandic Institute of Natural History, Hlemmur 3, P.O. 5320, 125 Reykjavík, has long been the centre for ornithology in Iceland. Basically all areas are open to access, although some protected areas have entry restrictions during the breeding season. Eider colonies should not be entered without permission from the local farmers. Permission should also be sought before crossing land and fences in the immediate vicinity of farms.

## GETTING THERE AND GETTING AROUND

Iceland can be reached either by air or sea. There is regular air traffic to and from Keflavík International Airport to major cities in Scandinavia, Western Europe, and USA. Passenger liners only operate during the summer months, but freighters, also open to a few passengers, call throughout the year.

## THE ICELANDIC SOCIETY FOR THE PROTECTION OF BIRDS

This comprises one national society (*see* Useful Addresses) and one regional division. A bird magazine, *Bliki*, is published by the Icelandic Institute of Natural History in cooperation with the Icelandic Society for the Protection of Birds and bird observers. Papers are in Icelandic with English summaries (1–2 issues per year). The Chairman of the editorial board is Guðmundur A. Guðmundsson. All enquiries should be made to him at the Icelandic Institute of Natural History (*see* address on previous page).

# BIRDWATCHING SITES

## GRÍMSEY
66°33N 18°00W

This 530-ha island is crossed by the Arctic Circle; it is 5.5-km long and about 2 km at its widest. The island slopes from a sheer cliff-face, about 100-m high on the eastward side, to near sea-level on the western side. The northernmost settlement in Iceland is on the island, comprising about 120 people. The vegetation is typically oceanic in character with rather few species (about 115), but with a luxuriant growth due to enrichment by seabird droppings and ocean spray. The island is not protected but a large part of it is listed as a site of special interest.

Being an oceanic island, seabirds dominate while a few moorland species, common in the rest of Iceland, are also to be found. About 22 bird species nest regularly. Grímsey has long been known as the only breeding site in Iceland of the Little Auk; now there is probably only one pair left and the breeding area is protected and should not be approached without prior permission from the Ministry of the Environment.

TIMING

A visit to Grímsey is basically a summer affair, from the arrival of the seabirds in April until August. Weather is most reliable in June and July which is the prime time for birdwatching. Mid-summer on the Arctic Circle is a memorable experience.

SPECIES

♦ *Breeding season* Fulmar, Kittiwake, Little Auk, Guillemot, Brünnich's Guillemot, Razorbill, Puffin, Snow Bunting.

ACCESS
The island can be reached in two ways; by near daily flights during the summer months from Akureyri, or by ferry departing from the same town. Most of the island can only be explored on foot. The continuous 5.5-km east-facing bird cliff is of particular interest. The coastline south of the village has interesting rock formations as well as varied bird life. Seals are frequently seen in the sandy inlet of Básavík, and the view from the lighthouse at the island's southernmost tip is worth enjoying. Make sure you visit the pond Sandvíkurtjörn near to the main road between the airstrip and the main part of the village.

# LÁTRABJARG
65°29N 24°28W
With a cliff-face area of some 330 ha, this is the largest bird cliff in Iceland, forming a 14-km long, uninterrupted wall of seabirds at the westernmost point in the country. The cliff reaches a height of over 400 m and boulder scree slopes are found in places at the foot of the cliff; these are important breeding habitats for some bird species. A central part of the cliff, called Bæjarbjarg, was bought by the Ministry of the Environment in 1993, and is now protected by law. The remaining part of the cliff is registered as a site of special interest by the Nature Conservation Council, while the entire cliff is listed as an Important Bird Area by BirdLife International.

TIMING
The cliff-nesting birds are found from late April, with breeding taking place towards mid- to late May. By mid-July the precocious young auks leave the cliffs with their parents for the high seas, while Shags, Puffins, Kittiwakes, and Black Guillemots mature and depart later. Fulmars remain into September. June and July are generally the best months for visiting the cliff.

SPECIES
◆ *Breeding season* Fulmar, Shag, Kittiwake, Glaucous Gull, Purple Sandpiper, Guillemot (300,000 pairs), Brünnich's Guillemot (120,000 pairs), Razorbill (230,000 pairs, over half the world population and certainly the largest colony anywhere), Puffin, Raven, Iceland Wren.

ACCESS
The cliff, which is 61 km from the nearest fishing town of Patreksfjörður (population 900), is easiest to reach by car along road no. 612. The town can be reached either by near daily scheduled flight from Reykjavík, by daily coach from Reykjavík or scheduled flight from Isafjörður.

The only proper road to the cliff takes the visitor to the lighthouse at Bjargtangar which is on the cliff edge, and also to the very westernmost tip of Iceland. Visitors who want to explore other parts of the cliff have to walk along the edge.

# VESTMANNAEYJAR
63°24N 20°18W (approximate centre of area)
This archipelago of rocky islands lies off the southern coast of Iceland and comprises a total area of some 24,000 ha. Only the largest of the 15 main islands Heimaey, is inhabited (population 5000). A third of the town was destroyed by ash and lava in a volcanic eruption in 1973. The second largest island is Surtsey, which emerged from the sea as a result of volcanic activity between 1963 and 1967.

The outer islands and many parts of Heimaey are surrounded by cliffs or steep slopes. Except on Surtsey, which is still essentially barren, the islands are dominated by dry meadowland and the so-called Puffin ground, which stays green most of the year.

Surtsey is a nature reserve and closed to visitors except for research purposes. Landing is not permitted without a permit from the Surtsey Research Society. Three other islands, Elliðaey, Hellisey, and Súlnasker, are listed on the Nature Conservation Council register as sites of conservation interest.

The islands' seabird colonies are of national and world significance. The only breeding colonies of Manx Shearwater in Iceland are on these islands (five sites, the largest at Ystiklettur on Heimaey), and the bulk of the Icelandic Leach's and British Storm-petrels breed here; Elliðaey has the largest colony of Leach's Storm-petrels in Europe (c. 50,000 pairs), and also the largest Icelandic colony of British Storm-petrels.

Approximately 9000 pairs of Gannets breed here and the largest Puffin colonies in the world are on these islands. Puffin-catching with pole nets is a common practice, with seemingly no harmful influence on the population noticeable as yet.

TIMING

Large numbers of seabirds are found all year round, although April–August is best for watching breeding birds. Puffins are active at their colonies until the beginning of September, but Fulmars stay all year round as do many of the Gannets. Manx Shearwaters and British Storm-petrels stay from April to September, and Leach's Storm-petrels even longer. Most of the auks leave the colonies in the latter half of July and Kittiwakes in August.

The islands are the first landfall for many migrants in spring, in April and May, and some use them as staging posts in autumn. These islands are particularly good for rarities and vagrants of all kinds, including North American ones, mainly in autumn (August to November).

SPECIES

◆ *Resident* Fulmar, Gannet, Eider.
◆ *Breeding season* Manx Shearwater, Leach's and British Storm-petrels, Oystercatcher, Great Black-backed, Lesser Black-backed, Herring and Glaucous Gulls, Kittiwake, Arctic Tern, Guillemot, Black Guillemot, Razorbill, Puffin, White Wagtail.
◆ *Passage* Waders, passerines.
◆ *Winter* Shag, Cormorant, Long-tailed Duck, Gyrfalcon, Merlin, Turnstone, Purple Sandpiper, Little Auk.

ACCESS

There are several scheduled flights daily from Reykjavík to Vestmanneyjar. The islands can also be reached daily by ferry from Þorlákshöfn, 50 km from Reykjavík. The ferry has a bus connection with Reykjavík.

Heimaey (13 km²) provides opportunities to watch most of the seabirds breeding on the islands. Some good sites are Heimaklettur north of the town, Dalfjall northwest of it, or the southernmost point of Stórhöfði which is easily reached on foot from the town.

Gaining access to the outer islands is difficult since there are no proper landing spots. However, they are open to visitors (except Surtsey). Puffin catchers' clubs own huts on most of the islands, and the clubs should be contacted before visiting these islands. Elliðaey, the third largest outlying

*Arctic Skua*

island, is the easiest to visit, lying about half an hours' sailing north-east from Heimaey harbour. An alternative is to take a trip with the tourist boats, sailing daily in the summer season around the archipelago.

## Staðarsveit-Lóndrangar area

**64°48N 23°24W**

The Snæfellsnes peninsula harbours examples of most types of landscape and wildlife to be found in Iceland. This magnificent area, which covers an area of some 20,000 ha, is dominated by the majestic central volcano, Snæfellsjökull.

The area described here can roughly be divided into two kinds of main habitats. The Hellnar–Arnarstapi–Lóndrangar area is mostly covered by post-glacial lava. Since the ground is so porous, vegetation is rather sparse and wetlands limited. The coastline is rocky, and there are no beaches or mud flats.

The other half, Staðarsveit, is mostly covered with wet marshland dotted with ponds and lakes, except for a recent lava field on the border with the above-mentioned area. This is called Búðahraun, renowned for interesting and rare species of flowering plants and ferns. Farms with cultivated fields are scattered all over the area. Drainage canals are prominent in the landscape as almost everywhere on lowland Iceland.

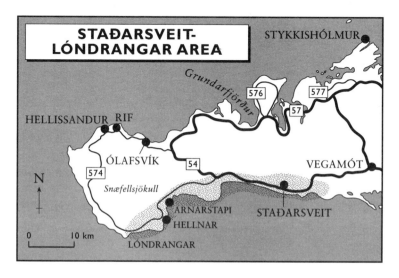

Three areas are nature reserves, for which special regulations apply: the Búðahraun lava field because of its plant life and the coast at Arnarstapi and Hellnar for curious landscape and interesting bird life.

Around 40 species of birds nest regularly within this area. Grey and Common Seals can be seen along the coast, and White-sided and White-beaked Dolphins are frequently seen offshore, sometimes pursued by Killer Whales.

TIMING
The best time to visit is from the middle of April to August. Migrants pass through the region in good numbers and are particularly abundant in April and May, and again in August and September.

SPECIES
◆ *Resident* Eider, Harlequin Duck, White-tailed Eagle.
◆ *Breeding season* Great Northern Diver, Slavonian Grebe, Black-tailed Godwit, Kittiwake, Arctic Tern, Guillemot, Brünnich's and Black Guillemot, Razorbill, Puffin.
◆ *Passage* Knot, Sanderling, Turnstone.

ACCESS
The best way to reach Snæfellsnes peninsula is to take a bus or rent a car. There are daily departures from the central bus terminal in Reykjavík. The trip takes about 3 hours along road no. 1 from Reykjavík.

On leaving Staðarsveit the most attractive vantage points are Arnarstapi, Hellnar, Svalþúfa, and Lóndrangar, and these are also the best birding spots in the area.

# MÝRDALUR

63°26N 19°08W

This lowland area, which covers roughly 7000 ha, has large glacial sands both to the west and east, the ice cap Mýrdalsjökull towards north, and is bordered by the Atlantic Ocean in the south. Glaciers and the volcano Katla (which is shielded by the ice-cap) have shaped much of the landscape. Two headlands are among the main attractions for bird-watchers, Dyrhólaey and Reynisfjall and most of the vegetated lowland is cultivated. Dyrhólaey is a nature reserve (510 ha) and the Nature Conservation Council restricts public access between 1 May and 25 June. Reynisfjall, Reynisdrangar, Dyrhólaós, and Loftsalahellir, as well as Skammadalskambar, are listed by the NCC as sites of conservation interest.

*Great Northern Diver, summer*

TIMING

The area is probably best known for its seabird colonies. The Puffins and Kittiwakes are active from April until towards the end of August, the Fulmars stay at the colonies more-or-less year round, most of the Guillemots have left by the end of July, and the Arctic Tern only stays from May into September. Few species are observed in winter.

SPECIES

◆ *Breeding season* Great Northern and Red-throated Divers, Fulmar, Leach's Storm-petrel, Greylag Goose, Mallard, Teal, Eider, Gyrfalcon, Oystercatcher, Whimbrel, Black-tailed Godwit, Dunlin, Great and Arctic Skuas, Great Black-backed, Lesser Black-backed, Herring and Black-headed Gulls, Glaucous Gull (non-breeder), Kittiwake, Arctic Tern, Guillemot, Black Guillemot, Razorbill, Puffin, Redwing, Raven, Snow Bunting.

ACCESS

Road no. 1 intersects the area with scheduled buses twice a day between Reykjavík and Kirkjubæjarklaustur and Höfn further to the east.

Dyrhólaey (or Portland) is the southernmost promontory in Iceland, made of palagonite tuff created in a submarine eruption. The headland and nearby stacks are renowned for their precipitous cliffs, teeming with bird life, and the huge, sea-eroded hole (or port), through which large boats can sail.

The mountains eastwards to Vík, in beautiful surroundings, are crowded with Puffins, Fulmars and Kittiwakes, but much care is needed. A steep 4WD track leads from Vík to the top of Reynisfjall. Reynisdrangar, which are prominent rock needles, rise from the sea a short way off Reynisfjall. The view from Reynisfjall and Dyrhólaey is magnificent. Boat tours from Vík to Reynisdrangar and Dyrhólaey give opportunities for bird- and whale-watching.

Many other places in Mýrdalur are worth visiting. Information is available at the information centre at Víkurskáli in Vík.

# MELRAKKASLÉTTA

66°28N 16°12W

Two principal peninsulas dominate the scene in north-east Iceland, the westernmost Melrakkaslétta, and Langanes some 30-km further east across the bay of Þistilfjörður. Both are very much of an Arctic character, sparse and low-growing vegetation, stony grounds, with obvious frost action, wind-swept, and foggy. Luxurious plant growth may be found at seabird cliffs and in many places on the inner Melrakkaslétta, with its numerous lakes and tarns; the whole covers some 50,000 ha. No part of this area has formal protection by law but the north-eastern part of Melrakkaslétta with its important coastline for birds, and the farm Gunnólfsvík, with interesting plant life, are listed as sites of special interest by the Nature Conservation Council. The seabird cliff at Rauðinúpur is listed as an Important Bird Area by BirdLife International.

TIMING

The summer months of June and July are the most ideal for birdwatching from the standpoint of the weather. However, migrating waders are particularly common on Melrakkaslétta in May when all kinds of weather can be expected. Far fewer species are found during the winter months but some high-Arctic species are frequent.

SPECIES

◆ *Resident* Eider, Gyrfalcon, Ptarmigan.
◆ *Breeding season* Great Northern Diver, Fulmar, Gannet (nesting at Rauðinúpur), Whooper Swan, Long-tailed Duck, Scaup, Teal, Whimbrel, Golden Plover, Redshank, Dunlin, Purple Sandpiper (densest breeding population in Iceland), Great Skua, Kittiwake, Arctic Tern, Guillemot, Brünnich's Guillemot, Razorbill, Puffin, Snow Bunting.
◆ *Passage* Knot, Dunlin, Turnstone.
◆ *Winter* Long-tailed Duck, King Eider, Glaucous and Iceland Gulls, Little Auk.

ACCESS

The general region can be approached by car along road no. 1 from Akureyri towards the west, or east from Egilsstaðir, i.e. with connection from Seyðisfjörður which is the berthing port of the ferry Norræna to and from Europe. The principal coastal road is no. 85. Scheduled flights are from Akureyri or Reykjavík into the two villages of the area, Kópasker and Raufarhöfn.

Numerous places on this peninsula can be visited, but some are a must. The seabird cliff at Rauðinúpur makes a good walk from the main road. The coastal lakes and lagoons towards the eastern part of the peninsula should be explored, which is easily done from the main road. So are the coastal areas, e.g. at Harðbakur, Ásmundarstaðir and Höskuldarnes, along which runs the main road. The stony moorlands abound in waders such as Golden Plover and Whimbrel, with Dunlins where the land is a little wetter and Redshanks principally nesting near human habitation. Walks over the moors to the inland lakes are rewarding. The lake at Raufarhöfn has various ducks, and the Sýlur or Ormarslónshöfði promontories are worth visiting for the seabirds.

# BREIÐAFJÖRÐUR

65°20N 23°00W

This 350,000-ha area comprises a large bay with numerous islands and skerries. The coast of the mainland is indented with fjords, and a staggering half of Iceland's coastline (by area) is found within the bay! The tidal range is as much as 6 m, resulting in extensive shallow sublittoral areas of seaweed forests which are harvested. Five areas, including a number of islands, are nature reserves where special regulations apply. Eight additional areas are listed as worthy of special protection. Furthermore, the Breiðafjörður Islands as a whole have recently been protected under special laws.

The area is important for breeding birds with 40 species nesting on the islands and a further ten on the adjacent mainland; Puffin and Eider are the most common seabirds, and this part of Iceland is the principal breeding area for Cormorant, Shag, Glaucous Gull, White-tailed Eagle, and Black Guillemot. Migrants also visit the area and stop off to feed and rest. Both Common Seal and Grey Seal occur in large numbers and several species of cetaceans, including Minke Whale, Killer Whale, and Harbour Porpoise, are seen on ferry crossings or boat trips in the bay.

TIMING

Large numbers of birds are present throughout the year. April to August are best for the breeding species while passage migrants, such as Red-necked Phalarope and other waders, are particularly abundant in April and May, and

again in August and September. The bay contains important moulting grounds for species such as Eider, Whooper Swan, and Greylag Goose in summer. In winter, hardy seaducks remain in the area.

SPECIES
- ◆ *Resident* Eider (25 per cent of Iceland's breeding birds), White-tailed Eagle.
- ◆ *Breeding season* Great Northern Diver, Cormorant, Shag, Whooper Swan (moulting in summer), Greylag Goose, White-tailed Eagle, Gyrfalcon, Eider, Grey Phalarope (rare), Glaucous Gull, Black Guillemot (400–500 pairs on Flatey Island), Puffin, Starling, Snow Bunting.
- ◆ *Passage* Brent Goose (up to 2000), Knot, Turnstone, Red-necked Phalarope.
- ◆ *Winter* Long-tailed Duck, Iceland Gull.

ACCESS
Roads follow most of the mainland coastline and are accessible year-round but, in the main, the islands are reached only in summer. There are scheduled flights to Patreksfjörður. The ferry Baldur crosses the bay from Stykkishólmur to Brjónslækur twice a day, stopping over on Flatey island. Trips to the islands are offered from Stykkishólmur, Flatey, and Reykhólar during the summer months. The region is easily approached on land from three sides: the south, north or the north-west peninsula. Easy access from the south is along road no. 1, from Reykjavík and Keflavík Airport (250 km). The region is most easily explored by car but some rental vehicles are excluded because of the location. Vantage points are numerous along the coast. A ferry crossing is a must, and boats from Stykkishólmur or Flatey allow a more intimate exploration of the islands.

*Grey Phalarope,*
*summer female*

# AKUREYRI AND SURROUNDINGS

65°41N 18°05W

Akureyri is the largest town in north Iceland (population 15,000), and is a centre of commerce and culture, situated on the shore at the head of the fjord Eyjafjörður. This town is more tree-clad than most other towns and villages in Iceland and the delta area of the river Eyjafjarðará is nearby with adjoining mudflats. Akureyri Airport is situated on this river system. Three areas in this region are listed by the nature conservation authorities as sites of special interest, of which one, the delta area of River Eyjafjarðará, is an important bird area (also registered by BirdLife International). The Akureyri Conservation Committee is working towards a legal conservation status for the delta.

TIMING

Birdwatching in Akureyri and its surroundings has attractions at all times of the year. Although fewer species are found during the winter period some species of more northern origin are common visitors. During the migration periods in the months of April and May, and from July to September, a number of species pass through the Akureyri area. The breeding season is at its peak during late May and June.

SPECIES

◆ *Resident* Eider, Harlequin Duck.
◆ *Breeding season* Scaup, Tufted Duck, Teal, Gadwall, Wigeon, Red-breasted Merganser, Snipe, Golden Plover, Whimbrel, Redshank, Dunlin, Red-necked Phalarope, Arctic Skua, Glaucous and Black-headed Gulls, Common Gull (nesting at Akureyri Airport), White Wagtail, Wheatear, Redwing, Redpoll, Snow Bunting.
◆ *Passage* Barrow's Goldeneye, Black-tailed Godwit, other waders.
◆ *Winter* Glaucous and Iceland Gulls, Long-tailed Duck, Little Auk, Snow Bunting.

ACCESS

Akureyri is on the crossroads to the south, west, and east Iceland, and as such has excellent communication to other parts of the country. Scheduled flights are several times a day to and from Reykjavík, and to various other towns albeit less frequently. Coach services are also daily. There are no specific restrictions on entering most areas, although Akureyri Airport is of course mostly closed to visitors. There is general access to land, but farmland should be avoided and permission sought for the more obviously sensitive localities in the vicinity of farms and private houses.

Many of the species may be seen during a stroll around Akureyri streets and along Glerárgil gorge. The two botanic gardens should be visited, and most of the water birds may be observed by walking along the shore or visiting the two ponds towards the southern end of town. The mud flats at the fjord's bottom are easily accessible from three sides. The delta areas are easily approached from the two roads leading south through the Eyjafjörður valley (nos 821 and 829). The old no. 1 road, across the delta south of the airport, is still open to the public. Make sure to look at the flooded areas directly below Kjarnaskógur public park, which itself is worth exploring.

# Skagafjörður

65°30N 19°00W (approximate centre of area)

Skagafjörður is a wide valley in northern Iceland covering an area of some 60,000 ha. It has particularly extensive flood-plains, inundated by glacial rivers which flood extensive areas, leaving nutrient-rich clay after the waters retreat. There are a few islands in the fjord. The principal town is Sauðárkrókur, while the small crossroad village of Varmahlíð is located on the main no. 1 road. The area of Skógar and Miklavatn is protected by law. It is an area which is important for breeding waders and also as a breeding and moulting area for wildfowl. Other areas, including Austara-Eylendið, a delta area of the river Eystri-Héraðsvötn, the island of Drangey, headland Þórðarhöfði and nearby lake, and the bird cliff Ketubjörg, are listed by the Nature Conservation Council as sites of special interest. Austara-Eylendið and Skógar are moreover listed as Important Bird Areas by BirdLife International.

The extensive and rather unspoiled wetlands with associated birdlife are the speciality of the area; the great numbers of geese found in spring are particularly noteworthy. The extensive marshes of Skagafjörður have few parallels in lowland Iceland, since farming practices have led to the drainage of a major part of all lowland marshes during the latter half of this century.

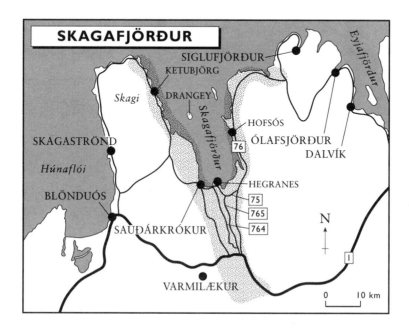

TIMING

The best period for birdwatchers in Skagafjörður is in May and June. In spring there are thousands of geese to be seen and the wetlands are teeming with birdlife. Those interested in seabirds or the Icelandic Sagas should visit the island of Drangey. There lived one of Iceland's most famous outlaws, Grettir Ásmundarson, as told in Grettir's Saga. It is best to visit Drangey during June and July when the auks are on the cliffs. In the second half of July the geese and swans begin to gather into moulting flocks, and the flock of Greylag Geese is impressive at Lake Miklavatn. During winter, the wetlands are frozen and most birds are to be found along the coast.

SPECIES

◆ *Resident* Great Black-backed and Glaucous Gulls, Eider, Raven, Snow Bunting.

◆ *Breeding season* Great Northern and Red-throated Divers, Slavonian Grebe, Fulmar, Whooper Swan, Greylag and Pink-footed Geese, Teal, Wigeon, Pintail, Mallard, Tufted Duck, Whimbrel, Black-tailed Godwit, Dunlin, Redshank, Arctic Skua, Lesser Black-backed Gull, Arctic Tern, Guillemot, Brünnich's and Black Guillemots, Razorbill, Puffin.

◆ *Passage* Barnacle and Pink-footed Geese, waders.

ACCESS

At Sauðárkrókur there is an airport with scheduled flights from Reykjavík. Coach services are daily, even twice a day during the main tourist season in summer. The coach stops at Varmahlíð with a connection to Sauðárkrókur in the morning. Another coach operates between Reykjavík and Hofsós-Siglufjörður three times a week. There are scheduled boat trips to Drangey from the Sauðárkrókur harbour but you must book in a advance.

A good route is to drive a circle around the lowlands north of road no.1, on roads nos 75 and 76. It is interesting also to drive around Hegranes where you take roads nos 764 and 765. The lakes at Hegranes and their surroundings harbour interesting birdlife as do the fertile marshes by the farms Keldudalur and Hróarsdar.

# LAKE ÞINGVALLAVATN AND ITS OUTLET

64°12N 21°08W (approximate centre of area)

Þingvallavatn is 35-km east of Reykjavík. It is a basin on the Atlantic ridge formed by fault movements and volcanic activities. The lake is 83 km² in area with a mean depth of 34 m and the catchment area is 1000 km². Half of the bottom is covered with post-glacial lava; the rest is glacial deposits. The river outlet of the lake, Sog, is about 20-km long and joins the glacial river Hvítá. Breeding waterbirds are plentiful but the main bird-watching attraction of the region is the collection of migrating waterbirds in early autumn.

In 1959 a dam was built at the south-east corner of •Þingvallavatn and blocked the lake; there were severe consequences for the balance of the entire ecosystem of this unique place. The flow of the river that drains the lake is narrow and swift for the first 1500 m. After that the water flow calms down and widens. This part of the river Sog is called Úlfljótsvatn. Further along the river narrows again until another wide and calm part is reached called Álftavatn.

The catchment area of Þingvallavatn has been used as a grazing field for sheep from the time of first human settlement; birch wood has been cut for

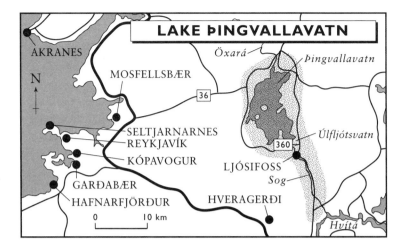

**LAKE ÞINGVALLAVATN**

AKRANES

N

Öxará

Þingvallavatn

MOSFELLSBÆR

36

SELTJARNARNES
REYKJAVÍK

KÓPAVOGUR

Úlfljótsvatn

360

LJÓSIFOSS

GARÐABÆR

Sog

HAFNARFJÖRÐUR

HVERAGERÐI

0        10 km

Hvítá

fuel as well. In recent times, other problems have appeared: increased traffic, power stations and summer houses, with all the contamination that inevitably follows man's activities, are of great concern to many.

The Þingvellir area has been protected by special law since 1928, and has from the beginning had the status of National Park, the first in Iceland.

### TIMING
The lake is usually covered with ice from January to April or May, with few waterbirds present. Spring migration takes place during April and May, but it is mainly terrestrial species that are common at that time. The most interesting time of year on the lake is perhaps the autumn to early winter when the lake is a staging post for migrating Great Northern Divers and wildfowl.

### SPECIES
- *Breeding season* Great Northern Diver, Fulmar, Harlequin Duck, Gyrfalcon, Merlin.
- *Passage* Great Northern Diver (10 per cent of Iceland's population congregate here in autumn), Red-breasted Merganser, Goosander, Barrow's Goldeneye, Long-tailed Duck.

### ACCESS
When travelling to Þingvellir from Reykjavík there are two possibilities. The first and shortest way to drive is to take road no. 1 to the north then, within 10 minutes, you turn to road no. 36. After about half-an-hours' drive road no. 360 is on the right. There you can drive on a gravel road quite close to the west coast of the lake and carry on to a point at Ljósifoss.

The lake can be explored rather easily from the ring road around it. In many places this passes at the water's edge which makes it easy to scan the lake with binoculars or telescopes. Be sure to study the bird life on the River Öxará and surroundings, and take a stroll among the dwarf birch along the water's northern edge. The opposite southern end is also worth exploring, but the best vantage points are from the western side. The thermal energy station at Nesjavellir, which supplies steam for Reykjavík houses 50-km away, is well worth visiting. Þingvellir National Park is one of the most important historic sites in the country, the site of the old Althing or parliament.

# MÝVATN – LAXÁ

63°36N 17°00W

Lake Mývatn is one of the largest lakes in Iceland (37 km²), and lies 278-m above sea level. The lake is quite shallow (average depth 2.5 m) and is spring fed; numerous islands are found in the lake. Many habitats, including lava fields, heathland, scrubland, and farmland border the northern and eastern shores of the lake, while to the south and west there are large wetlands with numerous sedge-bordered pools; these wetlands give way to heathlands and gravel flats.

In 1974, a law on the conservation of Lake Mývatn and River Laxá was enacted. The jurisdiction of the act extends over all of Skútustaðir district, the entire River Laxá down to its estuary in Skjálfandi bay, 59 km in length, and a 200-m wide border on both sides of the river. The main aim of the act is to protect the unique wildlife and landscape of Mývatn and Laxá. All construction and other disruption of land is subject to authorization by the Nature Conservation Council, and there are provisions for restricting tourist traffic so as to prevent disturbance of wildlife and damage to the protected area. The volcanic craters at Skútustaðir have been given special status as a natural monument.

The Lake Mývatn and Laxá River are famous for their wealth of breeding wildfowl. A total of 17 species of duck, c. 10,000 pairs, breed in the area including more than 95 per cent of the total European breeding population of Barrow's Goldeneye (c. 2500 birds). The most common duck species are Tufted Duck (3500 pairs in 1978), Scaup (c. 1800 pairs) and Wigeon (1000 pairs). The Lake is also immensely important for moulting and resting post-breeding birds which gather prior to migration.

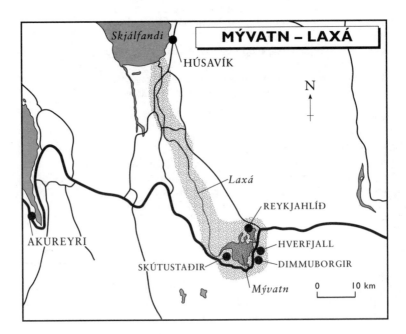

Black-throated Diver, summer

Red-throated Diver, summer

White-billed Diver, winter

Eider, adult male

Slavonian Grebe, summer

Smew, adult male

Steller's Eider, adult male

Long-tailed Duck, adult male winter

Harlequin Duck, adult male

King Eider, adult male

Lesser White-fronted Goose, adult

Goldeneye, adult male

Wigeon, adult male

Barrow's Goldeneye, adult male

Velvet Scoter, adult male

Common Scoter, adult male

Goosander, adult male

Red-breasted Merganser, adult male

Scaup, adult male

Pintail, adult male

Golden Eagle, juvenile

White-tailed Eagle, adult

Pygmy Owl

Hazel Grouse, adult male

Capercaillie, male

Hawk Owl

Tengmalm's Owl

Eagle Owl

Ural Owl

Great Grey Owl

Gyrfalcon

Rough-legged Buzzard

Snowy Owl

Ptarmigan,
male
winter
(above)

Willow Grouse, adult male winter

Broad-billed
Sandpiper,
summer

Temminck's Stint,
summer

Dotterel,
adult female

Great Snipe,
summer

Red-necked
Phalarope, summer

Little Gull, adult summer

Caspian Tern

Glaucous Gull, second winter

Iceland Gull, first winter

Puffin

Little Auk, adult summer

Guillemot, adult summer

Razorbill, adult summer

Brünnich's Guillemot, adult summer

Long-tailed Skua, adult summer

White-backed
Woodpecker,
adult male

Black
Woodpecker,
adult male

Three-toed
Woodpecker,
adult male

Grey-headed
Woodpecker,
adult male

Redwing

Fieldfare

Scarlet Rosefinch

Parrot
Crossbill,
adult male

Two-barred
Crossbill,
adult
male

Pine
Grosbeak,
adult male

Barred Warbler

Arctic Warbler

Greenish Warbler

Red-breasted
Flycatcher,
adult male

Blyth's Reed
Warbler

Yellow-breasted
Bunting, adult
male

Redpoll

Arctic
Redpoll,
adult male

Brambling,
adult male
summer

Penduline Tit

Shore Lark

Snow Bunting, adult
male summer

Red-spotted
Bluethroat,
adult male

Siberian Jay

Siberian Tit

Lapland Bunting,
adult male
summer

Little Bunting, adult male summer

Waxwing

Rustic Bunting,
adult male summer

Red-throated Pipit,
summer

J.Stenlund

TIMING

Birdwatching is possible all through the year, although during the winter few species are found. Parts of the lake and the river never freeze over and flocks of some wildfowl species remain throughout the winter; a few hardy landbirds remain in the uplands. Migrants arrive in April and May, but return migration starts for some species as early as July when the first waders leave. The last of the summer visitors have left by late October or early November.

SPECIES

◆ *Resident* Whooper Swan, Barrow's Goldeneye, Red-breasted Merganser, Mallard, Gyrfalcon, Ptarmigan, Raven, Redpoll, Snow Bunting.

◆ *Breeding season* Great Northern and Red-throated Divers, Slavonian Grebe, Whooper Swan, Pink-footed Goose, Harlequin Duck, Scoter, Long-tailed Duck, Mallard, Teal, Gadwall, Pintail, Shoveler, Goosander, Merlin, Red-necked Phalarope (thousands of pairs), Whimbrel, Snipe, Redshank, Golden Plover, Black-headed Gull, Arctic Tern, Meadow Pipit, White Wagtail, Redwing, Redpoll.

◆ *Passage* Geese, ducks, waders.

ACCESS

Road no. 1 runs through the area and is kept open all through the year. Coach services from Reykjavík to Lake Mývatn operate through the summer. The main airport serving Lake Mývatn is at Húsavík and a coach service operates to Mývatn (population 500). There is a small airport at Lake Mývatn and regular flights are offered from Reykjavík during summer. There is general access to land, but cultivated farmland should be avoided. The main breeding areas of ducks are also closed to all traffic from 15 May to 20 July.

Visitors should follow the main road around the lake where most of the wildlife can be viewed from the roadside. Points of interest include the banks of Laxá, several sites along the west shore of the lake, and Reykjahlíð, Norðurvogar and Skútustaðir along the east and south shores of the lake. To see some of the upland birds, a hike to Dimmuborgir, Hverfjall or Vindbelgjarfjall would be a good idea.

# HORNSTRANDIR

66°23N 22°36W

Hornstrandir is a heavily dissected basalt plateau, with short glacially eroded valleys covering some 58,000 ha. Lowland areas near the coast are usually wetlands with bogs, ponds and lakes rich with birdlife. The vegetation at higher altitudes is typically Alpine. The area has been a nature reserve since 1975. Between 15 April and 15 June all visits to the area have to be notified to the Nature Conservation Council, Hlemmur 3, P.O. Box 5324, IS-125 Reykjavík. It is best known for its two huge bird cliffs, Hornbjarg and Hælavíkurbjarg, which together hold about a 1,000,000 seabirds, mainly Guillemots and Brünnich's Guillemots (c. 400,000 pairs of each), and Razorbills (c. 70,000 pairs). The sea cliffs reach a height of 530m in places.

TIMING

Auks are present from April to the end of July, with decreasing numbers from mid-July onwards. Most other species are present from May to September.

SPECIES

◆ *Breeding season* Fulmar, Kittiwake, Puffin, Guillemot, Brünnich's Guillemot, Razorbill.

ACCESS
The area is difficult to reach as there are no roads. Accessible either by foot
(not recommended!) or by boat tours from Ísafjörður (June–August). You
need to bring a tent and your own food, as there is no accommodation
available on Hornstrandir.

# HORNAFJÖRÐUR AND LÓN

64°20N 15°00W

Hornafjörður and Lón are two lowland areas separated by a low-lying
mountain pass; in all, some 700,000 ha is included in the site. These areas are
mostly vegetated fluvio-glacial plains, intersected with glacial rivers, and
sheltered to the north by a heavily dissected mountain range. There are many
wetlands and extensive mudflats in the Hornafjörður area. The area has a few
dozen sheep and dairy farms, and the fishing town of Höfn (population
1,100) is situated on the rocky peninsula between the coastal lagoons
Hornafjörður and Skarðsfjörður. Ósland near Höfn is a country park;
Skarðsfjörður east of Höfn and Lónsfjörður further to the east are listed in the
Nature Conservation Register as sites of special interest.

The site is an important breeding area for swans, Greylag Geese and some
ducks and waders. Many species of migrant waterfowl and waders stop off in
spring, some in numbers of international importance.

TIMING
Spring to autumn is the best time for watching birds in this area, the start and
end of the season being best for migrants.
SPECIES
◆ *Resident* Harlequin Duck, Eider.
◆ *Breeding season* Whooper Swan, Greylag Goose, Teal, Redshank, Great
  Skua.
◆ *Passage* Whooper Swan (thousands), ducks, waders.
ACCESS
Road no. 1 runs through the area and is usually passable for all cars year-
round. Hornafjörður is connected to Reykjavík by daily bus tours and several
flights a week.

# JÖKULDALSHEIÐI

65°15N 15°30W (approximately)

Jökuldalsheiði is a highland plateau, 450–600-m above sea level, with bog-
filled depressions, and many lakes and ponds. Barren palagonite ridges run
through the area on a north–south axis, and palsas are found at several
localities. Jökuldalsheiði was inhabited in the late 1800s and early 1900s. It is
now a summer grazing ground for sheep, covering some 80,000 ha, and best
known as a breeding ground for tundra birds. A part of Jökuldalsheiði has
been assigned to the Nature Conservation Register as a site of special interest.

TIMING
Jökuldalsheiði is usually snow-covered from October to late May. The only
birds found at that time are Gyrfalcon, Ptarmigan, Raven and Snow Bunting.
Early migrants arrive in late April (Whooper Swans and Pink-footed Geese),
but most species arrive in May and onwards, depending on the spring thaw.
Swans usually start to breed around 20 May. Most upland species have left

by 10 August, but the waterfowl stay on until late September or early October. Visits to the area are recommended in June and early July.

SPECIES

◆ *Resident* Gyrfalcon, Ptarmigan, Raven, Snow Bunting.

◆ *Breeding season* Great Northern Diver, Whooper Swan, Pink-footed Goose, Scaup, Long-tailed Duck, Golden Plover, Purple Sandpiper, Red-necked Phalarope.

ACCESS

Jökuldalsheiði is the only tundra in Iceland that can be easily reached in early summer. A few hours hike from the main road is a rewarding experience for the serious naturalist! The area can be reached from Lake Mývatn or Egilsstaðir on road no. 1 (usually passable for small cars from late April to October), or from the Jökuldalur Road. The four-wheel drive tracks running through the area are usually open for traffic in late June.

# REYKJANES PENINSULA

63°50N 23°30W (approximately)

An active volcanic area, almost completely covered with rough post-glacial lava. The 75,000-ha area is low and rather flat, except for the mountainous eastern part. There are no surface streams or rivers, and there are few lakes and ponds. The coast is dominated by rocky shores. Part of the area is a country park, but many sites of special interest are listed in the Nature Conservation Register. Reykjanes is famous for its easily accessible seabird colonies.

TIMING

Rich birdlife can be found all year round, especially seabirds and shorebirds. It is one of the richest areas in terms of number of species in winter, due to the mild climate, relatively warm sea and large tidal range. Seabirds are present at breeding colonies from March to August. Auks are present at colonies from April to July, but numbers decrease from mid-July. Migrant shorebirds are numerous in spring (May) and late summer (July–September).

SPECIES

◆ *Resident* Eider.

◆ *Breeding season* Manx Shearwater (seen offshore), Fulmar, Gannet (seen offshore), Great Skua, Kittiwake, Arctic Tern, Guillemot, Brünnich's Guillemot, Razorbill, Puffin.

◆ *Passage* Waders, including Turnstone, Knot, Sanderling.

◆ *Winter* Great Northern and Red-throated Divers, Harlequin Duck.

ACCESS

This very accessible area lies close to the international airport Keflavík and within a short distance of the capital Reykjavík. The roads are good and open all year round, leading to most places of interest; the site is suitable for a one day round trip by car. The main seabird colonies are the sea cliffs Krísuvíkurberg, Hafnaberg and Reykjanes. Several large colonies of Arctic Terns are found in the area; the biggest and most spectacular one is at Reykjanes, the south-westernmost tip of the peninsula, among the hot springs. The most important sites for shorebirds, waterfowl and coastal birds are Þorkötlustaðavík and Arfadalsvík near Grindavík, Hafnir, Ósar, Sandgerði, Garðskagi, Garður, Njarðvíkurfitjar and Vogar. Garðskagi is an exceptionally good site for observations of seabirds flying by or foraging offshore. Kleifarvatn is the largest lake, with some wetlands at the south side.

# NORWAY

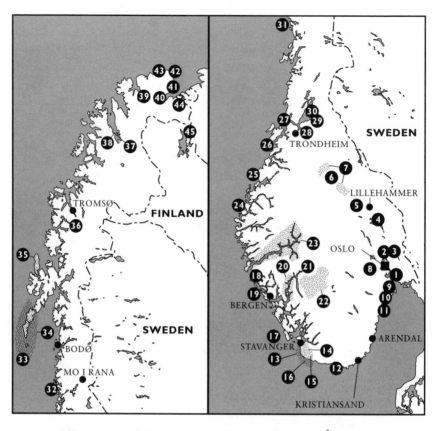

1 Kurefjorden, 2 Nesoddtangen, 3 Nordre Øyeren, 4 Åkersvika,
5 Lågendeltaet, 6 Fokstumyra, 7 Dovrefjell & Rondane,
8 Fiskumvatnet, 9 Ilene, 10 Mølen, 11 Jomfruland, 12 Lista area,
13 Jæren wetland system, 14 Grudavatnet, 15 Orrevatnet,
16 Jærstrendene, 17 Utsira, 18 Herdla, 19 Skogsøy,
20 Hardangerfjord area, 21 Bjoreidalen, 22 Hardangervidda National
Park, 23 Sognefjord area, 24 Runde, 25 Hustadvika, 26 Smøla,
27 Grandefjæra, 28 Gaulosen, 29 Vinge–Velvang, 30 Tautra, 31 Vega,
32 Lovunden, 33 Røst, 34 Lofoten, 35 Andøya, 36 Balsfjord,
37 Valdak, 38 Stabbursdalen, 39 Tanamunningen, 40 Nesseby,
41 Store Ekkerøy, 42 Hornøy & Reinøy, 43 Syltefjordstauran,
44 Neiden/Munkefjord, 45 Øvre Pasvik.

Norway covers 324,000 km², has a long coastline and is dominated by mountain areas. Only 3.6 per cent of the area is arable land, and 3 per cent is fully cultivated. Forests cover 37 per cent of the territory whereas 22 per cent is considered as productive forest. The Arctic group of islands, Svalbard, is part of Norway between 74° and 81° north.

Sited between 58° and 71° latitude in northern Europe you might expect the climate of mainland Norway to be dominated by harsh weather. However, the Gulf Stream continuously bathes the coast with relatively warm water. Thus living conditions in Norway are much better than at the same latitudes in other parts of the world.

Norway has 18 autonomous regions and a total population of 4,200,000 inhabitants. The Norwegian economy is strongly dependent on international trade, and the economy is open, with more than 50 per cent of the GNP as import and export. Income, education opportunities, and standard of living, are more evenly distributed in Norway than in many other European countries. The whole population gains from a comprehensive system of social security.

Offshore fisheries for species such as Cod, Capelin and Herring are especially important for the coastal population. Fishing is supplemented with fish farming, where Salmon is the most common species. Nowadays, people are gradually leaving rural areas along the coast, especially in northern Norway, due to the fisheries policy. Norway possesses significant amounts of oil and gas, but the topography of Norway, with huge mountain areas and numerous rivers and streams, makes it possible to gain 99 per cent of electricity from hydro-power.

There are two languages commonly spoken in Norway: Norwegian and Samiid. The latter is spoken among the Laplanders, mainly in the northernmost part of Norway, Finnmark. The Laplanders' traditional way of life, which revolves around keeping reindeer, is still practiced by 20–25,000 Laplanders in Norway. English is widely spoken among young and middle-aged people. Most regions are well served with camping sites as well as hostels and boarding houses. Larger hotels are mostly found in the cities.

## HABITATS

Norway is diverse in terms of its ecosystems and habitats. These vary from rich wetlands, bird cliffs, mountains and high plateaux, to large areas of boreal forest and bogs which all provide unique birdwatching opportunities. The rugged coastline, cut by fjords and consisting of numerous islands and islets, is also of great importance and interest.

The range of latitude across the country ensures that Norway has habitats similar to continental Europe (in southern parts) as well as the more unusual European habitats of Arctic tundra and taiga (in northern parts).

## IMPORTANCE FOR BIRDS

Norway holds globally important populations of several species of birds, as well as populations of European importance and interest. A breeding population of 1500 pairs of White-tailed Eagles and some 400 pairs of Gyrfalcons cannot be matched by any other European country.

The Norwegian coastline, with its bird cliffs, is important for seabirds. Here breed large populations of several species of auks together with Shags, Cormorants and Kittiwakes.

The presence of the westernmost part of the Eurasian tundra provides habitat for a range of rare breeding birds such as Jack Snipe, Broad-billed Sandpiper, Red-throated Pipit, Arctic Warbler and Little Bunting. Attention should also be paid to Norway's approximately 1500 pairs of White-backed Woodpeckers, which are found mainly in the west of the country.

The mountain ranges, including plateaux of unique quality in Europe, provide habitats for several hundreds of thousand pairs of Ptarmigan and Lapland Bunting as well as some 1000 pairs of Shore Lark. These areas are also important for several species of breeding waders, such as Dotterel, Temminck's Stint, Purple Sandpiper, and Red-necked Phalarope. Here you may find breeding Long-tailed Skua and, if you're lucky, also get to see Gyrfalcon and Snowy Owl.

Wetlands, especially upland bogs, are important for breeding waders, such as Great Snipe, together with a variety of other species; Common Cranes also breed in this habitat. The lowland wetlands, of which Norway has many, are of international importance for migrating ducks and waders.

You will find forests galore in Norway; most areas, however, are managed in some way. In southern Norway, look for Grey-headed Woodpecker, Icterine Warbler and Thrush Nightingale in pristine deciduous forest. In western Norway, there is a good chance of finding White-backed Woodpecker in coastal mixed forest. The boreal spruce forests, both in south and north, host a wide range of owls together with Black Grouse, Capercaillie and Hazel Hen. Birdwatchers should also expect Three-toed Woodpecker, Redstart, and Siberian Jay in good numbers. With luck, you will also find Pine Grosbeak.

The most famous and renowned part of Norway is probably also the most inaccessible, namely the tundra and taiga zone of northern Norway. Here, species breed which are rare elsewhere in Europe. These include Bean and Lesser White-fronted Geese, Smew, Jack Snipe, Broad-billed Sandpiper, Red-throated Pipit, Arctic Warbler and Little Bunting. If you miss these, at least you are sure to find Yellow Wagtail, Bluethroat and Arctic Redpoll.

In winter, the largest European populations of Steller's and King Eiders occur in the north (tens of thousands). Some 100 White-billed Divers over-winter too. Finally, Norway is on the eastern Atlantic flyway, having important staging and roosting posts for large numbers of ducks and Arctic waders.

# SEASONS

### SPRING
Spring is a good time to visit Norway. In April and May there are strong movements of geese, ducks and waders along the coast. Additionally, lekking Black Grouse and Capercaillie can be found, together with a variety of passerines returning from their winter quarters. Woodpeckers are most easily found at this time of the year.

### SUMMER
This is by far the best time to look for Norwegian specialities. Spring comes late, and the breeding season is short in northern Norway. June and July are the best months to visit these parts. Otherwise, in southern parts, woodpeckers and owls have become silent and are consequently difficult to find. A wide range of passerines are found, however, breeding in good numbers.

### AUTUMN
A good season to visit the southern parts. From August to October, a strong migration of ducks and waders occurs along the coastline. Also large numbers of passerines are everywhere. Northern Norway is deserted early and even by September most birds have left their breeding grounds. Those that are left could prove rewarding, but don't expect any miracles!

WINTER
In this season, concentrate your birdwatching efforts on the coastline. North of the Arctic Circle, birdwatching at this time is understandably difficult and demanding. However, both Steller's and King Eiders occur and Glaucous Gulls frequent the northern harbours at this time of the year. In the south, good numbers and a large variety of ducks overwinter. Look also for some of the typical species of boreal forests. Wear warm clothing!

## CONSERVATION

The country has many National Parks and nature reserves. Unfortunately, there is an unwillingness to protect other areas, except those that are unproductive such as mountain areas and regions free of conflict. Most of our National Parks are in mountain areas above the timber line. Important bird habitats like virgin forests and wetlands are only protected to a lesser extent. Several NGOs are engaged in conservation issues, among them the Norwegian Ornithological Society, World Wide Fund for Nature, the Nature Conservation Society and the Bellona foundation.

## GETTING THERE AND GETTING AROUND

Flights to Norway (the capital Oslo) are daily from many countries. From Fornebu airport near Oslo you can reach the cities of Kristiansand, Stavanger, Bergen, Ålesund, Trondheim, Bodø, Tromsø and Kirkenes by domestic flights every day. Svalbard can be reached several times every week from Tromsø. A car is necessary to reach most of the sites described in this book. All major international car hire firms are represented in Norway, and can be found in most good sized towns and at airports. If you arrive by car, there are several points where you can drive into the country from Sweden and, via car-ferry, from Denmark, Scotland and England. The highway E6 runs through the country from south to north, and is a good basis for reaching the sites in south-eastern, middle and north Norway. If you follow the western coast from south to north, you will need to take many car ferries. However, this route is recommended because of its beautiful scenery.

## NORWEGIAN ORNITHOLOGICAL SOCIETY (NOF)

More information about Norway and its bird life can be obtained from the Norwegian Ornithological Society (NOF). NOF is a vital link between conservation, research and birdwatching in Norway. NOF is also the Norwegian partner of BirdLife International. The domestic network consists of 17 regional societies and 53 local bird clubs. Twelve bird observatories are sited around the country. The society publishes several magazines: *Vår Fuglefauna* is a popular journal in Norwegian (five issues a year); *Cinclus (Fauna Norwegica. series C)* is a scientific journal in English and Norwegian; and *Ringmerkaren* publishes results and recoveries from bird ringing in Norway, in Norwegian.

Have you seen anything you want to report? Do not hesitate to contact NOF! (*See* Useful Addresses.)

# BIRDWATCHING SITES

## KUREFJORDEN

59°25N 10°30E

Kurefjorden is a marine wetland with some small areas of mainland and a few islets, in all comprising an area of 4000 ha. The tidal zone is dominated by seaweeds, but there are also areas with rush and sedge at Kokkholmsund. An alder forest grows in the south. The area is a nature reserve and a Ramsar site due to its importance for breeding and migrating wetland birds.

TIMING

An important area for migrants. From November to March, if the water is ice free, swans and ducks can be found. April and May see the arrival of large numbers of migrant ducks and Arctic waders. Most move on after a few weeks but a few remain to breed. Autumn migration, which lasts from August to October, comprises large numbers of waders, ducks and gulls.

SPECIES

◆ *Breeding season* Eider, Shelduck, Osprey, Redshank, Ringed Plover, Great Black-backed Gull, terns.

◆ *Passage* Great Crested Grebe, Wigeon, Mallard, Teal, Shoveler, Garganey, Goldeneye, Red-breasted Merganser, Goosander, Common Crane, Black-tailed and Bar-tailed Godwits, Whimbrel, Greenshank, Spotted Redshank, Ruff, Snipe, Dunlin, Temminck's Stint.

◆ *Winter* Mute Swan, Goosander, Goldeneye.

ACCESS

The site is situated 10-km south of Moss and 20-km north of Sarpsborg and Fredrikstad in Östfold county. The best way to reach the area is by car. Leave the E6 on Rv 119 (to Larkollen) or 116 (to Onsöy). Rv 119 will lead you to Kureskjær, at the 116 follow signs to Åven/Oven. Access to the reserve is prohibited 1 April to 10 July and again from 20 August to 1 October. However, most parts are easily viewed from outside. Two spots are especially good: Kureskjær and on the roadside to Oven. At Kureskjær in the north is a car park and a trail leading to an excellent observation spot. When following the road to Oven, observations in the south-eastern part of the reserve can be made if you park the car on the roadside when you see the coast again.

## NESODDTANGEN

59°50N 10°50E

This excellent migration site lies close to Oslo. From the northernmost point of the Nesodden peninsula you can view migration as well as airplanes arriving and leaving Oslo airport (Fornebu). Amongst houses and gardens, pine forest and grassy hills, Nesoddtangen provides excellent views over the inner Oslofjord area. Here almost anything can, and often does, turn up.

TIMING

This is one of the few sites in Norway where spring migration is good with flocks of geese, raptors, pigeons, swifts and passerines leaving to cross Oslofjord.

Summer is quiet but autumn migration lasts from August to November with passerines and seabirds in evidence.

SPECIES

◆ *Passage* Cormorant, Pink-footed Goose (mainly spring), Buzzard, Rough-legged Buzzard, Merlin, Kestrel, Osprey, Common Crane (mainly spring), Woodpigeon, Meadow Pipit, Nutcracker, Fieldfare, Redwing, Mistle Thrush, Ring Ouzel, Brambling, Chaffinch, Siskin, Lapland Bunting.

ACCESS

The locality lies 45 km by car, from Oslo. Take the E18 south from Oslo and turn off on Rv 156. This takes you north, on the western side of Bunnefjorden. The site is at the end of this road.

# NORDRE ØYEREN

59°53N 11°09E

*Merlin*

This is the largest inland delta in Scandinavia, formed by the river Glomma emptying into Lake Øyeren. Large mudflats are exposed at low-water level, attracting feeding waders and ducks. Muddy banks, containing vegetation dominated by sedge are also a dominant feature. Several large islands are found in the delta area. Otherwise, the vegetation is dominated by deciduous forest and willow scrub. Agricultural activity occurs close to the reserve which is also a Ramsar site.

TIMING

The best time for birding is during the migration periods. During April and May, especially when the water level is low, large numbers of migrating waders and ducks congregate. Birdwatching interest in the summer months comes mainly from the passerines that breed in the deciduous forests and scrub, but by August migrating birds have started to appear again. Waders and ducks dominate the scene through September and October although passerines can be found in the cut cornfields. From December to March, the area is almost completely frozen.

SPECIES

◆ *Resident* White-backed Woodpecker (rare).

◆ *Breeding season* Osprey, Common Rosefinch.

◆ *Passage* Great Crested Grebe, Whooper Swan, Bewick's Swan (late autumn), Pink-footed Goose (mainly spring), Wigeon, Teal, Mallard, Golden Plover, Ruff, Greenshank, Wood and Green Sandpipers, Snipe, Whimbrel, Yellow Wagtail, Red-backed Shrike, Thrush Nightingale, Bluethroat, Twite, Lapland and Snow Buntings.

ACCESS

Nordre Øyeren lies east of Oslo, approximately 30 km, in county Akershus. From Oslo, take Rv 159 to Strömmen/Fjellhammer. Rv 120 then leads you past the reserve. A trail from Årnes leads to an observation tower at Årnestangen. Do not venture off the trail! You could also view the area from the opposite side. From Strømmen/Fjellhammer, follow Rv 170 to Fetsund.

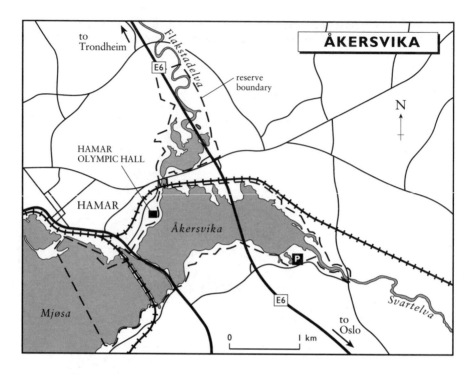

# ÅKERSVIKA

**60°50N 11°25E**

This delta area, comprising 4 km², is formed by the outlets of the Rivers Flakstadelva and Svartelva into Lake Mjøsa. Vegetation in the area is dominated by sedge and different species of grass. Surrounding the delta are areas of agriculture and pasture, although the latter have been abandoned, with willow scrub encroaching. The town of Hamar borders the area and a highway and a railway cross the reserve. The locality is both a nature reserve and a Ramsar site. A speedskating hall was built on part of the reserve for the 1994 Olympics.

### TIMING
This site is definitely best in migration periods, in April and May, and again from July to September. Arctic waders and ducks of many different species are numerous. This is a central stopover on their inland migration route through Norway. Areas bordering the reserve attract numbers of migrating passerines.

### SPECIES
◆ *Passage* Black-throated and Red-throated Divers, Great Crested Grebe, Mute Swan, Mallard, Teal, Wigeon, Garganey, Shoveler, Goldeneye, Goosander, Coot, Ringed and Golden Plovers, Ruff, Snipe, Whimbrel, Redshank, Greenshank, Green, Wood and Common Sandpipers, Temminck's Stint, Yellow Wagtail, Bluethroat, Icterine Warbler.

### ACCESS
The area is easily reached, lying as it does on the outskirts of Hamar in county Hedemark, with the E6 and the main railway between Oslo and Trondheim crossing the reserve. There is an observation tower overlooking

the delta area of Svartelva and this is especially good in the migration periods. A visit to Hamar Olympic Hall could be combined with a look at this reserve.

# LÅGENDELTAET

61°10N 10°40E

This area comprises a delta of 9 km² formed by the river Lågen emptying into Lake Mjøsa. Vegetation in the area consists mainly of sedge and different species of grass growing on mudbanks within the delta; several muddy islands have formed within the area. Agricultural land and pastures surround the delta which is also bordered by the town of Lillehammer; the E6 crosses the reserve.

TIMING

Best visited in spring, during April and May, and in autumn, from July to October. Then you will find concentrations of ducks and waders, stopping off on migration to rest and feed. In June and early July, the area is worth visiting for its breeding passerine species. In winter, from November to March, most of the area is frozen, although dippers and some ducks still remain.

SPECIES

◆ *Resident* Dipper.
◆ *Breeding season* Little Ringed Plover (occasional), Icterine Warbler, Common Rosefinch.
◆ *Passage* Black-throated and Red-throated Divers, Great Crested Grebe, Pink-footed Goose, Teal, Wigeon, Goldeneye, Goosander, Scoter, Pintail, Garganey, Shoveler, Golden Plover, Ruff, Redshank, Spotted Redshank, Greenshank, Red-necked Phalarope.

ACCESS

Lågendeltaet lies on the outskirts and close vicinity of Lillehammer in Oppland county. A visit here could well be combined with a visit to the several sports centres built for the Olympics in 1994. Car parks and resting places along E6, Rv 253 and 255 provide good viewpoints over the area. Visit the parts of the reserve that are accessible from these main roads.

# FOKSTUMYRA

62°10N 09°30E

Fokstumyra comprises 7.5 km² of mire complex, broken by ponds and creeks. The vegetation consists mainly of low wetland varieties with areas of birch and willow scrub; a railway crosses the area. Fokstumyra was among the first areas in Norway to be declared a nature reserve. It was protected in 1923 following damage from the building of the Oslo to Trondheim railway.

TIMING

Fokstumyra is almost exclusively a spring and summer site, the main interest coming from its breeding species; June and July are the best months. Migration in May and August may also be worth seeing, but seldom adds anything new to what may be seen during summer.

SPECIES

◆ *Resident* Willow Grouse.
◆ *Breeding season* Hen Harrier, Rough-legged Buzzard, Merlin, Kestrel, Common Crane, Golden Plover, Redshank, Wood Sandpiper, Snipe, Ruff, Red-necked Phalarope, Short-eared Owl, Yellow Wagtail, Bluethroat, Redwing, Redpoll, Brambling, Lapland Bunting.

ACCESS

Fokstumyra lies close to Dovrefjell and Rondane in Oppland county (*see* below). The nearest habitation of any size is Dombås, some 10 km to the south. You could go by train to Fokstua station, and the E6 runs nearby. During the breeding season, access to the area is restricted. However, there is a trail, leading to/from Fokstua Fjellstue, which is open for public access. This trail will lead you to all the specialities of the area. Do not leave this trail.

# DOVREFJELL AND RONDANE

62°00N 09°30E

These high mountainous plateaux both have outstanding wildlife and scenery; Dovrefjell covers some 256 km², Rondane 572 km². In Rondane, deep valleys and wide plains make the scenery picturesque; the scenery in Dovrefjell is less rugged, but only slightly less breathtaking. At this height (the peak Stortoppen in Dovrefjell reaches 2286 m above sea level), the vegetation is sparse, and the climate is harsh. Both areas are National Parks; Dovrefjell is divided into two, the areas being separated by a valley (Drivdalen), the E6 and three landscape protection areas. Several rare plants are recorded in this calcareous region.

TIMING

These two areas are visited only in the summer, from late May until July. The climate is too severe, and birds too scarce at any other time!

SPECIES

◆ *Breeding season* Golden Eagle, Rough-legged Buzzard, Gyrfalcon (rare), Merlin, Long-tailed Duck, Ptarmigan, Ringed and Golden Plovers, Dotterel, Dunlin, Purple Sandpiper, Temminck's Stint, Meadow Pipit, Shorelark, Dipper, Wheatear, Bluethroat, Brambling, Redpoll, Lapland and Snow Buntings.

ACCESS

These areas are part of the mountain range separating southern Norway from the counties of Trøndelag. Both form part of the border between Oppland and Hedemark. Access to Dovrefjell is from the E6 which divides the area into two; enter the mountains from Kongsvold Fjellstue. In Dovrefjell, there are marked trails, and a tourist hut in the western range. You could travel by train to Hjerkinn station, from where the mountain range is open for hiking.

Rondane is approached by car either from close to Otta (on E6), or from the opposite side near Stadsbuøyen and Straumbu (on Rv 27). Roads into the reserve are closed by barriers, but parking is possible.

At Dovrefjell, visit both the mountain areas within the National Park, and the landscape protection areas of Drivdalen and Hjerkinn. At Rondane, the valleys Illmanndalen and Dørålen are easily accessible.

# FISKUMVATNET

59°42N 09°50E

Fiskumvatnet is a shallow, mostly eutrophic lake, 3.2 km² in area, connected to the Eikern by a narrow strait. The river Vestfosselva, and two small creeks, empty into the lake. The eastern part of the lake is oligotrophic. Several small bogs around the lake add to the habitat variety. Vegetation is mainly reed and deciduous forest although there are large areas of sedge which are flooded in spring. In autumn, a broad mudflat often appears in the north-eastern part. Part of the area is a nature reserve and waterbirds are the speciality of the site.

TIMING

Fiskumvatnet is best visited at migration times with March to May and August to October being best. Large concentrations of ducks are found in all years but waders, which can be numerous, are only common when water levels are low. Several interesting species of passerines also occur on migration. Late spring and summer are the times to look for breeding passerines before autumn migration begins again. If the area near river Vestfosselva is open between November and February, both Goldeneye and Goosander may overwinter.

SPECIES

◆ *Breeding season* Osprey, Green Woodpecker, Icterine Warbler, Thrush Nightingale.
◆ *Passage* Black-throated Diver, Common Crane, Ruff, Greenshank, Green and Wood Sandpipers, Temminck's Stint, Great Snipe, Short-eared Owl.
◆ *Winter* Goldeneye, Goosander.

ACCESS

The locality lies 20-km west of Drammen and 15-km east of Kongsberg in Buskerud county. Follow Rv 11 and the lake is on the south side of the road and difficult to miss. A road, which runs along the south side of the lake, connects Rv 11 to Rv 35. This also passes beside the lake. There is restricted access to the nature reserve, but the area can be viewed from several spots. Good localities, with easy access, are the bridge crossing the strait between Fiskumvatnet og Eikeren, Sundhaugen, Måsnesmyrene and Høgstadmyrene. Several places along E76, passing the reserve, could also serve as vantage points.

# ILENE

59°18N 10°24E

Ilene is both a 905-ha nature reserve and a Ramsar site comprising a marine delta with a river emptying into a shallow bay. There is some scanty scrub and deciduous forest in the north.

TIMING

April and May are good months to visit the reserve, when you will find resting migrant geese, ducks and waders and perhaps Pink-footed Geese migrating overhead; a few interesting passerines also pass through in spring. Interest during summer is confined to breeding passerines and waders and, from August until October, migrant geese, ducks, waders and passerines pass through. From November to March, wintering swans and geese are present.

SPECIES

◆ *Breeding season* Little Ringed Plover, Caspian Tern (visiting only), Marsh Warbler.
◆ *Passage* Pink-footed and Greylag Geese, Shelduck, Eider, Pintail, Garganey, raptors, Curlew, Whimbrel, Ringed Plover, Ruff, Greenshank, Wood Sandpiper, Temminck's Stint (mainly spring), Snipe, Bluethroat, Snow Bunting.
◆ *Winter* Swans, geese, Smew.

ACCESS

Ilene lies within the city limits of Tönsberg in Vestfold county. The area is easily accessed from several places. Look for Jarlsberg Travbane jogging track when accessing the observation tower. The pier at Holmen is also a good observation spot. Rv 303, in the western outskirts of Tönsberg, will take you to within viewing distance of the area.

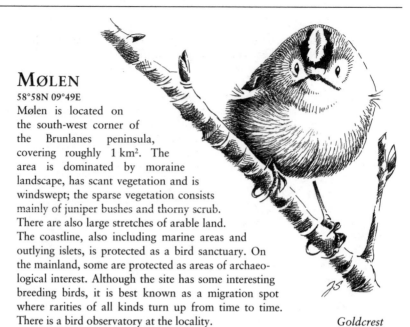

## MØLEN

58°58N 09°49E

Mølen is located on the south-west corner of the Brunlanes peninsula, covering roughly 1 km². The area is dominated by moraine landscape, has scant vegetation and is windswept; the sparse vegetation consists mainly of juniper bushes and thorny scrub. There are also large stretches of arable land. The coastline, also including marine areas and outlying islets, is protected as a bird sanctuary. On the mainland, some are protected as areas of archaeological interest. Although the site has some interesting breeding birds, it is best known as a migration spot where rarities of all kinds turn up from time to time. There is a bird observatory at the locality.

*Goldcrest*

### TIMING

Being primarily of interest during periods of migration, the area is most productive in spring and autumn. From April to early June and again from August to November, large numbers of ducks, waders, raptors and passerines turn up, the variety of waders being most pronounced in the autumn. Passerine migrants are also very much a feature of the area. There is little birdwatching interest from December to March although a few flocks of overwintering ducks may be present. Favourable winds bring passing seabirds close to shore.

### SPECIES

◆ *Breeding season* Barred Warbler.
◆ *Passage* Shearwaters, Fulmar, Gannet, Buzzard, Rough-legged Buzzard, Sparrowhawk, Merlin, Dunlin, Knot, Tengmalm's and Pygmy Owls (invasion years only), Swift, Woodpigeon, Tree and Meadow Pipits, Willow Warbler, Blackcap, Goldcrest, Red-backed Shrike, tits, Mistle Thrush, Redwing, Fieldfare, Nutcracker (autumn), Robin, Chaffinch, Brambling, Siskin, Yellowhammer, rarities.

### ACCESS

The site is situated approximately 10 km west of Larvik and Stavern in Vestfold county. From Larvik, follow Rv 302 to Helgeroa and continue towards Nevlunghavn. The road to Mölen will then be signposted on your right hand side. There is a car park, and a trail leading towards the west. Bird ringing and migration studies are carried out during most of the year.

## JOMFRULAND

58°52N 09°36E

The 6 km² island was formed during the last Ice Age as a terminal moraine; its coastline is dominated by boulders. The island is flat, and extensively vegetated with several rare plant species being found. Most of the central and northern parts are covered with oak and spruce forest while the southern half is dominated by agriculture. Parts of the oak forest are protected and there are several protected seabird sanctuaries near the island.

TIMING

The spring and autumn migration periods, March to May and August to October, are the best times to visit. At these times plenty of seabirds (during southerly gales), ducks, raptors and waders may be seen along with large numbers of Pink-footed Geese and passerines. June and July are generally quiet although a few interesting breeding passerines do liven things up. During the winter months, from November to February, ducks are seen in good numbers.

SPECIES

◆ *Resident* Eider.
◆ *Breeding season* Golden Oriole (probable breeder), Red-backed Shrike, Barred and Greenish Warblers, Thrush Nightingale.
◆ *Passage* Fulmar, Gannet, Cormorant, Greylag Goose, Velvet Scoter, Goldeneye, Buzzard, Rough-legged Buzzard, Great Skua, Lesser Whitethroat, Whitethroat, Garden and Willow Warblers, Goldcrest, tits, Brambling, Siskin, Twite, Linnet, rarities.

ACCESS

The island lies in Telemark county, in the skerries east of Kragerø. To get here, a daily boat connection operates from Kragerø. There is a bird observatory and an observation tower in the north. Bird-ringing and migration studies are carried out during most of the year.

# LISTA AREA

58°05N 06°30E

The area around Lista lighthouse is very diverse. The coastline is mainly moraine; in the western parts the inland area is dominated by heath. There are a few conifer plantations but large areas are agricultural. Gunnarsmyra and Slevdalsvann are reedbeds connected by a channel crossing the farmland. Near the lighthouse there is also a small area of intertidal saltmarsh (Våien).

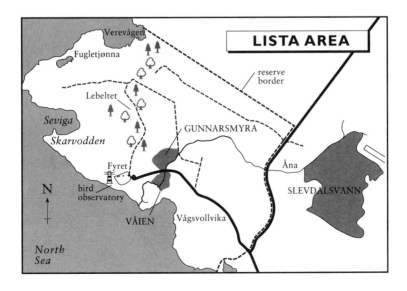

TIMING

The best time to visit is in migration periods, but most times of year are good. From March to May and again from August to November, visible migration can be impressive with representatives from most bird groups.

SPECIES

- *Breeding season* Marsh Harrier (occasional), Yellow Wagtail, Bearded Tit, Marsh Warbler.
- *Passage* Divers, Cormorant, Brent and Greylag Geese, Eider, Scoter, Long-tailed Duck, Sparrowhawk, Merlin, Peregrine, Gyrfalcon (scarce but annual), Hen Harrier, Oystercatcher, Golden, Ringed and Grey Plovers, Lapwing, Dunlin, Ruff, Snipe, Jack Snipe (autumn), Whimbrel, Curlew, Redshank, Green and Common Sandpipers, auks, Swallow, Tree, Red-throated and Meadow Pipits, Red-backed Shrike, Wheatear, Fieldfare, Redwing, Reed, Sedge, Icterine, Barred and Willow Warblers, Goldcrest, tits, Brambling, Chaffinch, Siskin, Redpoll, Crossbill, rarities.

ACCESS

The Lista lighthouse is at the westernmost end of the Lista peninsula, 20-km west of Farsund in county Vest-Agder. It is almost the most southerly tip of Norway. From Farsund, both Rv 463 and 43 will lead you straight there.

Firstly visit the lighthouse area (there is a car park here). Here you will also find the Lista bird observatory and you are certain to meet birdwatchers in the period March-June and July-November. They will tell you which areas to visit, and which to avoid. Except Slevdalsvann, which is excellent for reedbed birds, the lighthouse area itself is probably the best place to stay. From there on you can watch migration both at sea and over land.

# JÆREN WETLAND SYSTEM
58°40N 05°45E

Jæren is a large wetland complex, including Mølen, Jomfruland. It is also connected to the Lista area (*see* above). The wetland system covers a large number of small- to medium-sized wetlands, most of which are more or less densely covered by reedbeds. The wetlands were more than twice the present size only 100 years ago, but drainage has been carried out in most, and some of the largest ones are completely lost. Few of these areas are protected at present but a scheme is in progress to turn most of these wetlands into nature reserves.

TIMING

Birds can be seen here throughout the year, although spring migration is best. From March to May, there will be masses of ducks and waders and a good range of passerines. Breeding wetland birds are the main attraction in summer, but autumn migration soon starts again. From August to October, large numbers of ducks, waders and passerines can be seen. During the winter months, flocks of swans, geese and ducks can be found along with an array of raptors.

SPECIES

- *Breeding season* Mute Swan, Mallard, Shoveler, Reed and Sedge Warblers, Reed Bunting.
- *Passage* Gadwall and Garganey (spring), other ducks, Peregrine, Gyrfalcon, Oystercatcher, Golden and Ringed Plovers, Lapwing, Dunlin, Ruff, Snipe, Greenshank, Redshank, Green, Wood and Common Sandpipers, passerines.
- *Winter* Little Grebe, Whooper and Bewick's Swans, Mallard, Wigeon, Teal, Tufted Duck, Smew, Hen Harrier, Peregrine, Gyrfalcon, Water Rail.

ACCESS

The wetlands are scattered over most of the low-lying parts of Jæren in Rogaland county. Reach the areas by car, since most of them are situated close to Rv 44 or 510. Suggested wetlands to visit are, from the south, Lake Bjårvatn, Lake Søylandsvatn, southern parts of Lake Frøylandsvatn, Lake Ergavatn, Lonavatn (an enlargement of the river Figgjoelva) and Lake Horpestadvatn. Close to these are Lake Grudavatnet, Lake Orrevatnet and Jærstrendene (*see* page 122). In most cases, part of your journey will take you across private property or on private roads. Take care, and do not cross farmland or block the road with your car. You are advised to ask the farmer for permission to park your car before entering his property.

# GRUDAVATNET

58°47N 05°38E

Grudavatnet comprises two shallow, lowland lakes connected by a stream. Dense vegetation covers parts of the lakes due to the strong influence of organic material from the surrounding farmlands; there are pine plantations in the vicinity. Much of the area is a nature reserve with no access; adjacent to the reserve is also a larger bird protection zone. Visitors are however welcome to watch the birdlife from a distance, and there is an observation tower at the lake. It is one of the most important bird lakes in Norway.

TIMING

You will always find good numbers of birds at Lake Grudavatn, regardless of time of the year. From March to May, migrating dabbling ducks and waders predominate, and good numbers of passerines may also be seen. In June and July, breeding birds are the main attraction; these are typical of eutrophic lakes anywhere in this part of Europe, but include some species which are uncommon in Norway. The greatest numbers of birds appear from August to October during migration; especially ducks, geese and waders, as well as many passerine birds. The winter months from November to February can also be an exciting time, with wintering ducks and geese, and hunting raptors.

SPECIES

- ◆ *Resident* Mallard, Coot, Moorhen.
- ◆ *Breeding season* Great Crested Grebe, Shoveler, Avocet.
- ◆ *Passage* Geese, Wigeon, Teal, Gadwall, Ruff, Golden Plover, Bar-tailed Godwit, Snipe, Dunlin, Curlew Sandpiper, other waders, passerines, rarities.
- ◆ *Winter* Hen Harrier, geese, Smew and other ducks.

ACCESS

You may take a bus from Stavanger, but it is more convenient to use a car or even bicycle. Lake Grudavatn is c. 25 km south of Stavanger city, and a trip to this site could often be combined with visits to Jærstendene and other lakes in the Jæren region. Take the main road E18 from Stavanger, turn right before Sandnes and follow Rv 44 towards Bryne. Turn right when you see the sign to Voll, and follow this road for a few kilometres until you see Lake Grudavatn on your left. There are also several other roads leading to Lake Grudavatn.

Park at the car park at Vasshus skole (or nearby). From here cross the road, where a farm road leads to the lake. Follow this to a small gravel pit on your left, and an observation tower. From here there are good views over the entire area. You are not allowed to go nearer to the lake than this.

# ORREVATNET

58°45N 05°33E

Orrevatnet is a shallow eutrophic lake but without extensive plant growth. The area is surrounded by farmland, with some isolated conifer plantations. At the western part of the lake, you are within metres of Jærstrendene (*see* below). The nearby lakes Ergavatn and Horpestadvatn are also worth visiting.

TIMING

Although birds are present here throughout the year, migration times provide the best birdwatching. From March to May, the migration of ducks and waders can be good but, thereafter, the summer is rather quiet. Birdwatchers will find more of interest from August to October when ducks, raptors, and waders pass through. Migrant swans arrive late in the year and many remain for the winter. It is probably the most important bird lake in Norway.

SPECIES

◆ *Resident* Coot.
◆ *Breeding season* Great Crested Grebe, Mallard, Avocet, Black-tailed Godwit, Redshank, Lapwing, Black-headed and Little Gulls.
◆ *Passage* Wigeon, Teal, Gadwall, Buzzard, Rough-legged Buzzard, Sparrowhawk, Gyrfalcon (rare), Peregrine, Dunlin, Ruff, Greenshank, Redshank, Spotted Redshank, passerines, rarities.
◆ *Winter* Mute and Whooper Swans, Wigeon, Tufted Duck, Goldeneye, Smew, Pochard, Hen Harrier, Short-eared Owl.

ACCESS

Orrevatnet lies in the middle of Jæren, approximately 15-km south of Sandnes and 30-km south of Stavanger, in Rogaland county. Follow Rv 44 from Sandnes towards Bryne. From Klepp, turn on to Rv 510 for 3 km. Then turn into Rv 507, and the lake will appear on your left hand side. A visit to Orreosen and Malaneset is essential. Otherwise, it is difficult to find good viewpoints. Do not stretch the limits of private property. Roads make it possible to drive around the lake so stop the car whenever you see the lake.

# JÆRSTRENDENE

58°40N 05°40E

This comprises 16 km² of coastline north of Stavanger and to the south at Ogna. The sandy beaches and dune areas are the largest in Norway. Some isolated parts are more rocky and numerous islets and skerries occur in the northern areas. Outside the dune areas, shallow waters, important for feeding waterbirds, predominate. Seabird migration can be impressive here.

Most of the coastline is a landscape protection area. This means access is allowed, but care must be taken not to destroy or harm the area in any way (do not pick flowers!). Additional protection is given to some areas (bird protection zones), where access is prohibited during the breeding season. Parts of the area are Ramsar protection sites.

TIMING

There is excellent passage of divers, ducks, waders and auks offshore during April and May, the passage of Brent Geese in late May going almost unnoticed. During June and July, summering Arctic waders add to the interest provided by breeding waders and passerines. Heavy migration begins in August and lasts until October with good numbers of waders, ducks, raptors and passerines. From November to March, overwintering ducks, Cormorants, divers and grebes are present.

SPECIES
- *Resident* Shag, Eider.
- *Breeding season* Waders, Skylark, Meadow Pipit, Wheatear, Twite.
- *Passage* Red-throated Diver, Manx and Sooty Shearwaters, Brent Goose, Velvet Scoter, Long-tailed Duck, Merlin, Kestrel, Oystercatcher, Ringed and Grey Plovers, Lapwing, Ruff, Curlew, Whimbrel, Redshank, Dunlin, Peregrine, Gyrfalcon, Knot, Sanderling, Little Stint, Bar-tailed Godwit, Turnstone, Great Skua, passerines.
- *Winter* Great Northern and Red-throated Divers, Slavonian and Red-necked Grebes, Cormorant, Purple Sandpiper, Glaucous Gull.

ACCESS
The area is easily accessed from Stavanger. Alongside 44, 507, 509 and 510, small roads lead you to the North Sea and this locality. You should try at least some of them. Several spots along the coastline are recommended for birdwatching. Most famous is Revtangen and the Revtangen bird observatory, which is only metres away from Lake Orrevatn. You should also visit Børaunen in the north, Nærlandsstranden in the middle and Kvassheim in the south. In summertime, be prepared to fight your way between crowds of people. Jærstrendene is the most popular recreational area in the district.

# UTSIRA
59°18N 04°52E

This small, rocky island, 6 km² in area, lies 25-km west off the mainland (Haugesund, in Rogaland county). Farming on a small scale is practised in the central valley, this producing small plots of grassland and potato fields. There are also a few conifer plantations. In this valley there are many well kept gardens but most of Utsira is rocky outcrops and heathland. Some small islets to the south-west (Spannholmane) are bird protection areas.

TIMING
Best visited in spring, during April and May, and autumn, during September and October; then an astonishing number and diversity of small passerines may occur on the island, the sight of hundreds of Bluethroats and Redstarts leaving a lasting impression. The weather, and especially the wind direction, does determine what to look for and what you are likely to see. Seabird migration, especially in autumn can also be very impressive with up to 35,000 Fulmars recorded in a single day. In winter, November to March, and summer, June and July, you are probably better off birding elsewhere.

SPECIES
- *Breeding season* Fulmar, Shag, Puffin.
- *Passage* Fulmar, Manx and Sooty Shearwaters, pipits (including regular Richard's Pipit), wagtails, warblers (especially Barred and Yellow-browed Warblers), thrushes, Red-breasted Flycatcher, chats, Common Rosefinch, buntings, rarities.

ACCESS
You need to travel by boat from Haugesund. There are daily connections to Utsira. Be aware, some scheduled departures are from Karmøy. There are metalled roads on the island. Why, nobody has yet figured out. A bicycle, however, would be a good idea, allowing you to cover more of the island in a day.

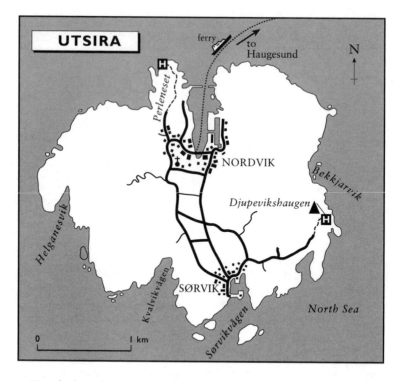

Keep looking for birds in the inhabited areas – the centre of the island. Check the gardens carefully, and also areas of farmland; the local inhabitants are used to this kind of activity. Just remember to keep outside the fences even if a rarity shows up. The conifer plantations are also worth checking.

If it is a bad day for passerines, seabird watching from the northern (Perleneset) or eastern (Djupevikshaugen) sides could prove profitable. Most of the rocky outcrops are less attractive to birds compared to the gardens, farmland and plantations of the inhabited areas. Birding at Utsira is very dependent on wind – and weather – conditions. With winds from the north-west to south-west sectors, opt for seabird watching. When the wind is from north-east, east or south-east, almost any Eurasian passerine could show up.

There is a bird observatory at Utsira. Assuming it is manned, there is a daily log held every night at the height of the season. This is the sacred highlight of the day, and will tell you how much you have missed!

## HERDLA

60°35N 04°55E

Herdla is a low moraine island surrounded by shallow marine waters, very different from the craggy landscape you see almost everywhere else in the region. Originally, the flattest parts were bogs and wetlands with high salinity. During World War II the Germans built an airfield here, and after the war the most interesting parts of the island became cultivated. The shallow shores remain, however, and these combined with the atypical nature of the island, make it extremely important for migrating birds. The lowest parts of Herdla are protected as a nature reserve. Some areas within the reserve (in the north-west) have access prohibited between April and September. Close to the nature reserve, in the north, is a large bird protection zone where no hunting is allowed.

TIMING

Herdla is an important stopover place for birds on autumn migration. This is due to the fact that there are very few, if any, other appropriate roosting sites of this kind for many species between Vigra (Møre & Romsdal County) and Jæren in south-west Norway. The best time of year to visit is from mid-August to mid-October with the first half of September as the optimum period. From November to February there are seaducks and Cormorants around, with a few Purple Sandpipers on rocky outcrops on the coast. From March to mid-May, bird numbers and diversity increase, and some days may be really good. The summer months are relatively quiet.

SPECIES

◆ *Resident* Eider.
◆ *Breeding season* Grey Heron, Red-breasted Merganser, Shelduck, Redshank, Ringed Plover, Lapwing.
◆ *Passage* Ruff, Golden Plover, Little Stint, Knot, Curlew, Bar-tailed Godwit, Twite, Linnet, Lapland Bunting, rarities.
◆ *Winter* Red-necked Grebe, Cormorant, Velvet Scoter, Long-tailed Duck, White-tailed Eagle (occasional).

ACCESS

Herdla is situated c. 40 km from the city centre of Bergen, in the northern-most part of Askøy community. You can reach the island either by bus from Bergen Bus Station or by car. Take Rv 555 from Bergen (marked Sotra), turn right on Rv 563 when you see the sign Askøy and drive north on Rv 562 as far as the road goes. When you cross the Askøy bridge on your return, you have to pay a toll. From the car park at Herdla it is only a short walk to the nature reserve where you should follow the marked trails. Please respect this as you will see all the birds either from the trail or from two observation towers. One tower is placed in the south end of the bay of Prestevika. This is inside a burned-out building but do not be put off as it offers you a good view over the bay and all the birds there. The other tower is not particularly high and is an old roofed bunker, but from here you can watch the diving ducks and other seabirds on the sea north of Herdla quite close by.

# Skogsøy

60°33N 04°32E

Skogsøy is an island with bridge connections with the mainland. The island is dominated by coastal heather moorland, with some areas of conifer plantations. For birdwatchers, the most interesting place is the westernmost part of the island, from where you have an excellent view to the North Sea and the massive bird migration which follows the outer coastal line of western Norway.

TIMING

The best time for watching birds here is the autumn, from August to October, but spring migration, from March to late May, can also be exciting. If you are there on the right day in May, most of the Spitsbergen breeding populations of Brent and Barnacle Geese will pass by, and species like Arctic and Pomarine Skuas may occur in good numbers. Another exciting aspect of spring seawatching is the chance to see all four species of divers fly by in breeding plumage.

In early August, nocturnal tape-lures on Skogsøy have attracted British Storm-petrels but otherwise the summer months are quite quiet apart from the typical moorland species. November to February can also be extremely disappointing from a birdwatching point of view.

SPECIES

◆ *Resident* Black Grouse.
◆ *Breeding season* Twite.
◆ *Passage* Divers (all four species), Sooty Shearwater, Fulmar, Cormorant, Shag, Gannet, Eider, other seaducks, White-tailed Eagle, Oystercatcher, Curlew, Grey Plover, Great Skua, auks, Grey-headed Woodpecker, thrushes, other passerines.
◆ *Winter* Little Auk.

ACCESS

The island is reached by car or bus from the city of Bergen. Take Rv 555 from Bergen and then turn left when you see the sign marked Herdlevær. Follow this road nearly to the end and park your car off the road before the last bridge (there is no car park), and from here you will have to walk a fair distance if you want to watch the bird migration. Make sure that your parked car will cause no disturbance to the traffic or local inhabitants!

If you intend to watch the bird migration, you will need to walk for about three quarters of an hour. The goal is the cairn on the south-west corner of the island, which is easy to see even from the road. There is a trail leading to the cairn, but this trail is not well marked and you will probably lose it at some point. If so, keep the south-western shoreline of the island in view, otherwise you may encounter some rough terrain. In order to watch the bird migration at its best, you have to start off from here very early in the morning, preferably at dawn. A good spotting scope will be very useful, as well as warm clothes! After 10 am migration activity may be very low, depending on wind conditions.

# HARDANGERFJORD AREA

60°15N 06°15E

The Hardangerfjord area is a popular tourist area in Norway, mainly due to the beautiful scenery, and the folklore attached to the region. The fjord itself is the most notable landscape feature. However, the rich (and often steep!) deciduous woods cloaking the valley slopes may offer good opportunities for birdwatchers and people interested in botany. South-facing slopes get more sunlight than other areas, hence these are usually the richest as regards birdlife and productivity generally. These are the native woods of this part of the country, with the niches provided by dead or dying trees adding to the biodiversity.

Some of the richest deciduous forests are protected as nature reserves, because of their botanical value. These areas are also rich in woodland birds, but you may find plenty of other attractive woods close to the roadside with the same species and bird densities.

TIMING

The most intensive bird activity in these woods will be throughout May and early June. Although resident birds may be more easy to find in early spring before most leaves appear, many of the inhabitants of these woods are late migrants and do not arrive until the second half of May.

SPECIES
- *Resident* Golden Eagle, Tawny Owl, White-backed, Green, Grey-headed and Lesser Spotted Woodpeckers, Jay and Nutcracker (both in areas of hazel), Wren.
- *Breeding season* Rough-legged Buzzard, Wryneck, Icterine Warbler, Blackcap, Pied and Spotted Flycatchers, Fieldfare, Brambling, Siskin, Redpoll.

ACCESS
Access is usually easy, as many interesting sites can be surveyed from the main roads. You may of course walk through the woods, but the steepest areas can be really dangerous as it is easy to slip. If you travel by car, a good way to see many different birds is simply to stop at signed picnic areas or other sites where you can park the car without obstructing traffic. Brief walks on the road will often be enough to see the interesting bird species, but of course a walk in a remote part of the forest is always likely to be the most rewarding.

Along Rv 550, about 8-km north of Odda, there is a bird station with a nature trail. You are welcome to use this trail on your own, and with some luck in this area you may encounter some of the most characteristic species mentioned above. There is a sign at the main road showing the direction to 'Ornitologisk stasjon' (bird observatory). The bird observatory is placed only a few hundred metres from the main road, but the road is poor and steep.

# BJOREIDALEN
60°20N 07°30E

Bjoreidalen is one of the best known mountain wetlands in southern Norway, primarily due to its rich birdlife and easy accessibility. However, it is vulnerable to disturbance, hence birdwatchers and other tourists are strongly requested to abide by the regulations in the area carefully. The richest parts for birds are the bottom of the valley, close to the river and the scrub vegetation along the shore. However, the valley slopes and mountain plains surrounding the Bjoreidalen area may offer many exciting experiences for foreign birdwatchers unfamiliar with Scandinavian mountain birds; at least 12 species of waders breed here.

TIMING
Bjoreidalen is interesting primarily as a breeding area, hence June and July are the best months to visit the place. However, some interesting species may stop over on migration for a few days and so August and even September can be exciting. Prior to 15 June you are not, however, allowed to enter the nature reserve at all; the snow which still lies at this time of the year would make hiking difficult anyway. You should see good birds in the mountains adjacent to the nature reserve as well, and even along the highway.

SPECIES
- *Breeding season* Teal, Scoter, Rough-legged Buzzard, Dunlin, Redshank, Snipe, Great Snipe, Temminck's Stint, Purple Sandpiper, Red-necked Phalarope, Ringed and Golden Plovers, Dotterel, Ruff, Long-tailed Skua, Shore Lark, Bluethroat, Lapland Bunting.

ACCESS
Park your car at Dyranut turisthytte close to the roadside of the main road (Rv 7). Follow the marked trail from this place, and stick close to it when you enter the reserve area. You may also enter the Bjoreidalen area from the toll road

from Tråastølen to Tinnhølen (*see* Hardangervidda National Park), but then be careful to park your car well off the road and away from vulnerable terrain.

In order not to disturb the birds too much, please stick to the trails within the nature reserve. You may get further information at 'Dyranut turisthytte' or 'Bjoreidalen turisthytte'. If you intend to stay in the area for some days, you should inform the warden in the nearby Hardangervidda National Park. The warden monitors human activity in Bjoreidalen nature reserve carefully, and if you violate the regulations, you risk an expensive fine. You should also be aware that Bjoreidalen and its near surroundings is one of the favourite places for egg collectors and bird poachers, so be careful that your behaviour can not be misinterpreted as such illegal activity. Otherwise, do not be surprised if you are reported to the warden!

The river is rich in tasty mountain trout, although most fish are fairly small. You are allowed to fish even inside the nature reserve, but only on certain sites (marked along the trail). You will need a nationwide angling licence (can be bought at any post office in Norway) as well as a local permit.

# HARDANGERVIDDA NATIONAL PARK
60°10N 07°10E

Hardangervidda is the largest mountain plateau in northern Europe (more than 5000 km²) and lies between 1000–1500 m above sea level. The entire area is virtually treeless, and freshwater lakes are numerous. Since 1981 the largest National Park in mainland Norway has been established here (3430 km²), with two adjacent landscape protection areas (combined area of 865 km²). Hardangervidda is well known among ornithologists for its rich bird life with 125 species having been recorded here, 56 of which have bred. Visitors who are fortunate enough to visit in a lemming year are in for the experience of a lifetime. Arguably, the area is most famous for the large population of wild reindeer; in winter, they number 10,000–12,000 animals. The area forms the south-western edge of the breeding range for several Arctic bird species and plants in Europe. Visitors are free to wander anywhere in the area as long as the wildlife is not disturbed. Several new nature protection areas are planned outside the existing areas, e.g. Bjoreidalen.

TIMING

At these high altitudes, the snow melts fairly late in the season, and the bird life is adapted to this. Late May and the whole of June can be very good for birds in areas where the snow has melted; the birds concentrate on these bare sites. However, at this time of the year it is difficult to move around due to the extensive snow-cover and the numerous fast-running (and cold!) streams. As a result, birdwatching is best from places near to main roads. During the last days of June the toll road to Tinnhølen is opened, and by then the entire area will have become accessible; July is a good month for birdwatching, especially the first half; it becomes quieter in late July and throughout August, although some early migrants will pass the area. In late August and September, migrants are common, but at this time there is much disturbance in the mountains due to the reindeer hunting.

SPECIES

◆ *Resident* Willow Ptarmigan.
◆ *Breeding season* Black-throated Diver, Scaup, Tufted Duck, Teal, Scoter, Velvet Scoter, Long-tailed Duck, Rough-legged Buzzard, Gyrfalcon (rare),

*Golden Plover, summer*

Common Crane, Dunlin, Temminck's Stint, Golden and Ringed Plovers, Ruff, Red-necked Phalarope, Purple Sandpiper, Dotterel, Long-tailed Skua, Snowy Owl (occasional), Bluethroat, Lapland and Snow Buntings.

ACCESS

If you take your own car, you will probably find Rv 7 crossing the northern part of the Hardangervidda most exciting. Also Rv 8 from Geilo to Uvdal is a popular starting point for bird excursions. These areas can also be reached by bus, but bus departures are not frequent. If you do not have transport of your own, you may take the train to Finse station (1222 m above sea level) and walk southwards towards Rv 7 from here. Finse is a remote place close to the glacier, and the bird life is characteristic of these altitudes, although not particularly rich. Alternatively, you can take the train to Haugastøl station and take the bus in a westward direction from here.

# SOGNEFJORD AREA

61°10N 06°40E

In terms of wildlife and scenery, there are many similarities between the Sognefjord area and the Hardangerfjord area (*see* page 126). Sognefjord is in most places characterized by very deep waters with limited value for waterbirds, but where large rivers meet the fjord, extensive deltas have built up. Unfortunately, most of them are now damaged or totally destroyed by industrial activity, but there are still a few places left for waders, gulls and other wetland birds. To foreign naturalists and birdwatchers, however, the many fragmented areas of deciduous woods in the steep hillsides may be of more interest.

TIMING

The best time of year to visit Sognefjord is in the spring when there are most birds and they are at their most active. Resident species are perhaps best searched for before the leaves appear on the trees. The greatest diversity of birdlife is present in late May, however, when migrants have arrived and the trees are in full leaf.

SPECIES

◆ *Resident* Golden Eagle, Tawny Owl, White-backed, Grey-headed and Lesser Spotted Woodpeckers, Jay, Nutcracker.

◆ *Breeding season* Wryneck, Icterine Warbler, Blackcap, Pied and Spotted Flycatchers, Redwing, Redpoll, Chaffinch, Brambling.

ACCESS

Access is easiest from roads into adjacent areas of forest, and you will have just as much chance of finding the more interesting species here as you would in more remote forest areas. South-facing slopes normally have the richest vegetation cover and hence also more birds, but you can still have good birding on the south side of the Sognefjord.

# RUNDE

62°24N 05°37E

Runde is an island connected to the other main islands in the area via a bridge, situated 70-km south of Ålesund. The island is famous for its seabird colonies. Runde has just over 100 local inhabitants, and the local community is geared to cope with the large number of summer tourists that come to see the seabirds. The most important seabird colonies are protected as nature reserves, where all kind of human activity is prohibited. It is, however, still possible to view the seabirds from outside these protection zones, and there are marked trails you can follow. A total of 222 bird species have been recorded on the island of which 77 have, or are suspected of having, bred.

TIMING

A visit to Runde is rewarding from April to August but if you want to see the breeding seabirds at their most active, you should be here in May or June. However, Runde is also a good place to see migrants in fairly good numbers, and may well be a good spot for unexpected records. A few seabirds linger on the sea around the island during the winter months, but not in very high numbers.

SPECIES

◆ *Resident* Fulmar (5000 pairs breed, many are present year-round), Eider.
◆ *Breeding Season* British Storm-petrel, Gannet (1600 pairs), Shag, Red-breasted Merganser, White-tailed Eagle, Great Skua, Kittiwake, Guillemot, Brünnich's and Black Guillemots, Puffin, Razorbill.

ACCESS

Most people drive to Runde, but there is also a bus connection (not many departures) and a passenger boat from Ålesund. Take Rv 61 either from Ålesund or from the opposite direction, then turn onto Rv 654 (marked Fosnavåg) from a crossroads some kilometres south of Ulsteinvik. This road ends at Runde. Drive past most of the houses to a car park, and leave the car. To see the seabird cliffs (from above), you have to follow a marked uphill trail for about 30 minutes. You will get a good view over some of the seabird colonies from the viewpoints along the trail, but this cannot beat the impression you get from the sea! A boat trip with a local sailor can be hired, and is not too expensive if you divide the cost between several people. More information can be obtained at the tourist office at Runde.

# HUSTADVIKA

62°98N 07°00E

The windswept and wave-battered shores of Hustadvika comprise shallow tidal areas and wetlands harbouring a rich bird life. In the bays and inlets, huge tangles of seaweed gather and, at low tide, vast areas of mud, sand and gravel are exposed. Away from the exposed tidal stretches are coastal meadows, saltmarshes and grass mires scattered with small pools and ponds. Further inland, the landscape is dominated by cultivated and enclosed pasture. The form and shape of the local mountain ranges which end at Farstad and Hustad, create a passage for migrating birds, which concentrate at Hustadbukta Bay and on the headland at Storholmen.

TIMING

The best time of year to visit is during migration time in autumn. Huge numbers of migrating waders congregate on the shores from the end of July, but August and September are best for the migration of passerines. Some rare passerines, Yellow-browed Warbler among others, are recorded on passage. Seawatching can be excellent in September and October during strong north-westerly winds; shearwaters, skuas and seaducks all pass in good numbers. In late October, the first flocks of migrant swans arrive and interesting wader species may be present. During the winter months, small groups of Purple Sandpipers are present along with the occasional White-tailed Eagle.

SPECIES
◆ *Resident* Eider.
◆ *Breeding season* Shelduck, Oystercatcher, Rock Pipit.
◆ *Passage* Manx and Sooty Shearwaters, British and Leach's Storm-petrels, Shag, Cormorant, Whooper Swan, Brent and Barnacle Geese, Red-breasted Merganser, Merlin, Gyrfalcon, Peregrine, Snipe, Jack Snipe, Dunlin, Little Stint, Curlew Sandpiper, Knot, Redshank, Ruff, Golden and Ringed Plovers, Meadow and Tree Pipits, Twite, Brambling.
◆ *Winter* White-tailed Eagle, Purple Sandpiper.

ACCESS
From Kristiansund, take Rv 64 (the Atlantic road) towards the south-west and Vevang (20 km). At Farstad (8-km west of Vevang), take a small road to the right, toward Solås. The first road to the right leads to the eastern side of the headland Storholmen, which is well worth visiting. You can also reach the western side of the headland by taking the second road to the right instead of the first. When you reach the end of the road, you can park the car. From this point you could follow the coastal meadows along the shore. If you drive further on the road towards Bud from the crossroads at Farstad, turn to the right at the first crossroads, and follow this road c. 1 km, you will reach Hustadbukta Bay. The outermost part of the western side of this bay, directly facing the rough sea of Hustadvika, is the best place for migrating waders. At this site, Male ornithological station is situated.

# SMØLA

63°20N 08°00E

The Smøla archipelago is made up of several hundred islands, and numerous small islets. Large areas of continuous shallow water exist at several localities. Smøla is partly cultivated, but is otherwise a huge wetland mosaic of open mire landscape and coastal heathland, with numerous small lakes, streams, ponds and pools. The coast of the main island consists of many inlets and bays. This is one of the biggest areas of marine wetlands in Norway, and some of the largest continuous mires are found here.

TIMING
The archipelago is best visited from late autumn until early spring. From September onwards, migrant waders start to appear in huge numbers, many remaining in the area for the winter. Seaduck and diver numbers build up through October and many of these also remain until the following spring. A visit to the region in early March can be particularly rewarding.

SPECIES
◆ *Resident* Eider, White-tailed Eagle, Willow Ptarmigan.
◆ *Breeding season* Red-throated Diver, Grey Heron (largest breeding colony in Norway), Greylag Goose, Ruff, Dunlin, Golden Plover, Arctic Tern, Sedge Warbler, Lapland Bunting.

◆ *Passage* Mallard, Shoveler, Wigeon, Teal, Goldeneye, Scoter, Gyrfalcon, Peregrine, Goshawk, Golden Eagle.
◆ *Winter* Great Northern and Red-throated Divers, Slavonian Grebe, Cormorant, Shag, Whooper Swan, Eider (up to 5400), King Eider, Long-tailed Duck, Velvet Scoter, Red-breasted Merganser, Purple Sandpiper, Redshank, Turnstone, Glaucous Gull.

ACCESS

Smøla is easiest to reach from the city of Kristiansand on the western coast of the county Møre og Romsdal in middle Norway. There are good connections daily, by car ferry (from Seivika) or by passenger boat from the centre of Kristiansand. Both arrive at Edøy, one of the southernmost islands of Smøla. The best areas for wintering and staging seabirds and waterbirds in general are the skerries in the south and on the northern and north-eastern shores of the main island.

# GRANDEFJÆRA

63°42N 09°35E

Grandefjæra is a shoreline with numerous shallow waters, situated on the western shore of Ørlandet. The area uncovered at low tide is the biggest in Norway (5–6 km²). The retreating tide leaves numerous small pools and the tidal zone itself is dominated by stones, sand and gravel. Formerly the area above the tidal zone consisted of huge areas of marshlands and mires; these areas are now cultivated. The flat countryside adjacent to Grandefjæra is the most bird-rich site in central Norway. The area is a Ramsar Site, roughly 21 km² of which has nature reserve status; 0.3 km² of this is dry land.

TIMING

This area is important as wintering grounds for numerous divers, seaducks, swans and gulls and so is best visited for these species from November to March. Migration times can also see huge influxes of passage waders and ducks with March to May and August to October being the best months.

SPECIES

◆ *Resident* Eider (up to 7000 moulting birds in summer), White-tailed Eagle.
◆ *Breeding season* Red-breasted Merganser, Shelduck, Black-tailed Godwit, Curlew, Oystercatcher, Dunlin, Ruff, Turnstone, Ringed Plover, Lapwing, Black-headed Gull, Short-eared Owl, Rock and Meadow Pipits, Twite.
◆ *Passage* Knot, Little Stint, Sanderling, Bar-tailed Godwit, Spotted Redshank, Jack Snipe.
◆ *Winter* Great Northern and Red-throated Divers, White-billed Diver (rare but regular), Red-necked and Slavonian Grebes, Whooper Swan, Mallard, Velvet Scoter (up to 5000), Surf Scoter (rare but regular), Long-tailed Duck, King Eider, Gyrfalcon, Peregrine, Redshank, Curlew, Dunlin, Knot, Purple Sandpiper, Herring, Great Black-backed, Common and Glaucous Gulls, Little Auk.

ACCESS

The area is reached from the city of Trondheim by car ferry (25 min), which runs continuously from 6am to midnight in summer from the ferry port at Flakk, 13-km west of Trondheim by Rv 715; you arrive at Rørvik. Follow Rv 715 from Rörvik 52 km to the end of Lake Krinsvatnet (at the right hand), from where you turn left at the crossroads and follow Rv 710 32 km to Brekstad. Follow the same road westward past Brekstad. You may also arrive at Brekstad by ferry (20 min) from Agdenes (Valset) which runs c. 15 times a day from Rv 710, or from

Steinkjer (from north) by following Rv 720, Rv 715 and Rv 710. Grandefjæra is accessible from the South (at Beian) and from the north (at Lakskløholmen west of Uthaug). Traffic in the area is restricted but in the north, at Hoøya and Lakskløsholmen, and in the south at Beian, there is organized access to the area. At these sites there are designated birdwatching sites with good views.

# GAULOSEN
63°20N 10°13E
This 312-ha area comprises the outlet of the river Gaula. In the middle of the estuary there is an islet 'Storøra'; the southern shores support saltmarsh, and closest to the river are sand dunes where grasses predominate. On the north side is another nature reserve, Leinøra, which is an area made of river deposits; there is a huge growth of Sea Buckthorn, and here you can see the tallest Sea Buckthorn trunks in the world. At low tide, a huge delta is uncovered, the haunt of thousands of waders. Six hundred and five hectares have Nature Reserve status and the rest of the area is a landscape protection area covering 2450 ha. Most of this area is covered by water. Access is prohibited only to the islet Storøra. A total of 205 bird species have been recorded in the area, 45 of which breed regularly. Migrant waders and wildfowl are also important.

TIMING
The area provides a good food supply for birds, and hence good birdwatching, all year round. In the winter, swans, geese and ducks are numerous and are best from November to March. As spring follows, huge numbers of migrant water-birds stop off to feed and rest, some of the birds remaining to breed in the area. The estuary is an important area in late summer for moulting seaducks and, from August to October, migrant waders and wildfowl pour through the region.
SPECIES
◆ *Resident* Eider, White-tailed Eagle.
◆ *Breeding season* Black-headed and Common Gulls, Common Tern, Little Ringed Plover, Temminck's Stint, Reed Bunting.

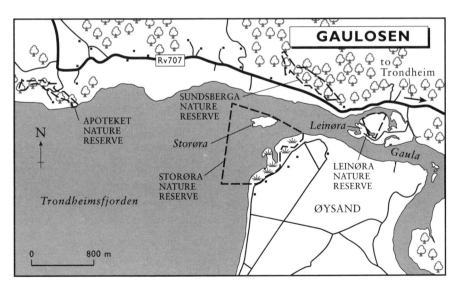

◆ *Passage* Wigeon, Teal, Goosander, Oystercatcher, Redshank, Dunlin, Golden Plover, Snipe, rarities (recent records have included White-winged Black Tern, Marsh Sandpiper, Great Snipe, Pectoral Sandpiper, Barrow's Goldeneye and Rustic Bunting).

◆ *Winter* Great Crested Grebe, Whooper Swan, Canada and Greylag Geese, Pink-footed Goose (mainly mid-April to mid-May), Mallard, Long-tailed Duck, Velvet Scoter, waders.

ACCESS

From Trondheim, follow highway E6 c. 12-km south. Go straight ahead at the roundabout at Klett on the Rv 65. Follow this road for 4.8 km, then turn right at the sign 'Øysand', where you will see a factory on your right. Follow this road 200 m before you turn left, then 1 km along the shore. Finally you will reach a signboard where there also is a car park. The north side of the estuary is accessible if you turn right at the roundabout at Klett, then follow the signs to Byneset on Rv 707. After a few kilometres, you will see the estuary on the left. Park the car at a small picnic area on the left side of the road. From the signboard, and the car park, you can follow the shore line all way out to the estuary, where you have a good view of the river mouth and Storøra.

# VINGE–VELVANG

63°29N 10°58E

The coastline between Vinge and Velvang is approximately 3-km long. This is mainly a shallow marine area, and at three localities extensive areas are uncovered at low tide. As far out as 1 km, the water depth is less than 10 m.

This is an important area for waterbirds with up to 9000 Eiders, for example, gathering here before migrating to Sweden; this is thought to be a significant proportion of the breeding population in Bottenviken. On late evenings in mid-April, you can also see smaller flocks of Eider leaving the fjord for the mountains between Norway and Sweden. If the spring migration of ducks and gulls coincides with Herring spawning, you are guaranteed a spectacular sight here.

TIMING

In spring, especially, this is an extremely rich area. The main reason for this is the huge amounts of Herring roe that drift ashore after the spawning in March and April. From this time and to the middle of May, thousands of birds have a feast; large flocks of Eiders and other seaducks gather at this time. Spring migration of waders is good and return migration, from August to October, of both wildfowl and waders is also impressive.

SPECIES

◆ *Resident* Eider, White-tailed Eagle.

◆ *Breeding season* Shelduck.

◆ *Passage* Eider, Red-necked Grebe, other seaducks, waders, Red-throated Diver.

◆ *Winter* Cormorant, Eider (3-5,000), King Eider, Velvet and Surf Scoters (rare), Long-tailed Duck, Red-breasted Merganser, Mallard, Tufted Duck, Black-headed, Common, Herring, Great Black-backed, Glaucous and Iceland Gulls, Purple Sandpiper.

ACCESS

This area is due north of the town of Stjørdal in Nord-Trøndelag county, which is easily accessible from the east by Highway E14, or from Highway E6 and otherwise by train or by airplane. The airport for Trondheim is situated here.

With a car the area can be reached by following Highway E6 past the centre of Stjørdal on the way north; a small road goes left at the signs 'Kvithammer' and 'Vinge'. Follow the sign to Vinge 5 km (follow this road until you see the shore). You are then at the northernmost part of the area, Vinge. Turn left at the cross-roads and follow the road along the shore. At some points the road is very close to the shoreline, and at others you can follow small roads down to the shore.

# TAUTRA

63°30N 10°40E

Tautra is a 2-km² island dominated by farmland and plantations (mostly spruce). There is an interesting eutrophic wetland (Måsdammen) in the middle of the island and nearby there is also a brackish water pool. The most interesting areas are perhaps the shallow coastal waters between Tautra and the mainland.

Tautra is a Ramsar Site and some parts are included in a nature reserve; the other parts are bird protection areas. Between 25 April and 15 July, access to the nature reserves and parts of the bird protection areas is not permitted.

### TIMING

Visit Tautra in spring, from March to May. Both in terms of numbers and diversity, this is a great season for divers, grebes, ducks and gulls. In late spring and summer, from May to July, there are impressive numbers of breeding wetland and coastal birds and the area is also important in late summer for moulting duck. From August to October, the shallow waters between Tautra and the mainland are important for migrating waders and ducks; numbers are not comparable, however, with those in spring. In winter, from December to February, the area still is important for wintering divers, grebes and ducks.

### SPECIES

◆ *Resident* Eider, White-tailed Eagle.
◆ *Breeding season* Shelduck, Common and Black-headed Gulls.
◆ *Passage* Ducks (including Garganey and Shoveler), waders.
◆ *Winter* Red-throated and White-billed Divers (rare but regular), Red-necked Grebe, Eider (up to 7000 in late winter), King and Steller's Eiders (rare but regular, the former even having stayed to breed), Velvet Scoter (up to 2000), Scoter, Surf Scoter (occasionally), Long-tailed Duck.

### ACCESS

Tautra is part of Frosta municipality in the county of Nord–Trøndelag. The closest urban localities are Levanger and Stjørdal. Take the E6 to Åsen and then turn off towards Frosta on Rv 753. Follow this road nearly to the end. When you see the island, turn right where the road is signposted.

An observation tower is situated near to, and overlooks, Måsdammen. Parking is possible near the breakwater leading to the island. Trails lead both to the observation tower, and into other parts of the nature reserve. Meeting places on the molo are excellent for watching the coast.

# VEGA

65°40–66°00N 11°30–12°00E

Vega is an archipelago consisting of several thousand small islands and islets and comprising an area of some 50,000 ha; some of the largest islands are inhabited and partly cultivated. The landscape is characterized by a mosaic of peat bogs and rocky outcrops and the extensive intertidal zone with areas of seaweed, nutrient-rich mud and stone, sand and gravel shores. Scattered

*Jack Snipe*

around are tarns with brackish water as well as fresh water ponds. The whole area is the site of a proposed National Park. The intertidal flats at Vikåsleirene are temporarily protected as a nature reserve, and the same is the case with the lakes Sveavatnet and Kjellerhaugvatnet. The area is good for nesting coastal and moorland birds and is an important staging post for migrants.

TIMING
Large numbers of wintering ducks can be found in the area from November to March and include some impressive statistics: 15,000 Eiders, 4500 King Eiders, 1800 Long-tailed Ducks and 1200 Velvet Scoters are among them. In spring, huge flocks of Barnacle Geese pause on spring migration; in fact, almost the entire Svalbard population passes through the area. Of course, there are plenty of other wildfowl species at this time along with migrating waders. From the end of July onwards, many waders stop off on passage before heading southwards and, from August to October, duck as well as wader numbers build up again.

SPECIES
◆ *Resident* Eider, White-tailed Eagle.
◆ *Breeding season* Red-throated Diver, Cormorant, Shag, Greylag Goose, Oystercatcher, Golden Plover, Lapwing, Curlew, Whimbrel, Snipe, Ruff, Common Sandpiper, Arctic Tern, Black Guillemot.
◆ *Passage* Barnacle and Pink-footed Geese, Greylag Goose (up to 4,000 moulting birds), White-fronted Goose (occasional), Knot, Grey Plover, Curlew Sandpiper, Sanderling, Dunlin, Spotted Redshank, Bar-tailed Godwit, Jack Snipe (late September and early October).
◆ *Winter* Great Northern Diver (up to 120 in February and March), Red-necked and Slavonian Grebes, Eider, King Eider, Long-tailed Duck, Velvet Scoter, Purple Sandpiper, Redshank.

ACCESS
Approaching from the south on the E6, turn left 22 km before Trofors, and follow Rv 76 to Brønnøysund. At Mosheim, near Brønnøysund, you must take Rv 17 to the right and drive 11 km to Horn at the end of the road, where there is a ferry; the crossing takes 45 min and runs 6 times a day. An express boat (40 min), also 6 times a day, runs from the centre of Brønnøysund. For tourist information on Vega, Tel. 75 03 53 88.

The most important intertidal flats are situated on the northern side of the main island, and should be visited. Some good small lakes with brackish water are situated between Viksås and Holand, and near Valen.

# LOVUNDEN

66°21N 12°20E

Lovunden consists of the island of Lovund with its distinctive and steep mountain of 619 m, towering above scree slopes below. Around the island there are numerous islets and skerries and on the north-east side there is a small village where the 300 island inhabitants live.

Lovunden is most famous for its breeding colony of Puffins, though the number of breeding pairs has unfortunately decreased dramatically in recent decades. In 1957, 60,000 pairs were breeding here (250,000 birds present in the colony); in 1977, 40,000 pairs, and by the end of the 1980s, 25,000 pairs. Although you can walk anywhere on the island, be considerate when you approach the colony of breeding Puffins.

TIMING

According to the locals, the island's Puffins return on 14 April, between 5pm and 7.30pm. From that time, the island is shrouded in a swarm of Puffins. Several species of gulls also breed here as well as a few passerines, migrants of which arrive in May. From the middle of August to the middle of September, the Puffins, and most of the other birds, begin to leave the island. In the winter months, there are seaducks at sea and a few waders on the shores.

SPECIES

◆ *Resident* Eider, White-tailed Eagle (groups of 15–20 are not unknown), Wren.

◆ *Breeding season* Shag (200–300 pairs), Greylag Goose, Shelduck, Golden Eagle (regular visitor), Peregrine, Gyrfalcon, Kestrel, Oystercatcher, Great Black-backed, Lesser Black-backed, Herring and Common Gulls, Black Guillemot, Puffin, Eagle Owl (regular visitor), Meadow and Rock Pipits, Wheatear, Ring Ouzel, Dunnock, Twite.

◆ *Winter* Long-tailed Duck, Purple Sandpiper.

ACCESS

From the town Mo I Rana municipality in Nordland county to which Highway E6 leads, take Rv 12 for 39 km to Utskarpen. Turn right and follow Rv 17 on the northern side of the fjord Sørfjorden 35 km to Stokkvågen, from where the car ferry (1 hour) leaves for Lovunden four times a day. An express boat to Lovund leaves from the same place twice a day.

A trip around the island will take you all day and enable you to see all that is worth seeing. There is much climbing on the route but, although strenuous, most people reach the top of the mountain. On a clear day it is definitely worth the effort. A boat trip to the surrounding skerries is also recommended.

# RØST

67°30N 12°00E

Røst is an archipelago consisting of numerous islands (more than 400) with a combined area of some 1500–2000 ha. Some of these islands have seabird colonies, the most important being Vedøy, Storfjellet, Ellefsnyken, Trenyken and Hernyken. These are steep sided, grass-covered islands (92–259-m high). The islands are also important as staging posts for migrants, most notably the inhabited island Røstlandet, with its numerous ponds, saltmarshes and mires; they have nature reserve status. Apart from Røstlandet, the only other island with unrestricted public access is Vedøya. Trips to Vedøya can be arranged from Røstlandet, where you may stay over night.

The islands of Røst are famous for having one of Europe's largest Puffin colonies, which recently was estimated to be c. 600,000 pairs strong. However, there has been a severe decline in the population during the last 30 years, due to a collapse in the food supply, and in the late 1960s the population was estimated to be twice this number. Thousands of other seabirds breed here and the islands regularly turn up rarities at migration times.

TIMING

Because of mild winters at Røst, several bird species overwinter on Røstlandet; these include landbirds, coastal species and seaducks. The bird cliffs themselves are tranquil until the end of February, when the first Kittiwakes return to their nests. To see the cliffs at their best, however, requires a boat trip between late May and early August. Later that same month, the seabirds begin to leave, making way for an influx of migrants in the autumn.

SPECIES

◆ *Resident* Eider, White-tailed Eagle.
◆ *Breeding season* British and Leach's Storm-petrels, Fulmar, Shag, Peregrine, Kittiwake, Guillemot, Brünnich's Guillemot, Razorbill, Puffin.
◆ *Passage* Ducks, waders, rarities.
◆ *Winter* Long-tailed Duck, Gyrfalcon, Redshank, Black-headed Gull, Starling.

ACCESS

There are daily boat connections between Røst and Bodø. The boat trip takes from 5 to 7 hours (stops also at Værøy). You may also go by airplane from Bodø (30 min). Alternatively, a ferry goes twice a week from Reine in Lofoten.

Access to the bird cliffs is prohibited from 15 April to 15 August. It is, however, possible to join arranged day trips to Vedøy, and here you can study most species. Visitors could also join boat trips to the outermost island in the archipelago, Skomvær, where a lighthouse is situated. The marshes on Røstlandet are situated close to the airport, and are easily accessible.

# LOFOTEN

68°00N 13°30E

The Lofotens are an archipelago comprising islands of varying sizes and covering, in total, some 1277 km²; most famous and best known are Vestvågøy, Værøy and Røst (*see* above). The islands are dominated by rugged mountains, with only a small strip of low-lying coastline. They are separated by broad fjords and narrow straits. Fishing is the main industry.

A visit to Røst is a must! Also visit Storeidvatnet, and several other small ponds, lakes and bogs on Vestvågøy. There are several shallow bays near Leknes at Vestvågøy, and birds are plentiful almost everywhere.

TIMING

The best time to visit the area is in late spring and summer, from May to August. The climate is then at its best and large numbers of breeding seabirds are present, especially at Røst and Værøy. Both spring, during March and April, and autumn, from September to November, can provide some migration, primarily of seabirds. In winter, the weather is generally more suited to indoor pastimes!

SPECIES

◆ *Resident* Eider, White-tailed Eagle, Peregrine.
◆ *Breeding season* Slavonian Grebe, Fulmar, British and Leach's Storm-

petrels, Shag, Greylag Goose, ducks, Black-tailed Godwit, Kittiwake, Arctic Skua, Guillemot, Razorbill, Puffin.
◆ *Passage* Spotted Redshank, other waders.
◆ *Winter* Glaucous Gull.

ACCESS

There is an air service from Bodø to Røst, or you may travel from Bodø by boat. There are airports in Svolvær and Leknes. Svolvær may also be reached by boat from Skutvik. If you have time, drive the longer, scenic route on the E6 to Bjerkvik, and from there on through Vesterålen to Lofoten on the E19. It is a long trip, but the stunning scenery will be reward enough for the effort. In summertime you may have to queue for the ferry.

# ANDØYA

69°00N 15°30E

Andøya is a large island of 490 km$^2$ in the north of the Vesterålen archipelago. A steep mountain range runs in a north–south direction and on the east coast there are some large areas of bog (Dverbergmyran). Off the northwest coast, the bird cliffs of Bleiksøya and Skarvklakken are found. The climate is mild for the latitude, but it can be very windy. Vegetation consists mainly of birch, but recently conifers have been planted in some areas. Dverbergmyran, Bleiksøya and Skarvklakken are protected by national laws.

TIMING

May to August is the best season, for both climate and birds. Several species of ducks, raptors, waders and passerines can be found in good numbers and the seabird cliffs have gulls and auks in abundance. In autumn and winter, expect interesting seaducks and gulls, but also chilling winds.

SPECIES

◆ *Resident* Eider, White-tailed Eagle, Willow Ptarmigan.
◆ *Breeding season* British Storm-petrel, Slavonian Grebe, Gannet, Shag, ducks, Rough-legged Buzzard, Merlin, Whimbrel, Black-tailed Godwit, Ruff, Snipe, Red-necked Phalarope, Kittiwake, Arctic Skua, Guillemot, Razorbill, Puffin, Redpoll, Brambling, Snow Bunting.
◆ *Passage* Pink-footed Goose, Peregrine, Spotted Redshank.
◆ *Winter* King and Steller's Eiders, Gyrfalcon, Glaucous and Iceland Gulls.

ACCESS

Andøya is the northernmost island of the Vesterålen archipelago in Nordland county. Follow the E19 from Bjerkvik. Turn north onto Rv 82. When you cross the bridge at Risøyhamn you have reached the island. Continue northwards and Dverbergmyran is a couple of kilometres. Further on and you reach Andenes, where there is a whaling museum, and sightseeing trips for whales can be booked. Follow the road to the west, past the rocket-launching field at Oksbåsen, then south to Bleik, from where you can take a boat trip around Bleiksøya. Further south you also find Skarvklakken.

# BALSFJORD

69°15N 19°15E

Balsfjord has several localities with large intertidal areas. The most important is Sørkjosen, which is the outlet of two rivers at the head of Balsfjord, consisting of extensive stretches of mud, sand and gravel banks. The fjord outside is an important spawning ground for Capelin and Herring. The intertidal zone of Sørkjosen stretches from Markenes in the east to Storsteinnes in the west, and as far out as 700 m from dry land. Along the shoreline, there are alder and birch woods in some places. In the eastern part of the area, there is a medium-sized coastal meadow. Elsewhere, the land is mostly given over to agriculture. This is the best site in Troms county for watching migrating waders, especially Knot, and wintering seaducks are also plentiful.

TIMING

In mid-winter, small flocks of waders are found along the shore and seaducks are seen offshore in sometimes sizeable flocks. In early May, the first Knots arrive, and their numbers reach several tens of thousands before they leave at the end of the month. They are, of course, found alongside numerous other waders, all of which stop off on return migration in smaller numbers from August to October; passerines are much in evidence in autumn.

SPECIES

◆ *Resident* Eider.
◆ *Breeding season* Arctic Tern, Oystercatcher.
◆ *Passage* Red-throated and Black-throated Divers, Slavonian Grebe, Gyrfalcon, Peregrine, Grey and Ringed Plovers, Sanderling, Dunlin, Bar-tailed Godwit, Knot (tens of thousands), Meadow Pipit (up to 600 per day in autumn), Fieldfare, Brambling (up to 5000 per day in autumn), Redpoll (up to 2500 per day in autumn), Snow Bunting.
◆ *Winter* White-billed Diver, Scoter, Velvet Scoter (up to 5500), Red-breasted Merganser, Long-tailed Duck (up to 7500), King Eider (among Eider flocks).

ACCESS

When approaching either from south or north by the Highway E6, you will reach the bottom of the fjord Balsfjorden where the highway E78 leading to Tromsø splits from E6. To reach Sørkjosen, follow E6 13 km southward from Nordkjosbotn to Sagelv, where you should take Rv 859 4 km to Storsteinnes.

In order to look for migrating waders, especially Knot, the largest concentrations are found on the shores at Sørkjosen; Kantornes and Kobbevågen are also well worth a visit, as well as the tidal areas at Nordkjosbotn.

# VALDAK

70°10N 24°40E

This coastal site covers some 1620 ha of saltmarsh and wet mires; most inland areas consist of peat bog and birch forest. The area is situated close to the headland Stabbursneset, made from glacifluvial depositions, which makes a natural view point with a height of 25 m over Valdak. Beyond the Valdak marshes the fjord Porsangen uncovers vast intertidal flats. Valdak is a Ramsar Site as well as a nature reserve where all human access is prohibited in the period May–September. However, the area is very easy to view from Stabbursneset during the prohibition period.

TIMING

Spring and early summer, during May and June, are the best times of year to watch birds at Valdak. This is particularly true for ducks and waders, both those which breed in the area and those that pause on migration; considering the high latitude, the diversity of duck species is good. The most spectacular sights at this time of year are, however, the huge flocks of migrating Knot, numbering up to 60,000 birds on the sandbanks exposed at low tide. There may also be good

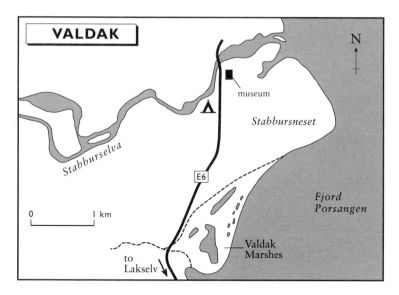

numbers of seaducks on the sea during their summer moult. The area is also a migration staging post for nearly the whole of the remaining Norwegian breeding population of Lesser White-fronted Goose. Together with other goose species, ducks and waders, they pass through on return migration in autumn.

SPECIES

◆ *Resident* Eider.

◆ *Breeding season* Shoveler, Garganey, Gadwall, Pintail, Wigeon, Red-breasted Merganser, White-tailed Eagle, Peregrine, Rough-legged Buzzard, Black-tailed Godwit, Dunlin, Temminck's Stint, Ruff, Wood Sandpiper, Lapwing, Curlew, Whimbrel, Snipe, Arctic Tern, Short-eared Owl, Lapland Bunting.

◆ *Passage* Bean and Lesser White-fronted Geese, Eider (up to 10,000 in summer moult), King Eider, Scoter (up to 3000 in summer moult), Bar-tailed Godwit, Long-tailed Skua (most mid-May to early June).

ACCESS

Valdak is situated about 20-km north of Lakselv in Porsanger municipality. The area is easily accessible, situated close to Highway E6. Valdak lies on the western side of the fjord Porsangen. Arriving from the south, the headland Stabbursneset is easy to see from the road, and finally the road crosses the headland. The wetlands are situated on the south side of the headland. 'Stabbursnes Nature House and Museum' close to the highway on the headland is well worth a visit.

## STABBURSDALEN

71°10N 24°30E

The lower areas of Stabbursdalen Valley are broad and flat and dominated by a terrace of sand and gravel deposits from the last Ice Age. The River Stabburselva winds slowly down the valley and, in places on the terrace, it makes a watercourse called the Lombola. It is also in this valley that we find the northernmost pine forest in the world, covering some 1000 ha. Further up the valley, birch forest dominates, and finally, at the far end of the valley we find bare rock. 9600 ha of Stabbursdalen is protected as a National Park. You are allowed to walk freely everywhere in the park.

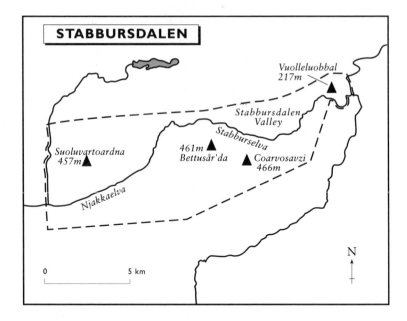

**STABBURSDALEN**

Vuolleluobbal
217m

Stabbursdalen
Valley

Stabburselva

Suoluvartoardna
457m

461m
Bettusår'da

Coarvosavzi
466m

Njakkaelva

N

0          5 km

**TIMING**

In mid-winter, gamebirds forage unobtrusively and flocks of foraging tits are active all day, making use of the short period of daylight. At the beginning of May, over a period of a few days, spring arrives, and, before long, summer will have started. An evening walk along the Lombola at this time of year can be a magical experience, the haunting calls of Black-throated Divers set against a backdrop illuminated by the midnight sun. The summer season is short, however, and, by late August, the area has lost many of its migrant bird species.

**SPECIES**

◆ *Resident* Capercaillie, Willow Ptarmigan, Three-toed Woodpecker, Siberian Jay, Willow and Siberian Tits, Pine Grosbeak.

◆ *Breeding season* Black-throated Diver, Pintail, Mallard, Teal, Wigeon, Velvet Scoter, Tufted Duck, Goosander, Red-breasted Merganser, Goldeneye, Long-tailed Duck, Golden Eagle, Rough-legged Buzzard, Merlin, Peregrine, Gyrfalcon, Osprey, Redshank, Greenshank, Wood Sandpiper, Long-tailed Skua (in good rodent years), Redstart, Pied Flycatcher, Waxwing, Great Grey Shrike.

**ACCESS**

From Highway E6 (*see* Valdak, page 140) a small road leads westward, to the left some 100 m after driving up the slope of the headland Stabbursneset when approaching from the south (Lakselv). If you arrive from the north on the E6, the road is about 2-km south of the bridge over the river Stabburselva. The road should be followed for 5 km, where there is a car park.

From the car park close to the Lombola, you may follow a marked track 500m to a small bridge which crosses the River Stabburselva. It is worth spending some time in the vicinity of the Lombola since the area is good for waders and wildfowl. However, the track leads on into the valley, where the old pine forest may yield some more exciting bird species. You should walk far up the valley to where the birch forest thins out.

*Pied Flycatcher*

# TANAMUNNINGEN

70°25–70°35N 28°20–28°35E

Tanamunningen is the estuary of the River Tana. Where the river flows into the Tanafjord, there is a large delta, with extensive areas of shallow water and sandbanks; the total area is 3450 ha, of which 180 ha is land. The delta area is inundated at high tide and when the river floods. Further out in the tidal zone, there is a grass-covered islet, Høyholmen, and in the river course, some of the sand and gravel banks are covered with wood and scrub. East of the delta, there is a small cove, Leirpollen. The river outlet has some of the biggest sub-Arctic coastal meadows in Finnmark, the largest ones being on the eastern side of the outlet. The site has been protected as a nature reserve since 1991. The area is proposed as a Ramsar Site.

This is an important moulting area for ducks and up to 30,000 Goosanders used to gather for this purpose in August and September. These are mainly males, making up most of the north-western European population; however, the number has decreased in recent years. The delta is also an important staging ground for migrating geese, ducks and waders; 22 species of the latter are regularly recorded. It is also important for wintering waterbirds.

### TIMING

The outlet of the River Tana holds huge numbers of wildfowl and waders in winter and early spring; up to 4000 Eiders, 4000 Long-tailed Ducks and 800 King Eiders are among them. Numerous ducks and waders breed on the coastal wetlands and are best from early May to July. From early August, huge numbers of ducks gather here for their summer moult and from then until October, migrant geese, ducks and waders pour through the region.

### SPECIES

- ◆ *Resident* Eider.
- ◆ *Breeding season* White-tailed Eagle, Peregrine, Temminck's Stint, Ringed Plover, Arctic Tern, Arctic Warbler.
- ◆ *Passage* Black-throated Diver, Little and Red-necked Grebes, Bean, White-fronted, Barnacle and Brent Geese, Shoveler, Surf Scoter (rare), Goosander, Coot, Red-necked Phalarope.

◆ *Winter* Long-tailed Duck, King Eider, Red-breasted Merganser, Purple Sandpiper.

ACCESS

Follow Highway E6 from Kirkenes to the bridge at Tana Bru, and take Rv 890 northwards, following the Tana river. Drive c. 25 km to the village of Austertana. You can also follow Rv 98 to the crossroads at Rustefjelbma, and take a small road northward on the western side of the River Tana to its outlet. If you arrive from Lakselv over the mountain pass, Ifjordfjellet, you can either cross the bridge at Tana Bru, and take the Rv890 as described above, or the small road to the left at the crossroads at Rustefjelbma.

From Austertana, you can drive on the eastern side of Leirpollen, to Geresgappe, from where you have a good view over parts of the area. The best view of the river outlet is from the headland before you reach Austertana, just passing Kirkenes. From here you can drive out to the islet Høyholmen, from where you can view the whole area. Leirpollen is easy to view from the road, when you have passed Austertana on the way north.

# NESSEBY

70°10N 28°50E

The area is situated close to Nesseby church, and is made up of a broad, shallow bay west of the church, the grass-covered islet Løkholmen, and the strait between Løkholmen and the mainland. The bay is highly influenced by tidal water; the tidal zone consists of mud and stones. Agricultural fields border the bay, and as protection against high tide, a sea wall of piled up stones has been built. A small lake is situated on the headland, and the surroundings are dominated by pasture and crags. In all, the land area comprises 90 ha while the marine area, protected as a nature reserve since 1991, covers 650 ha.

The area is important for migrant wildfowl and waders and also holds large numbers of wintering birds. The nearby Varanger fjord is an important wintering area for 10,000–20,000 Steller's Eiders, a major part of the European population; some are also found in the fjord right outside Nesseby.

TIMING

The best times to visit Nesseby are during migration periods in spring and autumn. From mid-April to late May, waders and wildfowl numbers build up and impressive flocks can be found. Summertime is relatively quiet although the first returning migrant waders appear in late July and August. Autumn migration extends from September to November, after which time numbers of overwintering duck species build up towards the end of the year.

SPECIES

◆ *Resident* Eider, Steller's Eider.
◆ *Breeding season* Redshank, Curlew, Turnstone, Arctic Tern, Wheatear, Bluethroat.
◆ *Passage* White-billed Diver, shearwaters (in northerly winds), British Storm-petrel, Bewick's Swan, Coot, Dunlin, Bar-tailed Godwit, Curlew Sandpiper, Little Stint, Ruff, Knot, Ringed Plover, Red-necked Phalarope, Little Gull, Black Tern.
◆ *Winter* King Eider, Long-tailed Duck, Purple Sandpiper.

ACCESS

Entering Varangerbotn via Highway E6, you should take Rv98 (Rv98 between Varangerbotn and Vardø. It will probably change to E75 during

1995) towards Vadsø at the crossroads at Varangerbotn. After 13 km, the idyllic view of the old Nesseby church appears on your right. A small road leads to the church, and a car park.

The tarn on the headland is a good place for phalaropes and ducks. The area is relatively small and you do not need to walk miles to get views of much of the coastal areas. In fact, you can see a lot by simply staying near the church.

## STORE EKKERØY

70°05N 30°10E

This 160-ha area comprises the southern and eastern half of the Store Ekkerøy peninsula, east of Vadsø; within the area, a 50-m cliff plunges into the sea, its ledges harbouring seabird colonies including some 10,000 Kittiwakes. On the north side of the peninsula, the ground slopes towards the sea. Except from the seabird cliffs, the area is covered by heather moorland.

*Turnstone*

TIMING

Several species of gulls are present in the area throughout the winter, their numbers building up towards early spring. The seabirds begin to return to the cliffs from March onwards and, in May, migrant passerines arrive. The season is relatively short, however, and most of the seabirds and passerines begin to leave from mid-August to mid-September. Store Ekkerøy can also be good during spring and autumn migration as a staging post.

SPECIES

◆ *Resident* Eider, White-tailed Eagle.
◆ *Breeding season* Cormorant, Shag, Gannet, gulls, Arctic Tern, Guillemot, Brünnich's and Black Guillemots, Razorbill, Puffin, Meadow Pipit, Wheatear.
◆ *Passage* White-billed Diver, British Storm-petrel, Fulmar, Temminck's Stint, skuas (all four species on occasions), Snowy Owl (rare), Red-throated Pipit, Shore Lark, Lapland Bunting.
◆ *Winter* Long-tailed Duck, Purple Sandpiper, Great Black-backed, Herring, Glaucous and Iceland Gulls.

ACCESS

At Varangerbotn take Rv 98 towards Vadsø at the crossroads at Varangerbotn. After 13 km you will pass Nesseby (*see* page 144), on the right. 49 km further east past the city of Vadsø, a small road to the right leads to Store Ekkerøy. You can drive almost all the way to the bird cliffs.

This seabird colony is particularly attractive because it is easily accessible. The colony of breeding Kittiwakes can be viewed very closely from the top of the cliff. From this point, there is also a good view over the sea.

## HORNØY AND REINØY

70°24N 31°10E

These important seabird colonies harbour thousands of breeding seabirds and have nature reserve status extending to the islands of Hornøya and Reinøya and the small islets of Prestholmen and Lille Avløysinga; access is controlled during the breeding season. The western part of Hornøya consists of a 65-m high hill, with steep cliffs facing westward. The eastern parts of Hornøya are flat; a lighthouse is situated at the northern part of the island. Reinøya has no steep cliffs. Hornøya is the easternmost point of Norway at 31°10E.

The islands possess Europe's largest colony of Herring and Great Black-backed Gulls (40,000–50,000 pairs). There are also 23,000 pairs of Kittiwakes, their numbers having declined during the 1980s. Puffins, on the other hand, showed a significant increase in the years 1980–83, and the breeding population numbered 6000 pairs in 1989. Other seabird populations include 6000 Guillemots, 400 pairs of Brünnich's Guillemots and 250 pairs of Razorbills.

TIMING
In the winter, Kittiwakes are numerous and mass around fishing boats heading for the harbour at Vardø. Other larger gull species are also present and seaducks gather in their hundreds, often just outside the harbour at Vardø. Large, dense flocks of Steller's Eiders, sometimes comprising more than 400 birds, are a highlight along with the 2500–3000 King Eiders present from February onwards. From early March, the auks start to return to the colonies, and from April on you can see them in thousands in the air around Hornøya and Reinøya. At this time the first migrants turn up, these invariably being Snow Buntings; other migrants arrive throughout May. Seabird numbers are plentiful from then until mid-August to mid-September when they begin to disperse from the cliffs.

SPECIES
◆ *Resident* Eider (1000 pairs breed), Black Guillemot.
◆ *Breeding season* Fulmar, Cormorant, Shag, Gannet, Oystercatcher, Herring and Great Black-backed Gulls, Arctic Tern, Guillemot, Brünnich's Guillemot, Razorbill, Puffin, Short-eared Owl, White Wagtail, Lapland Bunting.
◆ *Winter* Steller's and King Eiders, Purple Sandpiper, gulls, Little Auk.

ACCESS
At Varangerbotn take Rv98 (will probably change to E75 during 1995) towards Vadsø at the crossroads at Varangerbotn. After 13 km you will pass Nesseby (*see* page 144) on the right. 49 km further eastward past the city of Vadsø, Store Ekkerøy (*see* page 145) is close to the road. Follow Rv 98 a further 62 km northwards. The last 3 km is via a tunnel. You then reach the city of Vardø. The islands are situated just off Vardø in eastern Finnmark, only 2-km north-east of the city. It is possible to arrange boat transport at the harbour office or at the Tourist Office in Vardø (Tel. 78 98 82 70 in summer).

If you go ashore on Hornøya, it is possible to view most of the breeding seabird species from the slopes below the bird cliffs, except for Cormorant which nest only on Reinøya.

# SYLTEFJORDSTAURAN
70°35N 30°30E
Syltefjordstauran is on the north side of the fjord Syltefjorden, on the peninsula Makkaurhalvøya in Båtsfjord municipality. It is a coastline of some 11,600 ha. Rocky pillars ('*staurer*') and steep cliffs plunging into the sea from a height of 200 m, are features of the area, which has nature reserve status.

Norway's most impressive sea cliffs are found at Storalkestauren and, together with Hjelmsøya, these are the most important seabird cliffs in Finnmark. The Kittiwake colony is the largest in Norway, numbering 140,000 breeding pairs and the Gannet colony (400 pairs) is the only one in

Finnmark and the most northerly in the world. Other important species are Razorbill (1200 pairs) and Guillemot (12,000 pairs in 1985). Little Auk occurs regularly during the summer, albeit in small numbers.

TIMING
Hundreds of seaducks gather below the bird cliffs in the winter months, numbers of King Eiders in particular building up from February onwards. From early March, the auks return to the bird cliffs and, from April onwards, thousands swarm in the skies over Syltefjordstauran. Most landbird migrants arrive throughout May, and in the summertime this site possesses all the species and sights that a visitor could hope for at a north Norwegian seabird colony.

SPECIES
◆ *Resident* Eider, Black Guillemot.
◆ *Breeding season* Fulmar, Cormorant, Shag, Gannet, Kittiwake, Guillemot, Brünnich's Guillemot, Razorbill, Puffin, Little Auk (occasional), Meadow Pipit, White Wagtail, Snow Bunting.
◆ *Winter* Steller's and King Eiders, Long-tailed Duck, Little Auk, Purple Sandpiper.

ACCESS
Follow Highway E6 from Kirkenes to the bridge at Tana Bru, or follow Rv98 to the same point if you are arriving from Lakselv over the mountain passage Ifjordfjellet. Take Rv890 northwards, and follow the Tana river on the eastern side. After 74 km where the road splits, you must follow Rv891 for c. 28 km. Take to the left where a small road leads to the abandoned fishing station at Syltefjord after 30 km. From here you have to walk along a path for 2–3 hours to reach the seabird colony. Sometimes it is possible to arrange boat trips from the village/fishing station at Syltefjord out to the cliffs.

# NEIDEN/MUNKEFJORD

69°05N 29°35E

This site covers 10,800 ha of marine wetlands at the outlets of the Rivers Neidenelva and Munkelva; 1150 ha of dry land are also included in the site. The estuary of the River Neidenelva is characterized by tall terraces made from glacifluvial deposits together with numerous sandbanks beneath. The river is broad and calm, and is subject to tidal influences inland for several kilometres from the estuary. Munkefjorden is situated on the inside of the Neiden river estuary. In the bottom of the fjord, vast areas are exposed at low tide. In both areas there are several coastal meadows and saltmarshes. Munkefjorden is generally a shallow bay (most of it less than 10-m deep), ideal for waterbirds. Near both river outlets there are some farms. Since 1991 the area has been protected as a nature reserve.

The area supports one of the largest concentrations of divers in Norway, especially during spring. Red-throated Divers reach numbers of up to 100 birds and Black-throated Divers up to 400. The latter species remains in the area throughout summer and autumn in high numbers. 18 species of wildfowl and 20 species of waders are regularly seen in the area.

TIMING
During the winter, the outlet of Munkelva is frozen, and wintering ducks then frequent the Neidenelva estuary. Their numbers increase throughout the spring,

decrease in early summer and increase again in late summer when the birds are moulting. In spring, there are huge numbers of migrant Arctic waders, but probably the most spectacular sight is the high numbers of divers on the fjord.

SPECIES

◆ *Resident* Eider, Raven.
◆ *Breeding season* Arctic Warbler, Little Bunting.
◆ *Passage* Black-throated and Red-throated Divers, Bean Goose, ducks (including up to 4000 Goosanders in autumn), Bar-tailed Godwit, Knot (up to 2500 birds).
◆ *Winter* Long-tailed Duck, King Eider, Goosander, Red-breasted Merganser, Scoter and Velvet Scoter.

ACCESS

From Kirkenes, follow the E6 8 km to Bjørkheim, then a further 24 km to Munkelv. Approaching from west by E6, the Village of Neiden is situated 80 km from Varangerbotn. The small village of Munkelv is a further 7-km east at the bottom of Munkefjorden on the western side of the river Munkelva.

The area with the highest numbers of birds throughout the year is the estuary at Neidenelva, which is easy accessible from the village of Neiden. The area along Munkefjord is easy to view from the highway E6, which follows along the fjord along the eastern side. The bottom of the fjord, where the coastal meadows and saltmarshes occur, is best for migrant waders; it is best viewed from near the River Munkelva at the small village of Munkelv.

# ØVRE PASVIK

69°05N 29°00E

Pasvik is a valley close to the border of Russia and Finland in eastern Finnmark, 20 km² of which are protected as a National Park; within its boundaries can be found the largest virgin forest in Norway. In 1993 a common Russian-Norwegian nature reserve covering vast areas on both sides of the border was established. This is the westernmost limit of the Siberian Taiga, and the landscape is flat, with some drainage ridges, and covered by coniferous forest and peat bogs. There are numerous lakes, which are richly populated by several fish species, especially Pike. Several eastern plant species flourish here. There are no restrictions on ordinary access, which means you are allowed to walk anywhere you choose. On the Russian side of the border, 60 km is protected.

TIMING

Throughout the winter, hardy resident species remain, these having to survive the severe winters in Pasvik. Among the first spring migrants to arrive are Whooper Swans and Snow Buntings which sometimes appear in March. These are followed by Bean Geese at the end of April, first resting in the Pasvik River and then moving into the wilderness as the snow and ice gradually melts.

A visit to the area in May and early June is a great adventure. Snow and ice melts early in the valley, and large concentrations of birds gather here, waiting for their barren breeding grounds to thaw. In spring and summer the Pasvik river, wetlands and peat bog areas have numerous waterfowl and waders. The waders normally leave by mid-July, and ducks and geese normally disappear from the area in September and October.

SPECIES

◆ *Resident* Capercaillie, Hawk and Great Grey Owls (unpredictable), Three-toed and Black Woodpeckers, Siberian Jay, Siberian Tit, Pine Grosbeak.

◆ *Breeding season* Teal, Wigeon, Goldeneye, Smew, Rough-legged Buzzard, Osprey, Common Crane, Bar-tailed Godwit, Spotted Redshank, Wood and Broad-billed Sandpipers, Jack Snipe, Short-eared Owl, Waxwing, Sedge Warbler, Little Bunting, Pine Grosbeak.

◆ *Passage* Geese, ducks, waders, rarities.

ACCESS

From Kirkenes Highway E6, drive south 8 km to Hesseng from where you must turn left and follow Rv 885 further south into the Pasvik Valley for 34 km. Head for Svanvik, where you can stay overnight, then drive a further 18 km to Skogfoss where there is a petrol station. Follow the same road some 46 km more and you reach Nyrud at the end of the road.

The best areas are along the Pasvik river, where deciduous forest, scrub and thickets are dense, from Vaggetem and Kjerringneset in the north to Hestefossdammen in the south. These areas are all relatively close to the road. The most important areas for wading birds are between the Pasvik river and the National Park. The National Park itself is of less ornithological significance, consisting of uniform pine forest and peat bog. Recommended routes are, for example, a track from Gjøkåsen leading westwards to Gjøkvatn, or the small road from Vaggetem along the river Ellenelva to the mouth of the small lake Sortbrysttjern. It is also possible to follow the east side of the river passing a small lake Tørrfurutjern until you reach Lake Ellenvatn a distance of 2 km.

*Common Crane*

# SWEDEN

Sweden is a long country (1600 km from north to south) and covers an area of 450,000 km²; its size makes it the fifth largest country in Europe. The population, which numbers 8.7,000,000 inhabitants, is thinly spread with more than 30 per cent of the people living in and around the three largest cities of Stockholm, Göteborg (Gothenburg) and Malmö.

Sweden is a monarchy but the Royal Family today have primarily ceremonial duties. The Prime Minister is elected by a single chamber Parliament with different political parties, after public elections every fourth year.

Forestry, forestry technology and the engineering industry are the most important areas of business. Other industries include chemicals, machinery and food. Farming has become highly mechanized during the last couple of decades, which has caused a drastic decrease in the number of farmers and has transformed large areas of formerly diverse agricultural land into large monocultural fields.

Swedish is the national language but English in particular is widely spoken and easily understood by many Swedes; the older people are also quite good at German. More than 90 per cent of the population belongs to the Lutheran state church, but there are several independent churches and foreign religions in the country.

There is a tradition in Sweden called 'Allemansrätten' or Everyman's Right. In practice it means that everybody can walk, ski, pick flowers, berries or mushrooms on any land apart from private gardens. You are also allowed to use boats on lakes and rivers. But it also means an 'Everyman's Duty' not to cause damage to nature, walk across cultivated fields, disturb animals, pass too close to private houses and gardens and such like. In some nature reserves or National Parks there are restrictions to the Everyman's Right.

OPPOSITE: 1 FALSTERBO PENINSULA, 2 LAKE KRANKESJÖN, 3 FYLEDALEN, 4 LOWER REACHES OF THE RIVER HELGE WITH HAMMARSJÖN, 5 SOUTH SKÄLDERVIKEN & KULLEN, 6 KÄVSJÖN-STORE MOSSE, 7 LAKE ÅSNEN AREA, 8 BEIJERSHAMN, 9 OTTENBY, 10 KAPELLUDDEN, 11 STORA KARLSÖ, 12 HOBURGEN AREA, 13 STOCKVIKEN-FALUDDEN, 14 NORSHOLMEN-FÅRÖ, 15 MELLBYSTRAND AREA, 16 GETTERÖN, 17 MORUPS TÅNGE, 18 HÖNÖ, 19 SVARTEDALEN, 20 VÄNERSBORG BAY, 21 TIVEDEN, 22 LAKE HORNBORGASJÖN, 23 CAPE HAMMARÖ, 24 KILSVIKEN-ÅRÅSVIKEN, 25 LAKE KVISMAREN, 26 OSET, 27 TYSSLINGEN, 28 LAKE TÅKERN, 29 SVARTÅMYNNINGEN, 30 BÅVEN, 31 TYRESTA, 32 STOCKHOLM-EKOPARKEN, 33 BULLERÖ ARCHIPELAGO, 34 LAKE HJÄLSTAVIKEN, 35 LAKE ANGARN, 36 FLORARNA, 37 LEDSKÄR, 38 FÄRNEBOFJÄRDEN, 39 ASKÖVIKEN, 40 HOVRAN AREA, 41 TANDÖVALA-TISJÖN AREA, 42 KOPPÅNGEN AREA, 43 HORNSLANDET, 44 ÅSTHOLMEN, 45 STORNÄSET, 46 SKULESKOGEN, 47 FLATRUET, 48 LAKE ÅNNSJÖN, 49 STEKKENJOKK AREA, 50 UMEÄLVEN DELTA, 51 HOLMÖARNA, 52 GAMMELSTADSVIKEN, 53 HAPARANDA SANDSKÄR NATIONAL PARK, 54 ABISKO NATIONAL PARK, 55 AMMARNÄS, 56 MUDDUS NATIONAL PARK, 57 SJAUNJA, 58 VITTANGI-RIPAKAISENVUOMA, 59 PADJELANTA NATIONAL PARK, 60 KVIKKJOKK & TARRADALEN.

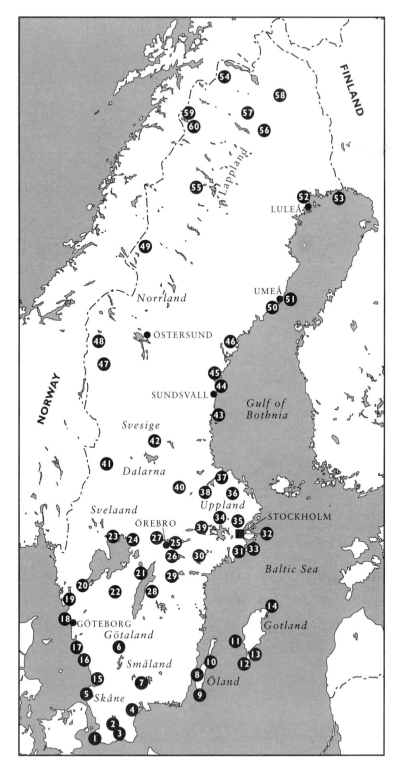

FINLAND

**54**

**58**

**57**
**59**
**60**
**56**

Lappland

**55**

**52**
LULEÅ
**53**

**49**

Norrland

UMEÅ
**50** **51**

ÖSTERSUND
**48**
**46**

**47**

NORWAY

**45**
**44**
SUNDSVALL
**43**

Gulf of
Bothnia

Svesige

**42**

**41**
Dalarna

**40**
**37**
**38**
**36**
Uppland
**34** **35**
STOCKHOLM
Svelaand
ÖREBRO
**39**
**32**
**23** **24** **27** **25**
**26** **30**
**31** **33**
**21** **29**
**22** **28**
Baltic Sea
**20**
**19**
**14**
**18** GÖTEBORG
Gotland
Götaland
**17** **6**
**11**
**16** Småland
**13**
**10** **12**
**15** **8**
**7** Öland
**5** Skåne **9**
**4**
**2**
**1** **3**

# HABITATS

In terms of habitat, Sweden is far from uniform. In the far north and at the high altitudes along the border with Norway is the Swedish Alpine region, or *fjeld* region. Between 800 and 1000 m there are a series of mountain plateaux with vegetation no more extensive than willow scrub. This is an exciting wilderness area studded with lakes and peaks, and crossed by watercourses and steep valleys. Then, of course, there are the forests, arguably the country's most dominating habitat, and lastly, there is the coast.

Sweden is a forested country and more than 65 per cent of the land can be classified as west Eurasian taiga (the boreal region). This area is dominated by conifers, mainly Norwegian Spruce on richer and productive ground, and Scots Pine in drier parts. Deciduous trees such as Aspen and birch also occur throughout the forest. Almost all of the productive areas are influenced by modern forestry and the amount of virgin forest is less than 0.5 per cent of productive land. The terrain varies from flat coastland in the east to hilly woodland further westwards.

The boreal region reaches a limit called 'Limes Norrlandicus' at the River Dalälven (80-km north of Stockholm). From this border southwards, in the boreo-nemoral region, the conifers become mixed with many species of deciduous trees. Agricultural land and reedbeds are also features of the boreo-nemoral region today. In earlier days the grazing of animals and haymaking were common practices in these areas. A drastic decrease in traditional activities over the last 50 years has changed many fields into scrub, creating a new forest generation. During the last 150 years most of the lakes in open farmland have been influenced by man, and in some parts of Sweden more than 90 per cent of the natural wetlands have been lost by drainage.

Changes in land use and agricultural practice have also affected the most southern part of Sweden, the nemoral region, whose character is similar to that of the northern part of the European mainland. The nemoral area in Sweden is highly cultivated and there is a lack of pure mature forests here. Many of the former Swedish beech forests have today been transformed into spruce stands. Despite this, the region offers many wonderful views together with excellent wildlife and several good sites for birds, especially species that are dependent on grazing and haymaking.

Finally, mention must be made of the long Swedish coastline which includes several archipelagos with thousands of islands and skerries. These stretch from Strömstad in the west to Haparanda in the north, a distance of 1860 km.

# IMPORTANCE FOR BIRDS

Around 290 species are regular breeders and another 20 species occur regularly on migration. In total 450 species have been recorded in Sweden.

There are good breeding populations of wetland and forest birds such as Black-throated Diver, Red-throated Diver (more local), Great Crested Grebe, Whooper Swan, Bean Goose, Goldeneye, Smew, Golden Eagle, Hen Harrier, Capercaillie, Black Grouse, Hazel Hen, Crane, Osprey (two-thirds of the European population), Tengmalm's Owl and Black Woodpecker.

The fjeld region with mountain plateaux, lakes, rivers and wetlands is a breeding area for Long-tailed Duck, Common and Velvet Scoters, Caspian Tern, Long-tailed and Arctic Skuas, Gyrfalcon, Dotterel, Temminck's Stint,

Dunlin, Great Snipe, Bar-tailed Godwit, Red-necked Phalarope, Shore Lark, Bluethroat, Ring Ouzel, Lapland and Snow Buntings, Red-throated Pipit, Willow Ptarmigan, Ptarmigan and Arctic Redpoll.

North Swedish forests and the mire mosaics are home to a large part of the European breeding population of Whimbrel, Greenshank, Spotted Redshank, Jack Snipe, Broad-billed Sandpiper, Ural and Great Grey Owls, Three-toed Woodpecker, Waxwing, Arctic Warbler (rare), Pine Grosbeak, Little Bunting and Siberian Jay.

*Hen Harrier*

During migration in April and May and September to November, large flocks of geese and ducks either pass or rest at several places. Notable are Brent, Barnacle, Bean and White-fronted Geese, Whooper and Mute Swans, Eider, Long-tailed and Tufted Ducks, Goosander and several species of dabbling ducks.

Thirty of the most valuable wetlands are listed in the Wetland Convention but many more are important as staging posts in the Nordic link of the European-African flyway of migratory birds.

Successful restoration programmes have resulted in increasing populations of White-tailed Eagle, Peregrine, Eagle Owl, and Red Kite. Also the Lesser White-fronted Goose shows signs of increasing, but is still an extremely rare breeder in Sweden, having been much more common 50-years ago.

## SEASONS

The weather varies markedly between the seasons and from north to south, and even from west to east. In the north, snow normally comes in late October or early November and can remain until the beginning of June or in some areas even longer. Spring and summer up here are short and intensive.

In south and mid-Sweden, winter normally starts in late November or December and ends in March to April. The snow conditions during this period vary considerably from year to year. The southernmost counties are without snow most winters.

### SPRING

March, April and early June are the best times for birdwatching in mid- and southern Sweden. This is when most migrants arrive and the breeding season starts. Many birds are singing and spring migration of passerines, geese, ducks, waders and raptors can be observed at many sites even if the spring migration is not as impressive as in autumn. Visit wetlands and bird lakes, and spend a few days and nights in the forest with owls and woodpeckers.

The second half of May to the first half of June is the time when most rarities from abroad can occur and many Swedish birdwatchers favour the counties of Öland, Gotland and Scania.

### SUMMER

During June and July, bird activity in the southern half of Sweden is decreasing as the breeding season comes to an end. Occasional rarities can occur and the autumn migration of waders starts. In the second half of July and in August, inland lakes with muddy margins and several coastal wetlands are excellent for waders. At some sites the concentrations of birds are high, and you can expect almost every species that normally occurs in Europe and perhaps something else too.

Late August and September are good months for a visit to the Falsterbo area in southern Scania. Here, the Swedish autumn migration of raptors and passerines can be followed perhaps better than anywhere else in the country.

Farther north, June and the beginning of July are the best months to hear birds singing. The activity decreases quite quickly, but even later on in July and August it is still nice to visit north Sweden. Be prepared, however, for the superabundance of mosquitoes!

### AUTUMN

September to November is the autumn migration period. Visit coastal wetlands, capes and some inland lakes. In September most of the raptors and several passerines migrate together with ducks, gulls, terns, waders and geese. October offers large flocks of geese, Golden Eagle and White-tailed Eagle at several places in southern Sweden. Common passerines seen foraging at migrating spots are Robin, Goldcrest and tits.

The middle of October is the best time to visit Öland. Today, this is a tradition for birdwatchers from Sweden and abroad. Many eastern rarities may occur and the birding combines with a vibrant social life in the evenings at Stenhusa Gård, the Swedish Ornithological Society's (SOF) trade centre and pub at Stenåsa. November can still offer good birdwatching opportunities even if the peak of the migration has passed.

In strong westerly winds a visit to Kullen, Mellbystrand, Morups Tånge, Getterön/Gubbanäsan or Hönö is strongly recommended from August to November. Late August and September are probably the best periods for watching seabirds.

### WINTER

Winter lasts from December to March in southern Sweden. Depending on the winter, overwintering species occur in varying numbers. In the southern counties, up to 150 species can be seen even in January compared to less than half that number in the Stockholm area. Golden and White-tailed Eagles, Goshawk, Raven, Great Grey Shrike, flocks of Waxwings, Redpolls, Siskin, Twite and Crossbill are typical winter birds. In some harbours, you can find the odd Glaucous Gull among the Herring and Great Black-Backed Gulls if you are lucky.

In February and March you should visit some good forest areas. Drumming woodpeckers and calling owls together with lekking Black Grouse and other early spring voices are highlights of the birdwatching year.

## CONSERVATION

Important nature areas are protected by the Nature Conservation Act. In 1995, 1588 areas, covering 2,800,000 ha, were protected as either nature reserves or National Parks. Besides the conservation legislation there are other laws regulating nature consideration within forestry, farming and industry. Still, many critics argue that this is not enough in order to secure biological diversity. SOF and other organizations are working hard to raise the profile of environmental impact among the many spheres of human activity that influence birds.

Sweden has ratified several international conventions including the Wetland Convention, the Bern Convention concerning species and habitats in Europe, and the Bonn Convention which deals with migrating species in Europe. The biggest problem for the conservation movement in Sweden is the lack of adequate follow-up in Swedish legislation needed to implement the aims of these conventions.

## GETTING THERE AND GETTING AROUND

It is easy to get to Sweden by air and there are several daily international flights to Stockholm-Arlanda, Göteborg-Landwetter, Malmö-Sturup and even other airports. The network of domestic flights is fairly well developed with connections between more than 30 airports. There are often weekend offers on domestic flights which can drastically reduce the high price. Combine a cheap flight with a car rental. Check the different rentals, however, as the prices can vary greatly.

There are several links to Sweden by train and boat. Within Sweden, the State Railway provides a widespread network with good connections. Going by train is also a good way to explore the country. A Nordic Railpass allows you unlimited travel in Sweden, Finland and Norway for three weeks. More information can be given by your travel agent.

As the Swedish coastline boasts numerous islands, there are many boat services, operating mainly in summertime; there are also services on many of the larger lakes. Regular year-round links also exist between the mainland and the largest island in the Baltic Sea, Gotland. The longest bridge in Europe leads to the island of Öland, a 'must' for birdwatchers.

If you drive, please remember that dipped highlights and the use of seat belts are obligatory. The Swedish road system is well maintained with around 98,000 km of trunk roads and 1000 km of toll-free motorways. Do not drink and drive; Swedish legislation is very strict on motorists who have consumed even a small volume of alcohol.

Hotels are available in all big cities and normally it is not difficult to find hotels, youth hostels or camping sites in southern Sweden; the distances between suitable places in northern Sweden are, not surprisingly, greater. Good information can be given by local tourist information offices. There are more than 400 such offices throughout the country.

## SWEDISH ORNITHOLOGICAL SOCIETY (SOF)

More information about the birdlife in Sweden can be obtained from the Swedish Ornithological Society. SOF is the national society for bird conservation, research and birdwatching in Sweden (*see* Useful Addresses). It is also the Swedish partner for BirdLife International. The domestic network consists of 25 regional societies and 70 local bird clubs. They run 20 bird observatories across the country and together they produce more than 50 regional and local bird publications. The society produces the following publications: *Vår Fågelvärld* is a popular journal in Swedish (eight issues a year); *Ornis Svecica* is a scientific journal in English and Swedish; and *Fågelåret* is an annual yearbook with bird reports in Swedish. For more information on birdwatching in Sweden, contact the SOF in Stockholm (*see* Useful Addresses).

# BIRDWATCHING SITES

## FALSTERBO PENINSULA

55°25N 12°55E

This flat peninsula, which comprises 7350 ha in the most south-westerly part of Sweden, is the best-known site for watching autumn bird migration in the country. It is a varied area with sandy beaches, sandbanks, lagoons, marshlands, grazed and lush meadows, forest stands and extensive heathland. The total area also includes three smaller communities, Höllviksnäs, Skanör and Falsterbo. If you make a visit, it is good to know of a couple of nearby locations, described below, which offer you added variety. The Falsterbo headland, including Fotevik Bay, is classified as one of the most important Ramsar Sites in Sweden. Several parts of the area are nature reserves.

A total of 333 species have been recorded at Falsterbo over the years, the bulk of species occurring during the autumn migration period. Waders, ducks and terns are all well represented, but it is perhaps the raptor migration for which the area is best known. Passerine numbers are also impressive with a staggering 1,100,000 Chaffinches and Bramblings having been recorded on a single October morning!

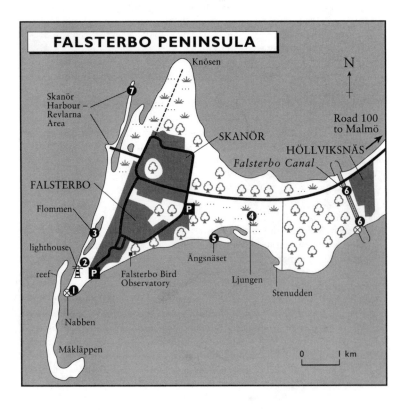

TIMING

In winter (December to February), some ducks, waders and passerines remain. Spring migration, from March to May, is not as spectacular as in autumn, but if you visit Falsterbo during the first half of April, you may witness impressive 'falls' of thrushes and other nocturnal migrants heading north.

Return migration can start as early as June with the passage of adult waders and seaducks. Late July to early August is a good time for different waders and you could see six tern species at Nabben.

From mid-August to November is the most exciting period of the year but sightings vary according to prevailing weather conditions. Wagtails and pipits pass through in August and September, with up to 10,000 Tree Pipits and 5000 Yellow Wagtails having been recorded in one morning. Raptors pass through in good numbers in early autumn and every European eagle species except Bonelli's has been seen.

Around mid-September is best for variety in raptor species, and numerous finches. In October, Woodpigeons pass through in incredible numbers, tens of thousands being seen on a good day; the maximum daily count is 120,000! Raptors are still numerous at this time of year and flocks of Branta Geese begin to pass through. The period from mid-October to mid-November offers large numbers of northerly passerines along with flocks of migrant swans and geese. The odd Siberian passerine sometimes turns up.

SPECIES

◆ *Breeding season* Kentish Plover, Avocet.
◆ *Passage* Whooper Swan, Bean, Brent, Barnacle and White-fronted Geese, Eider, Scoter, Gannet, eagles (White-tailed as well as rare but regular Lesser Spotted and other *Aquila* eagles), Marsh Harrier, Red Kite, Osprey, Buzzard, Rough-legged and Honey Buzzards (mostly between 15 August and 15 September), Peregrine, Hobby, Sparrowhawk, waders (including Curlew and Green Sandpipers), Arctic Skua, Little Gull, Woodpigeon (mostly October), Yellow and Grey Wagtails, Citrine Wagtail (rare), Tree, Meadow, Tawny (rare) and Red-throated Pipits, Richard's Pipit (rare), Woodlark, Dunnock, Great Grey Shrike, Waxwing, Pallas's and Yellow-browed Warblers (rare), Carrion Crow, Jackdaw, Nutcracker, tits, Goldfinch, Greenfinch, Chaffinch, Brambling, Twite, Redpoll, Lapland Bunting.
◆ *Winter* Little Grebe, Tufted Duck, Scaup, Eider, Long-tailed Duck, Rough-legged Buzzard, Buzzard, Redshank, Dunlin, Oystercatcher, Fieldfare.

ACCESS

The area is about 30-km south-west of Malmö in southern Sweden. Take the road E6 to Vellinge and then road 100 to Falsterbo. If you do not have a car, catch a bus from Malmö, but you will need a bike (can be hired at Falsterbo). Some of the best places to visit are as follows: **1. Nabben.** The south-western point is the best place to start birding in the morning during migration time. It is situated along the road through Falsterbo and ends up at the car park at Kolabacken. The track to Nabben passes over a golf course (also good for birds) so you have to watch out for flying golfballs. Off Nabben lies a sandspit called Måkläppen. Although prohibited to visitors between 1 February and 31 October, its breeding and resting birds can be seen from Nabben through a good telescope. **2. The lighthouse** is on the route to Nabben. Stop here if migrating passerines are passing close by. If it is windy, you hear bird calls better here than at Nabben. The lighthouse garden with its woodland is attractive to migrant birds. **3. Flommen** is reached by walking northwards from the lighthouse garden or taking the road called 'Fädriften' westwards from Falsterbo. Shelter among the bathing huts to watch raptors when the wind comes from the south-east. Passerines can be seen in the reedbeds. **4. Ljungen** is an area of open heathland, famous for its raptors. From late morning, when thermals start to rise, soaring and passing raptors can be seen. The south-western corner of the heath is usually good on bright, sunny days from August to October. **5. Ängsnäset.** This shallow lagoon and sand bank area is situated just south of Ljungen and is easiest to reach from the camping site at Ljungen. Ängsnäset is good for waders, ducks and raptors in northerly winds. **6. The Falsterbo Canal** is a good place for watching migrating raptors. Take the small road that follows the canal southwards, stop anywhere. In general, it is best in the north during southerly winds and in the south in northerly winds. **7. Skanör Harbour – Revlarna area.** From Skanör you take the road Hamnvägen to the harbour. The whole 1-km distance is good for birding so drive slowly and stop often. There are grazed fields and areas of shallow water on both sides of the road. **The Falsterbo Bird Observatory.** The Bird Observatory is run by the Ornithological Society of Scania, a regional organization of the Swedish Ornithological Society.

# LAKE KRANKESJÖN

55°42N 13°28E

This eutrophic lake with vast reedbeds and grazed meadows covers an area of 3970 ha. Close to the lake the grazing has ceased and the shores are encroached by Alder, willow and birch. The surrounding land supports varied agriculture with fields and stands of woodland. The area is a Ramsar Site and a national reserve. For two decades, waterplants declined causing waterbird numbers to fall. During the last few years, however, the lake has recovered and numerous waterbirds are now present. Lake Krankesjön is good for both migrant and breeding waders, ducks and passerines.

TIMING

From December to February, there are large flocks of diving ducks (unless ice-covered) and in March and April more than 1000 Bean Geese rest in the vicinity. Breeding ducks as well as other waterbirds and passerines are present from May until August after which time return migration can be seen until November.

SPECIES

◆ *Resident* Bearded Tit, Black Woodpecker.
◆ *Breeding season* Red-necked Grebe, Bittern, White-tailed Eagle, Marsh Harrier, Red Kite, Water Rail, Black Tern, Grasshopper, Icterine and Marsh Warblers, Thrush Nightingale, Penduline Tit, Golden Oriole.
◆ *Passage* Bean Goose, Garganey, Little Gull, Black Tern.
◆ *Winter* Goosander, Tufted Duck, Smew.

ACCESS

The area is 25-km east of the city of Lund, between the villages of Revinge and Silvåkra. Travel by car or bike, or take a bus to Revinge or Harlösa and walk from there. Start at the hide, signposted 'Fågeltorn' just north of the village of Silvåkra. Early mornings may be very productive here. Another possibility is to park at the ecological station Stensoffa, south-west of the lake. Follow a track to another hide where you also can view of the lake.

# FYLEDALEN

55°33N 13°52E

Covering an area of some 2000 ha, this site comprises a valley, slopes with beech forests; a small river, Fyleån, winds along the valley bottom. The valley is surrounded by farmland and patches of woodland. The area just west of Benstad is a nature reserve, mainly on account of its rich flora which includes several species of orchid. As well as woodland birds, the area can host lots of raptors in autumn and winter.

### TIMING

September and February are best for raptors and, at the same time, huge flocks of Bramblings and Chaffinches invade the forests; more than 100,000 birds occur in some winters. Breeding birds are at their best between mid-May and late June.

### SPECIES

◆ *Resident* Red Kite, Black Woodpecker, Hawfinch.
◆ *Breeding season* Wood and Icterine Warblers, Thrush Nightingale.
◆ *Passage* Eagles (including Lesser Spotted, Spotted, Imperial, Booted and Steppe Eagles), other raptors.
◆ *Winter* Golden and White-tailed Eagles, Rough-legged Buzzard, Goshawk, Hen Harrier, Merlin, Brambling, Chaffinch.

### ACCESS

Take the main road from Ystad and drive towards the village of Tomelilla. After 10 km, just before you reach Benestad, there is a sign 'Fyledalen' to the left; follow that road and you will come to the valley. Follow the small road along the bottom of the valley and stop at different places and look for raptors. Short excursions into the forest are recommended.

# LOWER REACHES OF THE RIVER HELGE WITH HAMMARSJÖN

56°00N 14°13E

This 5489-ha area includes the lower reaches of the River Helge and several lakes that have been drained in the past, resulting in reed and scrub colonization. The largest lakes are Hammarsjön and Araslövsjön. About 1000–1500 ha of the site comprise cattle-grazed wet grassland and hay fields that are regularly flooded in spring; these are good for breeding waders. More than 100 species of birds regularly breed here; the migration season can be exciting as well.

The whole area is a Ramsar Site and some sites are National Reserves. The management of the area is a good example of how co-operation between authorities, bird conservation groups and landowners can work. The Swedish Ornithological Society has bought 28 ha of land.

### TIMING

From December to February, sizeable flocks of swans and geese are present along with a few White-tailed Eagles. Bean Goose migration is good during March and April, but the best time for both migrants and breeding birds is in late May and early June, and the twilight chorus of songbirds is not to be missed. Waders begin their return migration in August and, from September to November, geese and duck numbers are impressive.

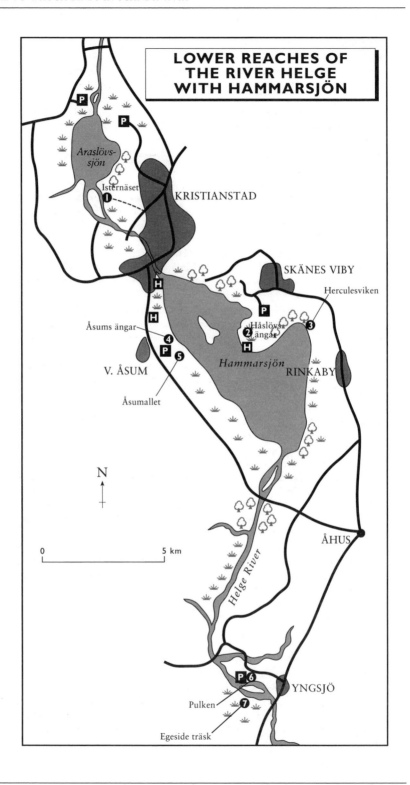

LOWER REACHES OF
THE RIVER HELGE
WITH HAMMARSJÖN

SPECIES
- *Resident* Bearded Tit.
- *Breeding season* Bittern, Garganey, Marsh Harrier, Hobby, Red Kite, Osprey, Spotted Crake, Quail, Ruff, Black-tailed Godwit, Black Tern, Nightjar, Woodlark, Golden Oriole, Savi's (rare), Marsh, River (rare), Grasshopper and Icterine Warblers, Common Rosefinch, Penduline Tit.
- *Passage* Bean Goose (up to 15,000 in October), ducks, waders, Caspian Tern (July and August), passerines.
- *Winter* Whooper Swan, Bean and Canada Geese, ducks, White-tailed Eagle, Rough-legged Buzzard, Hen Harrier.

ACCESS
Connections with Kristianstad, the nearest city, are good. There are direct flights from Copenhagen and many domestic flights to the local airport Everöd where you can rent a car. Kristianstad has a railway station and a good bus network. As the whole area is widely spread out, a car or bike is essential.

This is a great area to explore for yourself over a period of a few days. If you are pushed for time, however, the following sites should be visited. **1. Isternäset.** Grazed meadows with breeding ducks and waders. Resting geese and ducks in springtime, geese and White-tailed Eagle in winter. **2. Håslövs ängar.** This is an excellent area for breeding waders and good for wetland birds at any time of year. **3. Herculesviken.** Ponds and reedbeds with waterbirds. **4 Åsums ängar.** Grazed and cut meadows and reedbeds. There is a parking place and observation tower. **5. Åsumallet.** A swamp forest dominated by Black Alders which is good for woodpeckers and warblers. **6. Pulken.** Grazed meadows with breeding ducks and waders. There is an observation tower. **7. Egeside träsk.** A swamp forest with scrub.

# SOUTH SKÄLDERVIKEN AND KULLEN

56°13N 12°41–47E (South Skälderviken) and 56°18N 12°28E
South Skälderviken is a 5-km long stretch of coast from Jonstorp in the west to Utvälinge and the estuary of Vegeån in the east. Inland, there are grazed fields, small ponds and swamps while the shore itself shelves gradually and is good for waders and ducks; there are also a few areas of deciduous woodland. Kullen is an imposing headland which is situated 15-km west of South Skälderviken. The coastline here consists of cliffs and ravines, the highest point is 187-m above sea level.

The islands of Rönnen and Själrönnen are bird sanctuaries and visitors are not allowed. Sandön is also protected but parts of it can be visited. The whole of Kullen is a National Reserve. The South Skälderviken area is one of the best spots for breeding birds in Sweden, with more than 140 species recorded, including most wader and duck species you could hope to find in this part of Europe. Kullen, on the other hand is a place to visit during migration in spring and autumn; seabirds, waders, and raptors can sometimes be seen at close range.

TIMING
Good numbers of geese, ducks, divers and waders winter at South Skälderviken along with a few interesting raptors. Spring migration of waders, ducks and passerines lasts from late March to early June, by which time the breeding season is in full swing. Return migration of waders starts in August and from this month until late October, good numbers of birds pass

through the area. Kullen is best during migration times. In autumn, almost any European seabird could turn up during westerly gales.

SPECIES

◆ *Breeding season* Avocet, Little Tern, Tawny Pipit.

◆ *Passage* Shearwaters (five species have been recorded), British and Leach's Storm-petrels, Fulmar, Gannet, waders (including Broad-billed Sandpiper), skuas, Kittiwake, Woodlark, Ring Ouzel, Bluethroat, Thrush Nightingale, Common Rosefinch, rarities.

◆ *Winter* Divers, geese, ducks, White-tailed Eagle, Peregrine, waders, auks.

ACCESS

South Skälderviken lies 8-km west of Ängelholm and Kullen another 20 km to the west in the north-west of Scania in southern Sweden.

The best area of South Skälderviken is situated between the villages Jonstorp and Utvälinge along the southern shore. There are several parking places close to the coast and good observation points can be found at Sandön outside Utvälinge, Rönnen, and at the Farhult bay.

When visiting Kullen, just follow the road from Mölle to the most westerly parking place. The best place for seawatching is beyond the lighthouse. For woodland species, leave the main road 2 km before Mölle, and turn right to Björkeröd until the end of the road where there is a parking place. From here you will find marked trails through woodland and meadows, and past ponds.

# KÄVSJÖN-STORE MOSSE

57°18N 13°40E

This extensive mire complex covers 7580 ha and has the raised bog, Store Mosse, at its heart. Kävsjön is an oligotrophic lake with open water surrounded by fen areas. Sedge and rush cover much of the land and Scots Pine is the most common tree species.

The area is a Ramsar Site and a National Park. There have been some restoration activities to manage the area in a way typical of the last century; grazing and haymaking has been reintroduced in some areas. Two-hundred and eighteen species have been recorded here and 100 of these are regular breeders.

TIMING

Spring and early summer, from March to June, is the best time of year for birdwatching. When the ice has begun to thaw, small groups of Whooper Swans, geese and ducks can be found on the lake; waders follow a little later in the season. In April, Cranes start displaying and, in late evenings in May and June, Jack Snipe can be heard. Returning migrant waders appear again in July and August and, from September to November, geese, ducks and passerines pass through.

SPECIES

◆ *Breeding season* Whooper Swan, Shoveler, Osprey, Hobby, Water Rail, Spotted Crake, Common Crane (a few pairs), Jack Snipe, Whimbrel, Wood Sandpiper, Golden Plover, Ruff.

◆ *Passage* Whooper Swan, geese, ducks, Common Crane (large flocks), waders, passerines.

◆ *Winter* Golden and White-tailed Eagles, Great Grey Shrike.

ACCESS

The site lies 15 km from Värnamo in southern Sweden. Drive to the car park and information site at Kävsjön, 4-km south-east of Hillerstorp.

A large observation tower, with an elevator for people in wheelchairs, offers a good view over the lake and mires. There is a 2-km walk to a smaller observation tower closer to the lake for better views of waders and ducks. During 1 March to 30 September, access to Kävsjön is restricted but the trails can still be walked. Visit Lakes Horssjön and Häradsösjön as well; these are marked on the information boards.

# Lake Åsnen area

**56°37N 14°43E**

Åsnen is a shallow oligotrophic lake with a great number of islands. The average depth is 3 m and the deepest part 13 m. The lake shore is indented with headlands and bays giving a long shoreline. The surrounding land supports conifer woodlands, but also includes deciduous forests with beech and oak common. In the northern parts and around Lidhemsjön are wetlands and grazed meadows. The whole site embraces an area of some 16,800 ha. The whole area is a Ramsar Site and 1580 ha of it are protected in four nature reserves; 108 ha are also Bird Sanctuaries. A great many waterbirds and wetland species breed here, but migration times and even winter will produce outstanding birdwatching.

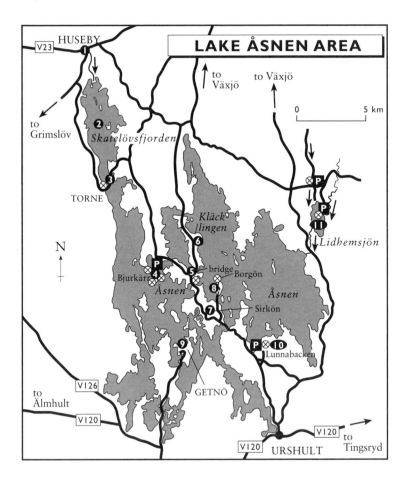

TIMING

As winter approaches, huge flocks of Goosanders (up to 10,000) gather and are joined by raptors whose numbers build up as spring approaches. Early March gives flocks of migrant swans and geese, and the weeks that follow are good for ducks and waders. Breeding species are best seen between late April and early July, after which the return migration of waders begins. Geese, ducks, raptors and passerines pass through from September to November.

SPECIES

◆ *Resident* Capercaillie, Black Grouse, Hazel Hen, Pygmy and Tengmalm's Owls, Black and Lesser Spotted Woodpeckers, Nutcracker, Crested Tit.

◆ *Breeding season* Black-throated Diver, ducks (including Goosander, Goldeneye), Osprey, Buzzard, Honey Buzzard, Marsh Harrier, Hobby, Goshawk, Sparrowhawk, Red-backed Shrike, Red-breasted Flycatcher.

◆ *Passage* Whooper Swan, Bean, Greylag and Canada Geese, Nutcracker, Red-throated Pipit, Lapland Bunting.

◆ *Winter* Goosander, Smew, White-tailed Eagle (more than 20 in some winters), Waxwing.

ACCESS

Drive 25-km south of Växjö in southern Sweden. Several roads lead to and around the lake. It is possible to travel by bus from Växjö to Urshult but a car is the best option. Some of the small roads are closed to traffic by landowners, but you are welcome on foot. You need a telescope since the birds are often distant. Several days are needed to do the site justice, the following being just some of the places to visit: **1. Huseby.** A large estate and an outdoor museum with a Nature Information Centre. **2. Skatelövsfjorden** is surrounded mostly by farmland, and is the part of Åsnen where the most species have been seen. The road on the western side gives good access and there is a small observation tower overlooking the northern part of the lake. **3. The bridge at Torne** offers good views of the lake. **4. Bjurkärr** is an old deciduous forest and a National Reserve, good for woodpeckers and other woodland birds. The yellow-marked path along the shoreline has several good viewpoints, where breeding waterbirds can be seen in summer and eagles in winter. **5. The bridge.** In November it is the best spot for ducks and eagles. **6. Kläcklingen** is the second largest island with interesting deciduous woods in the southern part. Good views of the lake can be obtained from the road on the northern part. **7. Sirkön** hosts excellent deciduous woodland. Good views of the lake can be obtained from the bridges. **8. Borgön** is a good place to see breeding birds, and in winter ducks and eagles. Park the car immediately after the bridge and from there walk to the northern tip. **9. Getnö** is a tourist centre with self-catering cottages, canoe and boat hire. **10. Lunnabacken** is a viewpoint in pleasant surroundings with orchards. **11. Lidhemsjön** is a lake dominated by reedbeds and adjacent farmland; it is particularly good for geese. The small observation tower on the eastern side gives opportunities for raptor observation.

# BEIJERSHAMN

56°36N 16°24E

Beijershamn has a special history. In the middle of the nineteenth century, a 2-km long pier was built with the aim of creating a harbour. The project failed but the pier remains, decayed and overgrown with vegetation. North of the pier are marshes and reedbeds, while to the south are muddy banks favoured by waders. The area is a National Reserve and during the 1990s restoration work began. The biggest threats have been the encroaching reeds and the lack of grazing. Much of this restoration work is done by the regional ornithological society of the island of Öland which has its own highland cattle.

TIMING

In the first week of April, Eider migration peaks, and on good days about 100,000 birds could pass by. Other wildfowl, wader and diver species pass through in the next few weeks, the next birdwatching highlight occurring in mid-May when 20,000–30,000 Brent Geese pass through in the space of a few days. May to July is an extra breeding period. The return migration of waders begins in August. From September to October the pier provides good views of migrating geese, ducks, waders and seabirds.

SPECIES

◆ *Resident* Lesser Spotted Woodpecker, Bearded and Long-tailed Tits.
◆ *Breeding season* Garganey, Shoveler, Shelduck, Marsh Harrier, Water Rail, Dunlin, Caspian and Sandwich Terns, Icterine, Grasshopper and Barred Warblers.
◆ *Passage* Divers, Brent Goose, Eider, Collared Flycatcher.

ACCESS

The site is situated about 10-km south of Färjestaden on the west coast of Öland. If you come by car from the north, turn right just north of St Frö where there is a sign 'Hagapark'. When you reach the coast turn to the right; after about 500 m you will find a parking place and an information map. You could start with the southern observation tower close to the track or follow the pier stopping along the way. The shallow bay south of the pier has good numbers of waders and ducks when the water level is not too high. From the outermost part of the pier you can watch birds migrate through the sound.

# OTTENBY

56°12N 16°24E

This flat, southernmost part of the 170-km long island of Öland has open grassland, bays and sandbanks. Grazing and haymaking have been carried out in the area for the last 1000 years. In the centre of the site is a large deciduous wood harbouring small ponds and clearings. West of the wood is heavily grazed scrub, while to the north are cultivated fields and *alvarsmark* (a sort of heathland). The Ottenby area is a Ramsar Site and a National Reserve. One of the most important conservation aims is to keep the meadows open by grazing. During breeding season there is restricted access.

This is one of the classic birdwatching sites in Sweden and even in the nineteenth century the Ottenby area was a focal point for studies of migratory birds. In 1946 a bird observatory was built by the Swedish Ornithological Society. In total 342 bird species have been recorded in the Ottenby area and 27 of these had their first Swedish record here. Around 90 species are regular breeders and among them you will find 12 species of waders and 14 species of ducks and geese.

TIMING

From November to March, swans, seaducks and raptors occur in good numbers. Passerines are numerous from the end of April and during May,

*Purple Sandpiper*

migration also include waders, geese and ducks. Rare visitors from the south can always occur, the best opportunities being during the last week in May and the first week of June.

Breeding birds are the other feature of late spring and early summer. By the time the breeding season has finished, in early August, the first returning migrant waders have appeared and 25 species can sometimes be seen at this time of year. Intensive autumn migration lasts until October. Depending on the weather, it can be a spectacular affair with vast numbers of common migrants pouring through along with a fair share of rarities.

SPECIES

◆ *Breeding season* Greylag Goose, Barnacle Goose (occasional), Eider, Velvet Scoter, Montagu's Harrier, Avocet, Dunlin, Curlew, Redshank, Oystercatcher, Ruff, Sandwich and Arctic Terns, Short-eared Owl, Golden Oriole, Barred Warbler, Red-breasted and Collared Flycatchers, Common Rosefinch, Thrush Nightingale.

◆ *Passage* Barnacle Goose, Red-breasted Goose (almost annual), ducks, raptors (20 species recorded annually), Dunlin, Little Stint, Temminck's Stint, Knot, Ruff, Curlew Sandpiper, Broad-billed Sandpiper, Whimbrel, Spotted Redshank, Greenshank, pipits, including Red-throated, wagtails, thrushes, Robin, Goldcrest, other passerines (almost every Swedish migrant species has occurred), rarities (including rare but regular White Stork, Black Kite, Red-footed Falcon, Turtle Dove, Pallas's, Yellow-browed, Radde's and Dusky Warblers, Siberian Stonechat).

◆ *Winter* White-billed Diver (rare), Whooper Swan, Eider, King and Steller's Eiders (both scarce), White-tailed and Golden Eagles, Rough-legged Buzzard, Gyrfalcon (rare), Purple Sandpiper, Shore Lark, Twite, Snow Bunting.

ACCESS

The island of Öland is situated in the Baltic Sea in south-east Sweden. From the city of Kalmar, on the mainland of Sweden, there is a 6-km long connecting bridge to Öland. The Ottenby area is 50-km south of the bridge head. A bus service exists (once a day), but a car is a better bet because sites are spread out.

Start your morning's birdwatching at the Cape and lighthouse garden to catch the early morning migration; this is also a good place to meet other birdwatchers and get the latest news.

A walk in the wood and scrub can be good at any time of year. There are several marked tracks and also ponds and observation towers in this area. From 1 April to 31 August access to some areas is prohibited. At midday during days with good thermals, raptors can be seen at the Kungsstenarna soaring over the wood.

# KAPELLUDDEN

56°51N 16°50E

This 4000-ha site consists of three shallow, coastal bays with shingle ridges and sand banks. The adjacent land comprises open pasture and grazing meadow and at Cape Kapelludden there is a pebble shoreline. The area has high national protection status and the fields are managed by grazing and periodic physical removal of rank vegetation. There are plans to set the whole area aside as a bird sanctuary. This is an excellent area for watching both migration and breeding waders. Around 330 species have been recorded and 130 of these have bred; at least 12 species of waders nest here.

TIMING

Kapelludden is worth visiting throughout the year. From December to February, flocks of swans and seaducks are the highlights, with good numbers of raptors as well. Spring migration starts with the arrival of migrant duck and wader flocks in mid-March and, for the next few weeks, large numbers of birds pass through the region. Birdwatching interest in June and July is mainly confined to local breeding birds, but autumn migration starts again in early August with the arrival of returning waders. Ducks and passerines pass through in September and, in late October, skeins of geese appear.

SPECIES

◆ *Breeding season* Cormorant, Montagu's Harrier, Corncrake, Common Crane, Avocet, Dunlin, Black-tailed Godwit, Caspian and Sandwich Terns, Short-eared Owl, Barred and Marsh Warblers.

◆ *Passage* Brent and Barnacle Geese, Red-breasted Goose (rare but almost annual), ducks, eagles, Montagu's Harrier, Buzzard, Honey Buzzard, Merlin, Hobby, Knot, Curlew and Broad-billed Sandpipers, Red-necked Phalarope, other waders, pigeons, passerines.

◆ *Winter* Whooper Swan, Eider, Steller's Eider, White-tailed Eagle, Hen Harrier, Peregrine (rare), Gyrfalcon (rare), Snow Bunting.

ACCESS

Kapelludden is situated on the east coast of Öland island. From the town of Borgholm at the middle of Öland you drive north-east to a small village called Bredsätra. In the village there is a sign 'Kapelludden 4'. The road takes you over flat agricultural land until you come to a small parking place with a tiny red cottage. Please leave your car here. The best point for overviewing the area is 200-m east of the parking place. Walk along the road that follows close to a number of small summer cottages, and beyond them is an open area just before the bridge. From here you can see migrating birds and also watch the bay.

# STORA KARLSÖ

57°17N 17°58E

Stora Karlsö is a rocky, 246-ha island in the Baltic, 6.5-km west of Gotland and boasts the only sizeable seabird cliffs in the Baltic. The island is dominated by a horseshoe-formed plateau with the opening to the north. The highest part of the plateau is 50-m above sea level and there are gullies and cave formations mainly along the west and north-east coasts. On top of the island there are areas of juniper scrub and scattered deciduous trees. Not far from Stora Karlsö is a similar but smaller island called Lilla Karlsö.

The site is a nature reserve, and parts of the island as well as the surrounding sea have access restrictions from 15 March to 15 August. A warden is present from 1 April to 30 September. Around 240 species have been recorded on the island, of which 50 breed regularly.

TIMING
Although the Guillemots return early to their ledges, from February onwards, it is not until May that the breeding gets under way. The months of May and June are ideal for a visit to Stora Karlsö, not only for the seabirds but also for the singing passerines and the carpet of orchids to be found here; there is always the possibility of a rarity turning up as well. The Guillemot chicks leave the cliffs in July and from then onwards the seabird colonies are left vacant. In autumn, passerine migration can be interesting and, during the winter months, flocks of seaducks grace the island's seas.

SPECIES
◆ *Breeding season* Eider, Scoter, Lesser Black-backed Gull, Guillemot (7000 pairs), Black Guillemot, Razorbill (2000 pairs), Rock Pipit, Red-backed Shrike, Barred and Greenish Warblers (rare), Common Rosefinch.
◆ *Passage* Passerines, rarities.
◆ *Winter* Cormorant, Long-tailed Duck, Goldeneye.

ACCESS
From the beginning of May until the end of August there are daily boat services to the island from Klintehamn, which is located 30-km south of Visby. The boat trip takes 45 minutes and you can make reservations by phone, Tel. +46(0)498–240500 or +46(0)498–240567. Further information is available at the tourist office in Visby. At other times of the year you need private arrangements to reach the island.

As a day visitor, you are not allowed to walk freely and you will be shown around by a guide. This tour offers you much interesting information on the history and nature of the island and also brings you to the cliffs where the seabirds breed.

# HOBURGEN AREA
56°55N 18°11E
Hoburgen is the southernmost cape on the island of Gotland in the Baltic. It is a 2-km long rock, covering around 200 ha, which at the highest point is 35-m above sea level; the bedrock is dominated by limestone. East and north of Hoburgen there is agricultural land with fields and grazed meadows. Small ponds, that dry up in summer, dot the landscape.

At Hoburgen 275 bird species have been seen and of these are 40 regular breeders. Both spring and autumn migration is exciting.

TIMING
Spring migration extends from March until June and is dominated by ducks, geese, divers and passerines. There is little bird activity during July and

August but numbers and variety of migrants, especially passerines, pick up again from September to November. The winter months are rather quiet.

SPECIES

◆ *Passage* Barnacle Goose, ducks, pipits, wagtails, thrushes, finches, rarities (including rare but regular Richard's Pipit, Yellow-browed and Pallas's Warblers).

ACCESS

Take the main road south from Visby and you will find Hoburgen at the end of the road from Burgsvik. The best place to watch migration in both spring and autumn is at Cape Rivet about 1-km south of the Hoburgen rock. A walk in the scrub south of Hoburgen can also be productive for passerines.

# STOCKVIKEN-FALUDDEN

57°00N 18°21E

Faludden is a 800-ha headland comprising large grazing meadows and smaller fields. Stockviken Bay is located along the southern shores and can be divided into two parts: the innermost part is nowadays a eutrophic lake with rushes, reeds and sedges while the outermost part is a shallow bay with muddy banks and grazed meadows along the shore. The area is a Ramsar Site.

TIMING

In April and the first half of May up to 5000 Barnacle Geese roost here and provide the birdwatching highlight of early spring. July and August have migrating waders and, from September to November, an excellent autumn migration of seabirds can be seen from the Cape. Flocks of swans grace the area during the winter months.

SPECIES

◆ *Breeding season* Little Grebe, Greylag Goose, Garganey, Shoveler, Gadwall, Avocet, Ruff, Black-tailed Godwit, Little Tern, Bearded Tit.
◆ *Passage* Barnacle Goose, Eider, Scoter, Velvet Scoter, Scaup, waders, Little Gull.
◆ *Winter* Whooper Swan.

ACCESS

Five-kilometres south-east of Burgsvik in southern Gotland; a car is invaluable. Just north of the lake is a parking place and a marked trail leads to a bird observation tower with views of the lake. It is possible to follow the shore line both on the south and north coasts of the peninsula (restrictions) and here you may see waders during migration in July to September. Seabird migration is best observed from the small fisherman's cottage at the horn of Cape Faludden.

# NORSHOLMEN-FÅRÖ

58°00N 19°14E

This 120-ha cape has pebble beaches and very sparse low vegetation. The area is a bird sanctuary, mainly for its breeding terns and gulls. Migrant birds also stop off here and the site can be visited throughout the year.

TIMING

The winter months are generally quiet although a few Purple Sandpipers and seaducks remain. Passerines migrate in the second half of May, and spring and summer offer several breeders. Autumn migration starts in September and continues through November with passerines comprising the main focus.

SPECIES
◆ *Breeding season* Hobby, Golden Eagle (occasional visitor), Avocet, Little Tern.
◆ *Passage* Waders, Little Gull, passerines (including Red-throated Pipit, Bluethroat and Rustic Bunting).
◆ *Winter* Seaducks, Purple Sandpiper.

ACCESS
This is one of the most northerly capes on the island of Fårö in north Gotland. From Sudersand, take the road north to Ajkesvik. After about 1 km there is a parking place and then you can follow the coast northwards. The innermost part of Norsholmen, the strip of land between Tällevika and Ajkesvik, has the highest concentrations of birds.

## MELLBYSTRAND AREA
62°70N 13°23E
Mellbystrand is the name of a small part of the shoreline of Laholm Bay. The sandy beach itself is 20–50-m broad and away from the sea, there are sand dunes and meadows; the whole area covers some 5 km². It is not the beach, however, that is of prime interest to birdwatchers but rather the seas offshore. The bay is rather shallow (10–20-m deep) and is a popular tourist spot in summer. The area can provide good birdwatching throughout the year although spring and autumn migration times are best.

TIMING
Spring migration starts at the end of March with the passage of seaducks: up to 60,000 Eiders have occurred in one day along with many other species of ducks, divers and geese. Arguably the most spectacular event occurs in May when Red-throated Divers pass by just after sunrise. Parties of several hundred are not uncommon, the largest recorded being 2200 birds.

SPECIES
◆ *Breeding season* Tawny Pipit, Redpoll.
◆ *Passage* Red-throated Diver, Black-throated Diver (scarce), White-billed Diver (rare), Red-necked and Slavonian Grebes, Sooty and Manx Shearwaters, Leach's Storm-petrel (among the best places to see this

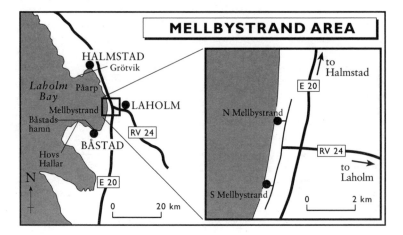

species in Sweden; autumn), Fulmar, Gannet, Barnacle and Brent Geese, Teal, Wigeon, Scoter, Velvet Scoter, Eider, skuas (all four species), waders, Little Auk.

◆ *Winter* Red-throated Diver, Razorbill, Little Auk, Shore Lark, Twite.

ACCESS

From the main road E20 take the road to Mellbystrand. The hotel 'Strandhotellet' is found in the north of the area and the restaurant 'Stallet' in the south. Walk to the shore and good places for bird watching can be found along the whole beach. Thanks to the sand-dunes you can find viewpoints 10–20-m above the sea level. Two of the best places are the dunes just outside the hotel at north Mellbystrand and outside the restaurant Stallet in south Mellbystrand. Other good sites for birdwatching in the Laholm bay area during strong westerly winds are Hovs Hallar and the harbour of Båstad in the southern part of the bay where seabirds can come close to land. In the northern part of the bay is Påarp, good for spring migration, and Grötvik, good for autumn migration during easterly winds.

# GETTERÖN

57°08N 12°14E

This 350-ha coastal area was created when a road was built between the mainland and an offshore island in 1930. The former bay became more isolated from the sea and today the water is more brackish than saline due to an inflow of freshwater. The vegetation is dominated by reeds and sedge but there are also both wet and dry meadows. The area is a Ramsar Site and also a National Reserve. The reserve is managed for the benefit of breeding and resting birds. The reeds have been cleared, some small islands in the freshwater have been built and most of the wet meadows are grazed by cattle. The water level is managed by means of embankments and pumps, which allow the salinity to be controlled. The area is good for both migrants and breeding birds. Migrants, too, are often abundant and a total of 320 species have been recorded.

TIMING

In mild winters, numerous geese, ducks and waders are present from December to February along with a selection of overwintering raptors. The passage of seabirds starts in mid-March with fair numbers of Eiders being seen, along with more unusual duck species. Divers pass by in April and May which are also the best months for waders and passerines. June is the best month for breeding birds and by late July, most birds have finished and the first Arctic waders are beginning to return. Their numbers build up into September after which time flocks of migrant geese and ducks begin to appear. Windy days in September to November can offer spectacular seabird watching at the coastal Point Gubbanäsan.

SPECIES

◆ *Breeding season* Avocet, Dunlin, Redshank, Black-tailed Godwit, Teal, Wigeon, Gadwall, Osprey, Peregrine, Marsh Harrier, Little Tern (40–45 pairs).

◆ *Passage* Geese, Eider, King Eider, other ducks, waders, passerines, rarities.

◆ *Winter* Bittern, Eider, White-tailed Eagle, Peregrine, Water Rail, Purple Sandpiper, Kingfisher.

ACCESS

The Getterön area is on the west coast of Sweden near Varberg and about

60-km south of Göteborg. You can reach the area by car or take the train to Varberg; if you take the train there is a 1-km walk before you reach the area.

In 1994 a new Nature Centre was built and it includes an exhibition and a cafe with a view over the bird area. There is also a shop, Naturbokhandeln, owned and run by the Swedish Ornithological Society. There are observation towers, hides and a bird observatory run by a local bird club.

Gubbanäsan is at the end of the road which runs west to the sea. During migration times when the winds are right, this can be good for migrants.

# MORUPS TÅNGE

56°55N 12°23E

This 90-ha coastal area has shallow bays and sand-dunes. The grassy fields are heavily grazed and some shores comprise shingle and rocks. The area is a Ramsar Site and a National Reserve. There is restricted access during the breeding season but birding is still good.

Morups Tånge is a good area for both breeding and migrating birds. In all, 266 species have been recorded here, of which 54 are annual breeders. In May and at the beginning of June there are opportunities to observe migrant Arctic waders in summer plumage.

TIMING

From December to February, waders, gulls and ducks can be found, their numbers and variety influenced by the severity or otherwise of the winter weather. Eider migration extends from the end of March to the beginning of April with plenty of other seabirds to be seen as well. Return wader migration begins in July and lasts through August and September when passerines begin to turn up. September to November is the most intensive migration period with raptors (in easterly winds), ducks, waders and passerines much in evidence. In strong westerlies, seabirds come extremely close to the cape at Glommen.

SPECIES

◆ *Passage* White-billed Diver (rare but regular in spring), Leach's Storm-petrel, Eider, King Eider (rare but regular in spring), Merlin (mainly autumn), Dotterel (mainly August and September), Spotted Redshank, Greenshank, Bar-tailed Godwit, Ruff, Golden and Grey Plovers, Little Stint, Dunlin, Curlew Sandpiper, Knot, Sanderling, Little Auk, Tawny Pipit, wagtails, finches, buntings.

◆ *Winter* Peregrine, Purple Sandpiper, Shore Lark, Twite, Snow Bunting.

ACCESS

The area is located on the west coast, 20-km south of Varberg and 9-km north-west of Falkenberg. In order to get there, take Highway E6 towards the town centre if you come from the south. You then go north on the access road outside the town. Seven-kilometres north there is a junction that takes you left to Morups Tånge. From the north take the turning directly to Glommen or to Morups Tånge from the main road E20.

From the parking place at Korshamn, the best bay for waders and ducks, you will also get a good view over the grazed meadows. A little further to the north is a lighthouse with a parking place. Around the lighthouse there are some low growing pines and bushes which harbour passerines during migration. From here you also can reach the shore and the north bay Brevik for more waders. The best place for seawatching is at the western cape of the village of Glommen, just north of the reserve.

# HÖNÖ

57°N 11°E

Hönö is a low rocky island in the Göteborg Archipelago, covered with sparse and low vegetation. The outermost part of Hönö is a nature sanctuary.

Hönö is one of the best sites in Sweden for watching migrating seabirds. Strong winds from the south-west to the north-west force the birds to fly nearer the coast allowing excellent viewing. Migration times are obviously most productive, the best period for watching pelagic seabirds being between August and November.

TIMING

From December to February, divers, grebes, ducks and auks can be found around the island's coast and interesting gulls sometimes turn up. From the middle of July onwards, strong westerly winds can bring an impressive southward migration of waders, and this is also a good time for seabirds such as Manx Shearwater. Seabirds are still good during September and October but geese and ducks become dominant among the migrant birds.

SPECIES

◆ *Passage* Red-throated Diver, Sooty Shearwater, Leach's Storm-petrel, Fulmar, Gannet, Brent Goose, Eider, Scoter, Velvet Scoter, Long-tailed Duck, skuas (all four species), Little Gull, Puffin, Little Auk.

◆ *Winter* Divers, grebes, seaducks, auks, Purple Sandpiper, Glaucous Gull.

ACCESS

The ferry to Hönö operates from Lilla Varholmen, Torslanda in north Göteborg. To reach Kråkudden, drive left at the bridge leading to Öckerö. Turn right twice, and then take the first road to the left (Ersdalsvägen). Follow this road to its end, where there is a small parking area. Walk along the small track leading towards the sea. Kråkudden and the observation tower are to the south-west when you reach the sea.

The western point of the island, Kråkudden, is the best site for watching seabirds and wildfowl. There is an observation tower at the point, which gives you an excellent view over the open sea. The fishing harbours at both Hönö and the nearby island Öckerö, as well as the strait between the two islands, may be worth a visit in winter.

# SVARTEDALEN

58°N 12°E

Svartedalen is a large woodland area, of which 550 ha is a nature reserve. It is located about 40-km north of Göteborg. The landscape is hilly with several lakes and bogs, and conifers predominate in the forests although deciduous trees occur in the outskirts of the area. Svartedalen is partly affected by forestry, which in some areas has been intensive. In the nature reserve in the north-east, forestry is not permitted and some of the trees here are now about 100 years old. One-hundred or so species are regularly found here.

TIMING

From late February to early April, is the best time to listen for drumming woodpeckers, calling owls and displaying forest gamebirds. Migrants arrive from late March until early June and the forest chorus of songbirds can be impressive. July and August are quiet months and the autumn may provide views of passing migrants but is best enjoyed for the scenery alone.

*Nutcracker*

**SPECIES**
- ◆ *Resident* Capercaillie, Black Grouse, Black Woodpecker, Pygmy, Eagle and Tengmalm's Owls, Nutcracker.
- ◆ *Breeding season* Black-throated Diver, Osprey Honey Buzzard, Goshawk, Nightjar, Grey Wagtail, Icterine Warbler, Red-backed Shrike, Dipper, Crossbill.

**ACCESS**
Svartedalen can be reached from the Highway E6 at Järlanda and Stora Höga. Also, the road between Kungälv and Lilla Edet has several small roads leading into the area. Svartedalen is reserved for outdoor pursuits and there are many tracks and signs. Nevertheless, a detailed map of the area is probably a good investment. The nature reserve, and especially the area east of Lake Härsvatten, will provide you with most of the conifer forest species. The area around the Lakes Hungersvatten and Aborrvatten is also a good site for gamebirds and woodpeckers. Ranebo Lund, about 7-km east of Järlanda, is a rich deciduous forest with a wealth of passerines; the small river here holds breeding Dippers and Grey Wagtails.

## VÄNERSBORG BAY
58°23N 12°19E

This site is the south-westerly part of Lake Vänern, the largest lake in Sweden. The area is defined by the outflow of the River Göta Älv and the Halleberg mountain. It is lowland in character with an archipelago of small low rocks. In the south there are reedbeds and close to the outflow is a lakeside forest with good habitat for many passerine birds. The reedbed and adjacent shoreline comprise a bird sanctuary with no access between 1 April and 31 July. Two-hundred and seventy species have been recorded here and 80 are regular breeders.

**TIMING**
In spring, the visible migration is poor compared to autumn but groups of Ring Ouzels are a regular feature from late April to early May. Songbirds can be good in May and June and in July and August, Arctic waders, gulls and terns begin to appear on passage. The best migration is from September to November when geese, ducks and passerines are found in good numbers.

**SPECIES**
- ◆ *Breeding season* Osprey, Marsh Harrier, Lesser Spotted Woodpecker, Grey Wagtail, Dipper, Grasshopper Warbler, Red-breasted Flycatcher, Bearded and Long-tailed Tits, Hawfinch, Common Rosefinch.
- ◆ *Passage* Geese, ducks, Arctic, Pomarine and Long-tailed Skuas, Little Gull, terns, Red-throated Pipit, Bluethroat.
- ◆ *Winter* Little Grebe, White-tailed Eagle, Rough-legged Buzzard, Waxwing.

ACCESS

The area has links with Vänersborg: from the central part of the city, it is only some 100 m to the bay. The city is easily reached by bus or train if you do not have a car. Close to the reedbed there is an observation tower which gives you a good view over the area. The north cape also provides good views.

# TIVEDEN

58°37–48N 14°30–45E

This is certainly a place to visit for a wilderness experience. Out of a total of 1353 ha, almost 1000 ha comprise conifer forest with the remaining areas harbouring bogs and open water. Despite its primeval feeling, the forest has been managed in the past by human activities such as felling and replanting. Today, the area is a National Park with free development for the forest. Tiveden is located on a ridge between two large lakes, Unden and Vättern and the terrain is undulating with rocky outcrops.

The conifer forest is around 100 years old, and together with its size is a unique area in southern Sweden.

TIMING

If you want to look for owls and woodpeckers then the time to visit is in March and April when they will be calling and drumming respectively. Migrant forest species usually arrive in late April and May and thereafter is a brief period of song. July and August are quiet months but from September to November there is a chance of seeing the occasional migrant. A few hardy species remain throughout the winter.

SPECIES

◆ *Resident* Goshawk, Capercaillie, Hazel Hen, Pygmy and Tengmalm's Owls, Black and Green Woodpeckers, Nutcracker, tits.
◆ *Breeding season* Black-throated Diver, Goldeneye, Osprey, Honey Buzzard, Hobby, Common Crane, Nightjar, Woodlark, Redstart.
◆ *Passage* Waxwing, Redpoll.
◆ *Winter* Golden Eagle, Great Grey Shrike, Dipper.

ACCESS

There is good access from both the north and the south. Take highway 49 between Askersund and Karlsborg and drive northwards to Bocksjö which leads you to the central part of the area.

If you come from the north, drive to the parking place close to Vitsand beach just north of the lake Trehörningen. At Vitsand beach you will find many marked paths and tracks into the area. Though it is a wilderness park it is possible to explore the area with basic equipment. Coming from the south drive to the parking place with information signs and toilets at Stenhällebergen mountains. From this point the 'Tivedsleden', a wide track, leads into the forest.

# LAKE HORNBORGASJÖN

58°19N 13°33E

This site is a freshwater lake surrounded by arable land with fields and meadows; the wetlands comprise 6370 ha and dry land 3300 ha. The lake has been lowered artificially several times leading to encroachment by reeds, sedges, scrub and deciduous trees. Since 1970 a restoration plan by the Swedish Environmental Protection Agency ensures that both the water level and the surroundings are managed in order to restore the area.

The area is a Ramsar Site but only a part of it is so far protected as a National Reserve. Lake Hornborgasjön is one of the classic bird areas in Sweden and of high international value. The restoration work is the most ambiguous for wetlands in Sweden and is connected with the Ramsar Monitoring Procedure. During the period 1992–95 the water level in the lake was raised 0.85 m and huge areas of previously overgrown shoreline have been cleared.

Lake Hornborgasjön is well known for the number of Common Cranes that stop off on migration. It is also an excellent spot for breeding wetland birds; five species of grebe, dabbling ducks and harrier occurs here, for example.

TIMING
The peak season for birdwatching starts in the second half of March when the migrating Common Cranes arrive in large flocks from Rügen in Germany. Until the end of April around 10,000 birds rest at Bjurum in the southern part of Lake Hornborgasjön; you can see them from the information centre 'Trandansen'. This is a well-known event and is visited by more than 100,000 people every year. The springtime and early summer, April to June, are also highly recommended for studying birds at the lake; 50 wetland species breed and a further 40 are regularly seen during migration.

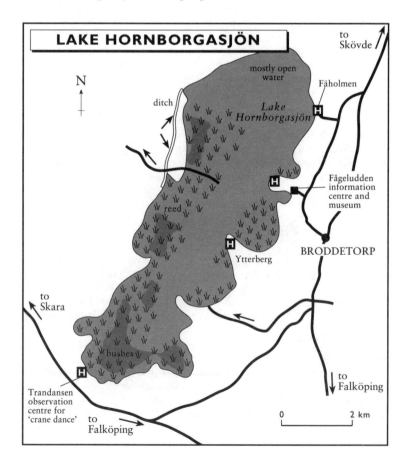

*Marsh
Harrier*

In autumn
flocks of ducks
and Greylag
Geese visit the
lake. Many remain
late into the year and
attract the attentions of
overwintering raptors.

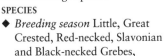

SPECIES
◆ *Breeding season* Little, Great
  Crested, Red-necked, Slavonian
  and Black-necked Grebes,
  Bittern, ducks, Marsh and Montagu's Harriers, Water Rail, Black-headed
  Gull, Black Tern, Great Reed Warbler, Bearded Tit.
◆ *Passage* Greylag Goose, ducks, Common Crane.
◆ *Winter* White-tailed Eagle, Peregrine.

ACCESS
The lake is situated about 20-km south-west of Skövde in the county of
Skaraborg in central southern Sweden. If you do not have a car, you can take a
bus from Skövde to the village of Varnhem and another bus for the village of
Broddetorp. From Broddetorp (*see* the map) there is a 3-km walk to the
information centre at 'Fågeludden'. A car is, however, invaluable. .

In the information centre is an exhibition, a coffee shop, bookstore and
toilets. There are several towers and hides around the lake and a second
information centre 'Trandansen'.

# Cape Hammarö

59°15N 13°31E
This peninsula is situated on the northern shore of Lake Vänern and covers
an area of some 2 km². The peninsula is mostly covered with conifer forest,
but there are also areas with deciduous trees. The main observation point is
at the lighthouse island in the south of the peninsula. This island is connected
to the mainland by a track and a footbridge. Around 240 species have been
recorded here, including all the Swedish woodpecker species, and some 60
species breed regularly.

TIMING
The best times of the year are spring and autumn migration seasons from the
end of March to May and from August to mid-November.
SPECIES
◆ *Resident* Black Grouse, Tengmalm's and Pygmy Owls, Black, Great Spotted,
  and Green Woodpeckers, Crested, Bearded and Long-tailed Tits, Crossbill.
◆ *Breeding season* Black-throated Diver, Red-breasted Merganser, Osprey,
  Sparrowhawk, warblers, Common Rosefinch.
◆ *Passage* White-backed, Lesser Spotted, Three-toed and Grey-headed
  Woodpeckers (rare but regular).
◆ *Winter* Goldeneye.

ACCESS
The site is about 15-km south of Karlstad in the county of Värmland. Take the road to Takene and then on for another 1 km to the parking place. From the parking place you have a 500-m walk to the lighthouse island. During the walk you will pass through deciduous forest where you may see woodland birds. Not far from the lighthouse is a small bird observatory run by Karlstad Ornithological Club. Ringing and studies of migrants occur from March to mid-November.

# KILSVIKEN–ÅRÅSVIKEN

59°03N 14°04E

This 8910-ha wetland area is in the north-east corner of the Lake Vänern. The site is divided into three main bays: Kilsviken, Kolstrandsviken and Åråsviken. Within these bays a number of small islands also occur. Kilsviken is the best known one for birdwatching, with swampy meadows, reedbeds, open water and areas of dense aquatic vegetation. Kolstrandsviken is more oligotrophic with less vegetation while Åråsviken again is rich in nutrients. Adjacent to Åråsviken are some interesting deciduous woodlands.

The area is a Ramsar Site and a total area of 2459 ha is protected as a nature reserve. A total of some 245 species have been recorded here and of these 115 are regular breeders.

TIMING
From December to February, diving ducks and raptors can be found on the lake. From March onwards, numbers of migrant birds build up with ducks, geese and waders being well represented. By late July and early August, many of the waders are beginning to return and numbers of ducks and geese build up during September and October.

SPECIES
◆ *Resident* Hazel Hen, Black and Lesser Spotted Woodpeckers, Bearded Tit.
◆ *Breeding season* Black-throated Diver, Bittern, Garganey, Red-breasted Merganser, Honey Buzzard, Marsh Harrier, Osprey, Hobby, Common Crane, Wryneck, Red-backed Shrike, warblers, Red-breasted Flycatcher, Common Rosefinch.
◆ *Passage* Geese, ducks, Rough-legged Buzzard, Hen Harrier, Merlin, Common Crane (up to 3000), Ruff, Spotted Redshank, Greenshank, Broad-billed Sandpiper (rare), Red-throated Pipit, Bluethroat, Lapland Bunting.
◆ *Winter* Goldeneye, Goosander, White-tailed Eagle, Great Grey Shrike, Dipper.

ACCESS
Kilsviken is about 30-km south of Kristinehamn. A car is essential because there is no public transport; you also need a good map. Take the road 64 to Nybble and turn off to Ed. After 6 km there are parking places on each side of the road. From here there is a marked pathway (900 m) to the observation tower.

In the reserve Nötön-Åråsviken are several marked tracks which can be reached from any of the parking places. In winter, the outlet of the River Gullspångsälven, close to Årås, is a good observation point for watching eagles and ducks. An early morning visit should start either up in the north at Kilsviken or in the forests close to Åråsviken, depending on your interest in forest or wetland birds.

# LAKE KVISMAREN

59°10N 15°23E

The central part of this 780-ha site consists of two lakes that have been subject to drainage activities since the nineteenth century. Today 15 years of management and restoration have created a really good wetland area where besides the lakes there are flood meadows, woodland and pastureland. The main vegetation in the lakes is reed and willow thickets. The arable land is protected from flooding by a series of embankments and channels. Kvismaren is a Ramsar Site and 720 ha a National Reserve. It is excellent for breeding wetland birds: 100 or more nesting species having been recorded here; a further 150 have been seen.

TIMING

In winter, the lake and wetlands hold many raptors. Geese and ducks occur in high numbers in March and April when up to 6000 Bean Geese and 1000 Teal feed in the fields. Migrant waders pass through in May, and later that month and early in June the twilight songs of birds is wonderful. Return migration of waders occurs mainly in July and August while from September to November up to 25,000 Bean Geese and 1500 Common Cranes visit the area.

SPECIES

◆ *Breeding season* Little, Slavonian and Red-necked Grebes, Black-necked Grebe (occasional), Bittern, Greylag Goose, Gadwall, Garganey, Shoveler, Marsh Harrier, Common Crane, Quail (rare), Water Rail, Spotted Crake, Great Snipe (rare but regular), Black Tern, Lesser Spotted Woodpecker, Great, River and Blyth's Reed, Savi's (rare) and Grasshopper Warblers, Bearded and Penduline Tits.

◆ *Passage* Bean, White-fronted, Lesser White-fronted and Pink-footed Geese, Wigeon, Teal, Common Crane, Ruff, Wood Sandpiper, Greenshank.

◆ *Winter* White-tailed and Golden Eagles, Rough-legged Buzzard, Merlin, Great Grey Shrike.

ACCESS

The site is 15-km south-east of Örebro in south-central Sweden. Take the road 207 from Örebro towards Odensbacken. Two-kilometres south of Odensbacken is a sign 'Kvismaren', which is 14 km further on.

*Wood Sandpiper*

Park in the parking place at Öby Kulle where you also will find information boards. Go to the observation tower where you will get good views of the waterbirds. If you want close views of Slavonian Grebe and various ducks, visit the hide, 200-m north of the observation tower. A walk along the embankment in the north part of 'Fågelsjön' is recommended as well as stops to view the grazing meadows in the south. In springtime the restored wet meadows at Fiskinge are good and here you will find the largest concentrations of ducks.

# OSET

59°17N 15°16E

Oset is a wetland area around the estuary of River Svartån and the shallow, western bay of Lake Hjälmaren. There are reedbeds, meadows, swamps, groves of deciduous trees and open water; in total, the site covers 180 ha. The site is a National Reserve and parts of it are protected from April to October. Rynningeviken Bay just north of Oset is a bird protection area, which has recently been restored.

The area is good for breeding wetland birds and for migrant geese, ducks and waders. It is also one of Sweden's best known bird sites and a fair share of rarities have been observed here.

TIMING

A visit to Oset is best between March and early June. At this time you will not only be able to see migrants but also encounter some of the region's numerous breeding species. From the time the ice melts in early April, ducks start arriving and, in late April and early May, migrating waders pass through. The breeding season is at its peak in late May and early June. Return wader migration occurs in July and August and geese and ducks arrive from September to November.

SPECIES

◆ *Breeding season* Bittern, Garganey, Pintail, Shoveler, Marsh Harrier, Osprey, Goshawk, Sparrowhawk, Honey Buzzard, Kestrel, Corncrake, Spotted Crake, Great Snipe (rare but regular), Snipe, Temminck's Stint, Redshank, Little Ringed Plover, Lapwing, River Warbler (scarce), Grasshopper and Marsh Warblers.

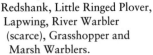

*Ringed Plover*

◆ *Passage* Hen Harrier, Rough-legged Buzzard, Merlin, Canada and Greylag Geese.

◆ *Winter* Grey Heron, Smew, Goosander, Goldeneye, Goshawk, Kingfisher, Great Grey Shrike, Siskin, Redpoll.

ACCESS

The area is situated some 20-km east of Örebro city. From the central parts of Örebro you will find road signs specifically for 'Oset'. The golden rule is to follow the River Svartån eastwards on its south side.

From the parking place at the sewage-treatment plant there are tracks leading eastwards to the meadows. You can walk along the River Svartån to the northern observation tower and follow the bicycle road to the old, southern observation tower. Along the road there are two platforms where you can scan the meadows. Rynningeviken is 10-km north-west of Oset, so you have to go back to the city to get there.

# TYSSLINGEN

59°18N 15°02E

Tysslingen is a partly overgrown shallow lake with reedbeds and extensive growths of sedges and rushes, in all covering around 600 ha. It lies in arable land but close to the taiga forests at Kilsbergen.

Around the lake there is a mixture of fields, grazed meadows and forests. Around 230 species have been recorded here, 90 of which regularly breed.

TIMING

From December to February, a few ducks remain in the area and raptors pay regular visits. In springtime, more birds arrive and, at the end of March, up to 2000 Whooper Swans and 1000 Bean Geese can be found along with several duck species. The breeding season is under way from late April to late June and autumn migrants pass through from September to November.

SPECIES

◆ *Breeding season* Bittern, Osprey, Corncrake, Spotted Crake, Quail (rare), Great Snipe (rare but regular), Marsh and Grasshopper Warblers.

◆ *Passage* Whooper Swan, Bean Goose, ducks, waders.

◆ *Winter* Golden Eagle, Goshawk, Great Grey Shrike.

ACCESS

The site is 10-km west of Örebro. If you follow the road to Eker and Garphyttan and then turn to Frösvidal you will reach the north side of the lake. The southern part can be reached directly from the road between Örebro and Garphyttan.

There are two observation towers, one in the north-east and one in the south-western part of the lake. Kilsbergen lies 5-km west of Tysslingen. Follow the roads in the area and stop where it looks good and explore the forest.

# LAKE TÅKERN

58°21N 14°49E

Tåkern is a 5650-ha eutrophic lake with extensive reedbeds and open wet meadows, located in arable land east of lake Vättern. It is a classic Swedish bird lake and like many others in agricultural areas it suffered from attempts at reclamation during the nineteenth century. The adjoining meadows are becoming overgrown as a result of decreasing haymaking and grazing.

The area is a Ramsar Site and also a National Reserve. Tåkern is of great international importance for migrating and resting geese and ducks. Fishing is still allowed and, regrettably, in most parts hunting continues.

TIMING

The most productive period for birdwatching is in spring and early summer, from mid-April to mid-June. At this time of year, numerous species of ducks, grebes, waders and raptors typical of this wetland habitat are easy to see. Large numbers of swans, geese and ducks gather in July and August to undergo their post-breeding moult and these are joined, from September to November, by migrant wildfowl from farther afield. Bean Geese numbers are particularly impressive with some 25,000 birds being present in mid-October; this is a decline on numbers formerly seen in the 1980s.

SPECIES

◆ *Breeding season* Red-necked Grebe (100 pairs), Bittern, Mute Swan, Greylag Goose, Pochard, Mallard, Gadwall, Coot, Black Tern, Great Reed Warbler, Bearded and Penduline Tits.

◆ *Passage* White-tailed Eagle, Mute Swan (2000–3000 birds in October and November), Bean, White-fronted, Lesser White-fronted and Pink-footed Geese, Pochard (2000 birds in autumn), Bearded Tit (up to 10,000 birds in October).

◆ *Winter* Rough-legged Buzzard, Hen Harrier, Great Grey Shrike.

ACCESS

The site is 40-km west of Linköping in central southern Sweden in the county of Östergötland. To visit the southern part of the area, take the E4 and turn off at the signpost 'Kyleberg 2'. From Kyleberg, turn left and after l km you will find a sign that shows the area. The northern part is reached if you follow National Highway 50 and turn off at sign 'Strå 7'. After having passed the Tåkern canal drive 2-km more and you will find more information signs about the observation towers.

There are five observation towers in all. From 1 April to 30 June visitors have restricted access to certain areas and should follow the marked tracks. Using the tracks it is possible to come close to the birds at certain places. The Tåkern field observatory is located at Kvarnstugan near the south-western shore of the lake. Here you can get information on the current bird situation at the lake.

# SVARTÅMYNNINGEN
58°29N 15°34E

This 325-ha site lies on the estuary of the River Svartån in the south-west part of Lake Roxen in the county of Östergötland. It comprises a gently shelving shore with flood meadows, which are partly inundated in spring, and reedbeds. The area is a nature reserve. From 1 April to 30 June you have to follow the marked tracks, but you will see everything from there.

In total, 200 species have been recorded on the reserve. Of those 30 are annually breeding wetland birds. The number of resting migrant ducks and waders on the flood meadows during migration is strongly influenced by the water level.

TIMING

The breeding season occurs from mid-April until late June. Returning migrant waders begin to appear in July and August, but for sheer numbers, September to November are the most impressive months. More than 10,000 Goosanders may be present, large flocks gathering on the west side of the lake in the afternoons. There are plenty of other wildfowl species present at this time and some of them stay throughout the winter months. December to February is a good time to look for overwintering raptors.

SPECIES

◆ *Resident* Bearded Tit.

◆ *Breeding season* Bittern, Gadwall, Garganey, Osprey, Black-tailed Godwit, Little Gull, Black Tern, Short-eared Owl, Great Reed Warbler.

Great Grey Shrike

- ◆ *Passage* Goosander, Smew, White-tailed Eagle, Jack Snipe, Little Gull, Red-throated Pipit, Bluethroat.
- ◆ *Winter* Rough-legged Buzzard, Hen Harrier, Great Grey Shrike.

ACCESS
The area is 7-km north-west of Linköping and is easily reached by car or bike. Follow the road towards Berg (road 36 towards Motala). 1 km before the road passes the River Svartån there is a sign 'Svartåmynningens naturreservat' to the right and after about 1 km you reach the parking place. You can also take a bus from Linköping and get off at the approach to the reserve.

From the parking place you can easily reach an observation platform. If you walk another 600 m you reach the observation tower.

# BÅVEN

59°00N 16°55E
Båven is an oligotrophic lake with 360 small islands and skerries forming an archipelago; the whole area covers some 50 km². The lake itself has suffered remarkably little human disturbance or industrial pollution. It is even possible to drink the water directly from the lake! The surroundings consist of hills covered with conifer forests and open arable land. The area is a Ramsar Site and includes several nature reserves and bird sanctuaries with restricted access from April to July. Please respect the signs! Around 100 species regularly breed here and a further 50 have been recorded.

TIMING
Best time is from mid-April to late June.
SPECIES
- ◆ *Resident* Black Woodpecker, Nutcracker.
- ◆ *Breeding season* Black-throated Diver, Grey Heron, Goosander, Red-breasted Merganser, Osprey, Hobby, Honey Buzzard, Common Sandpiper, Woodcock.
- ◆ *Passage* Goosander, White-tailed Eagle.
- ◆ *Winter* Raven.

ACCESS
The lake lies 30-km north of Nyköping and 100-km south of Stockholm. From Sparreholm you can take road 222 southwards to Oxbro where you can park and boats may be hired. An alternative way is along road 223 from Gnesta towards Nyköping. Turn off to Sofielund and carry on to the parking place at Dagsnäsön.

If you have hired a canoe, sites for entering the lake include the Sparreholm bathing place, Oxbro and the Sibro bathing place. Ådö in western part of the area is also a good starting point.

# TYRESTA
59°05N 18°20E

Tyresta comprises 5000 ha of old growth forest dominated by conifers. Some pines are more than 300 years old. Mires and lakes are also part of the scene.

The central area of Tyresta is a National Park (2000 ha) and in the east it has nature reserve status (3000 ha). No logging or other modern forestry practises are allowed.

TIMING
Although there are some birds present throughout the year, the best time to visit Tyresta is in early spring when you can hear drumming woodpeckers and calling owls.

SPECIES
- *Resident* Capercaillie, Great Spotted, Lesser Spotted, Green and Black Woodpeckers, Pygmy Owl, Nutcracker, tits, Crossbill.
- *Breeding season* Black-throated Diver, Goshawk, Sparrowhawk, Osprey, Woodlark, Mistle Thrush, Redstart, Jay.

ACCESS
The amazing thing about this exciting area is that it is only 20-km south-east of Stockholm. Travel to Brandbergen and follow signs to the National Park. Tyresta village, the main entrance, can also be reached by bus from Handen.

There are several possible entrances to Tyresta. One idea is to start at Tyresta village where you can get detailed information on the park, but from Åva you can enter directly into the area. There are many marked tracks through the forest.

# STOCKHOLM-EKOPARKEN
59°15N 18°02E

This unique area, covering some 32 km², comprises a mosaic of water, islands, forests and meadows all located in the central part of Stockholm. The total area includes the islands Fjäderholmarna in the east, south and north Djurgården, Brunnsviken, Hagaparken and Ulriksdals park.

In 1995 the area was established as the first 'City National Park' in the world. The idea is to create a national nature and culture park for biodiversity in the most urban part of Sweden. As the area is located in the capital of Sweden it also offers good possibilities for the citizens to experience nature on their doorstep. Most of the park is open all year and only some small, vulnerable spots such as the bird colonies at Fjäderholmarna, have restricted access during the breeding season, 1 April to 15 July. The main threat to the area is the relentless expansion of the city. This includes not only new roads and industrial sites but also plans for future Olympic Games! Two-hundred and fifty species have been recorded in the area, 100 of which regularly breed.

TIMING
From early April to late July is an excellent time to visit the park; both woodland and waterbirds are well represented. Returning migrant waders

start to appear in July and August and duck flocks build up later in the autumn. Depending on the ice situation, many remain throughout the winter.

SPECIES

◆ *Breeding season* Great Crested and Little Grebes, Grey Heron, Barnacle Goose, Gadwall, Goldeneye, Teal, Goshawk, Kestrel, Coot, Oystercatcher, Common Sandpiper, Lesser Black-backed Gull, Eagle Owl, Lesser Spotted Woodpecker, Skylark, Grasshopper, River and Marsh Warblers, Thrush Nightingale, Red-breasted Flycatcher, Long-tailed Tit.

◆ *Passage* Ducks, Ruff, Wood Sandpiper, Dunlin, Temminck's Stint.

◆ *Winter* Ducks, Glaucous Gull (rare but regular).

ACCESS

The park is easily explored on foot or by bike, the following areas being worth a visit (buy a map in Stockholm): **1. Fjäderholmarna.** Regular boats run to these four islands from central Stockholm. The trip itself is very pleasant and takes about 30 minutes. Colonies of seabirds and Barnacle Geese are present from May to July. **2. South Djurgården.** An area of wooded parkland, formerly a Royal hunting ground. The area east of 'Manillavøgen' and around Isbladskärret is the best one for birding. **2a. Isbladskärret and Isbladsviken.** A swamp where the water level is regulated in order to favour breeding birds and passage migrant waders. **4. North Djurgården.** A rest area in an ancient deer park. **4a. Hundudden-Kaknäset-Kaknässkär-Lidingöbro.** Fine forests with passerines and breeding Goshawk. Kaknässkär is a small island with breeding waterbirds, viewable from distance. **4b. Ladugårdsgärde.** A large, open meadow. **4c. Lill-Jansskogen.** Deciduous forest with passerines such as Hawfinch and Wood Warbler. **4d. Ugglebacken-Uggleviken.** An alder swamp with interesting plants and birds. **4e. Björnnäset-Fiskartorpet.** A conifer forest area with an observation tower. **4f. Stora Skuggan.** An information centre called 'Naturens hus' (the house of Nature) with information about Ekoparken but also lots of other things. Open grassland and forest in the surrounding area offer many good birding possibilities. **5. Haga and Ulriksdal.** Both areas are old Royal parks with a rich and varied bird fauna.

# BULLERÖ ARCHIPELAGO
59°10N 18°40E

10,000 islands make up the Stockholm Archipelago. These vary from larger forested ones near the coast to low, rocky islets in the east. Bullerö Archipelago itself includes 900 islands and skerries. On the main island, Bullerö, birches and alders are dominant free species; wind-pruned pines and junipers are also widespread.

The area is a nature reserve and some parts are bird sanctuaries with no access during the breeding season. Traditional means of managing the land, such as haymaking and grazing, are part of the management at Bullerö and Rågskör.

TIMING

Best time is from late April until early July. Seabirds and ducks are much in evidence and family parties can be seen towards the end of the season. Flocks of ducks and other migrants can be found in the autumn with a few birds lingering into the winter months.

SPECIES

◆ *Resident* White-tailed Eagle, Black Grouse.

◆ *Breeding season* Velvet Scoter, Red-breasted Merganser, Goosander,

Eider, Tufted Duck, Redshank, Oystercatcher, Turnstone, Arctic Skua, Great Black-backed Gull, terns, Razorbill, Lesser Whitethroat, Black Guillemot, Rock Pipit.

◆ *Passage* Brent and Greylag Geese, Wigeon, Pintail.

◆ *Winter* Long-tailed Duck.

ACCESS

From 'Slussen' in central Stockholm you can take the bus to Stavsnäs and then a taxi boat to Bullerö. Order the boat in advance by phone: Tel. +46(0)766–50100 ('Sjötaxi'). In summer there are regular boat connections with Bullerö.

Bullerö field centre has information about the wildlife and where to go; it is open to the public from May to September.

# LAKE HJÄLSTAVIKEN

59°40N 17°23E

This 77-ha lowland lake has broad reedbeds, water meadows and grazed areas close to the lake. The surroundings host woodland types from conifer to deciduous forests. The area is a nature reserve and a Ramsar Site. As with many other lowland lakes in Sweden, it has become overgrown during the

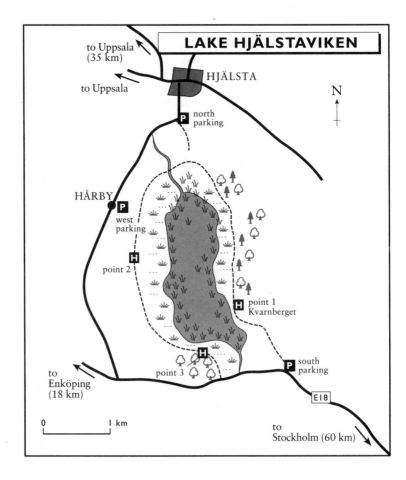

last two decades. The management plan for restoration includes raising the water level and cultivation of the shore meadows. Two-hundred and forty-five species have been recorded in the area, 100 of which are regular breeders.

TIMING
The best time is from late March to late June. Geese, ducks, raptors and passerines are well represented during both spring and autumn migration.

SPECIES
◆ *Breeding season* Bittern, Gadwall, Garganey, Marsh Harrier, Osprey, Goshawk, Sparrowhawk, Honey Buzzard, Hobby, Coot, Great Snipe (rare but regular), Great Reed and Grasshopper Warblers, Bearded Tit, Common Rosefinch.
◆ *Passage* Greylag Goose (up to 5000 in September and October), Bean Goose (numerous), White-fronted and Pink-footed Geese (occasional), White-tailed Eagle, Hen Harrier, Rough-legged Buzzard, Merlin, Peregrine, Red-throated Pipit, Bluethroat, other passerines.
◆ *Winter* Golden Eagle, Rough-legged Buzzard, Great Grey Shrike.

ACCESS
The lake is about 60-km north-west of Stockholm and 35-km south-west of Uppsala. Public transport is poor so you need a car. Take the road E18 from Stockholm towards Enköping. At Bålsta turn right at the sign 'Skokloster/Arlanda' and follow the road to Enköping. After driving 10 km from Bålsta you will come to the southernmost parking place on your right hand side. It is a 15-minute walk to the view point at Kvarnberget (point 1) where you get the best views of open water. Point 2 is a low hill where you have a good view of the grazed meadows. Point 3 lies at the border of a small deciduous forest. You can view a part of the lake and also look for birds in the forest.

There is a well marked track running around the lake which takes about five hours to complete, including breaks. The total route is 6 km and quite easy.

# LAKE ANGARN
59°33N 18°10E

This shallow, 140-ha lake is sited in mixed forest and agricultural land. Since the mid-nineteenth century, the water level has been lowered several times. There are extensive reedbeds and marshy meadows which flood in the spring. The surrounding land has been cultivated for centuries but areas of conifer forest add another dimension to birdwatching.

The area is a nature reserve. Since the end of the 1960s, a local conservation group, 'the Angarn group' has been working to protect and restore of the area.

TIMING
Spring is probably the best time to visit the lake. Birdwatchers will then be able to study the breeding ducks, grebes and waders as well as see resting passage migrants; the flocks of Ruff are particularly good in spring. Summer is a quiet time, livened up only by family parties of locally breeding birds. Waders begin to return on migration in late July and August and numbers of ducks build up as the autumn progresses.

SPECIES
◆ *Breeding season* Whooper Swan, Greylag and Canada Geese, Slavonian and Little Grebes, Garganey, Gadwall, other dabbling ducks, Marsh

Harrier, Osprey, Hobby, Water Rail, Spotted Crake, Black Tern, warblers, Ortolan Bunting.
◆ *Passage* Wood and Curlew Sandpipers, Redshank, Spotted Redshank, Greenshank, Little Stint, Curlew, Whimbrel, Golden Plover, Bluethroat, Rustic Bunting, other passerines.
◆ *Winter* Rough-legged Buzzard, Goshawk, Great Grey Shrike.
ACCESS
The area is 25-km north of Stockholm. From Stockholm by car take the road E3 northwards towards Norrtälje and turn left at Gillinge to Angarn. A good place to stop at is at Örsta. By bus from Stockholm to Norrtälje it is possible to get off at Angarn church, Örsta or Hacksta.

The area has many tracks, viewing points, shelters and information boards. For a first visit, start at Örsta where there is good parking, information maps and also an information hut, manned every weekend from April to September.

# FLORARNA

60°18N 17°40E
Although this amazing site covers nearly 5000 ha, only 20 per cent is dry ground, the remaining 80 per cent comprising mires or lakes. The mosaic of mires which dominates the scene, is studded with islands of solid ground, both large and small; these are mainly covered by conifers although, in wetter areas, birches and Aspen are frequent. Dead and decaying trees have been left and are good for the woodpeckers and other hole-nesting species. Around Lake Vikasjön the woodlands are more complex and comprise Ash, limes and many species of orchid.

The area is a nature reserve where there are some restrictions on modern forestry. The area holds many bird species associated with taiga forest. This means that numbers of individuals are quite low and they are scattered rather than concentrated.

TIMING
The first interesting period occurs from late February through March. Normally there is snow on the ground and all mires are frozen, which means that the best way of getting around is on skis. In early mornings just after sunrise, you may hear drumming or calling woodpeckers; lekking Black Grouse and calling owls. Common Cranes can be seen over the next few weeks during which time the frozen ground is beginning to thaw. Later in spring it can be difficult to move around as the mires are flooded.

Displaying waders and singing passerines are best in June. In late summer and autumn, a scattering of migrants stop off in the area to rest on passage.
SPECIES
◆ *Resident* Capercaillie, Black Grouse, Hazel Hen, Pygmy and Ural Owls, Black and Three-toed Woodpeckers, Crested and Long-tailed Tits, Raven, Jay, Crossbill, Parrot Crossbill, Goshawk.
◆ *Breeding season* Hobby, Common Crane, Wood and Green Sandpipers, Snipe, Jack Snipe, Woodcock.
◆ *Passage* Whooper Swan.
ACCESS
The area is approximately 50-km north of Uppsala and the usual way to approach the site is by car along road 290 from Uppsala; you should then

take minor roads to a parking place 'Stormo', south-west of Lake Vikasjön. You can also drive to the marked parking place 'Risön' north of Vikasjön.

At the two parking places mentioned above, there are information boards showing marked tracks, toilets, small hides and barbecue sites. If you are a group travelling in two cars, why not leave one car at the north parking place and then start from the south one and work your way north? A good map and compass are essential since this is a wilderness area where you can easily get lost.

# LEDSKÄR
60°30N 17°43E

This 100-ha shallow bay on the Baltic Sea has a gently shelving shore and grazed meadows inland; the meadows are easily flooded depending on the sea level. Open scrub with wooded patches, along with arable land, reedbeds, canals and conifer forest, make the Ledskär area a really varied location and one well worth visiting.

The area is classified as being of national importance for the birdlife although it is not protected. Some of the coastal meadows undergo hay-making and are grazed in order to make them suitable for waders and ducks. About 250 species have been recorded here.

### TIMING
Ledskär is an excellent spot for watching migrant wetland birds and waders, ducks, raptors and passerines which are well represented from March to June. Many of the birds stay here to breed but considerable numbers pause only for a short while to rest and feed. Family parties of locally breeding birds provide interest in July and August and Arctic waders begin to return on migration. Geese and passerines pass through from September to November.

### SPECIES
◆ *Breeding season* Greylag Goose, Garganey, Gadwall, Montagu's and Marsh Harriers, Common Crane, Dunlin, Redshank, Little Gull, Grasshopper Warbler, Common Rosefinch.
◆ *Passage* White-tailed Eagle, Whooper Swan, Bean Goose, Smew, Shelduck, Sanderling, Greenshank, Broad-billed Sandpiper, Red-necked Phalarope, Arctic Skua, Little Gull, Little and Black Terns, Red-throated Pipit, Bluethroat, Twite, Lapland Bunting.
◆ *Winter* Whooper Swan.

### ACCESS
The area is 90-km north of Uppsala and 40-km south-east of Gävle. Coming from the south on road 76 you pass the village of Skärplinge and after about 4 km there is a sign 'Ledskär' to the right. After some 100 m you see the bay to the right.

A trip through the wet meadows in the east leads you to an observation tower from where you get a good view of the bay. This spot repays patient and lengthy observation. Please stick to the track to the tower and do not stray into the actual meadows themselves. The bay can also be checked from the small harbour. Westwards on the road (Fladen) are larger reedbeds which are good for harriers. The fields around Ledskär could host large flocks of geese during migration.

## FÄRNEBOFJÄRDEN

59°15N 16°50E

Färnebofjärden is where the River Dalälven expands into a lake. The area (with 6000 ha of land and 4000 ha of water) is bounded by the runwaters at Tyttbo in the west, and Gysinge in the east. The flat lands are flooded annually by the river which has created mires, swamp forests, river meadows and shoreline forests dominated by deciduous trees. The river is the natural geographical border between the north and south taiga region. This offers a rich and varied fauna and flora as elements from each region meet here. Some parts are today nature reserves and most of the area will be a National Park in 1997. Some sites have restricted access during the breeding season.

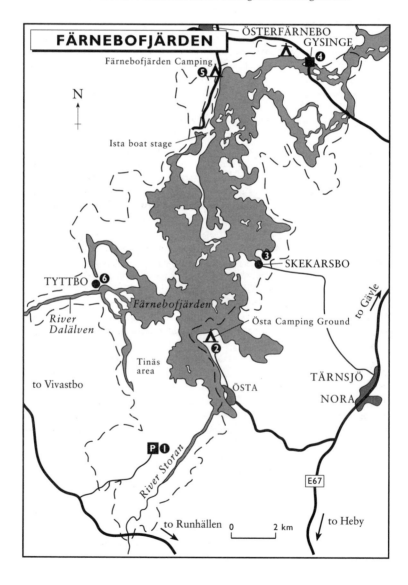

TIMING

The best time for owls, woodpeckers and grouse is March to early April. There is snow and ice during this period, but spots of bare land and open water offer many possibilities for arriving migrants. Whooper Swans, Common Cranes, Ospreys, thrushes and other passerines arrive at this time of year. May and June is also a wonderful time here with a long list of birds of forest, mires and water. In July to August there is a lower activity of birds, but there is a fair chance of seeing Hobby with fledglings, and migrating waders and ducks. September to November, raptors and passerines migrate. There are about 100 breeding species, but in total more than 225 species have been recorded here.

SPECIES

◆ *Resident* Capercaillie, Black Grouse, Hazel Hen, all resident Swedish woodpeckers (7), Ural, Pygmy and Tengmalm's Owl, Raven, crossbills, tits.

◆ *Breeding season* Black-throated Diver, Common Crane, Osprey, Hobby, Woodcock, Wood and Green Sandpipers, Red-breasted Flycatcher (rare), Goldeneye, thrushes, warblers and other passerines.

◆ *Passage* Whooper Swan (several 1000 in April), Dipper (best in winter), Hen Harrier, Waxwing, Redpoll.

ACCESS

The area is 60–70-km north-west of Uppsala. With a car there are good opportunities to explore the area, either by skiing in the winter, canoeing in spring and summer, or walking any time of the year. Some key points are marked on the map. The roads in and around Färnebofjärden are mostly good, but some forest roads can be impassable in winter and early spring.

**1. Entrance place in the Tinäs Area.** A forest road with a parking place and information of the Tinäs Area Nature Reserve. Study the information closely as some parts are bird sanctuaries with no entrance in late winter and the breeding season. **2. Östa Camping Ground.** Cottages and canoes can be rented here. **3. Skekarsbo.** Observation tower; possible to put in a canoe. **4. Gysinge.** A beautiful old foundry and impressive runwaters. The nearby area is excellent for birdwatching and a walk to the island of Storön with its large oaks and riverine forests is highly recommended. Gysinge Inn offers food and accommodation. Tourist information. **5. Färnebofjärden Camping.** Camping ground and youth hostel on the shoreline. It is easy to put in a canoe here and there is a good view over the water areas. **6. Tyttbo.** Fishing camp and tourist information.

# ASKÖVIKEN

59°30N 16°30E

This shallow bay, partly covered with reedbeds, occupies a corner of Lake Mälaren. Some meadows are pastured and the drier parts host scrub dominated by juniper. The site lies in an interesting historical district with Tidö castle just south of the bay as the highlight.

The area is a nature reserve, and has recently been restored to its former importance as a wetland area for birds.

TIMING

The best time to visit is from late March to late June. Migrant birds pass through in good numbers and breeding birds can be seen. July and August are quiet but geese, ducks and raptors pass through on migration from September to November. In the winter months, raptors are found in good numbers.

SPECIES
- ◆ *Breeding season* Slavonian and Great Crested Grebes, Bittern, dabbling and diving ducks, Marsh Harrier, Osprey, Water Rail, Black Tern (rare), Yellow Wagtail, Sedge and Grasshopper Warblers, Thrush Nightingale, Common Rosefinch.
- ◆ *Passage* Greylag Goose, ducks, waders.
- ◆ *Winter* White-tailed and Golden Eagles, Goshawk, Great Grey Shrike.

ACCESS
Asköviken lies 12-km south-west of Västerås. Take road 537 towards Tidö and Lindö and turn off at road 536 to Barkarö church. At the church, turn right at road 534 and 535 until you come to Askö farm. Here you will find a parking place and an information board.

There are three main spots to visit, all of them with parking places, marked tracks and good observation points. **Askö side.** North of the Bay. Parking close to Askö farm. A pleasant walk through a mixture of forests and open grazed land leads you after 2 km to an observation tower with a good view over the bay. **Rudöklippan.** After five minutes walk you are at the viewpoint from where you can see the shore meadows and the reedbeds. **Tidö Castle.** From the parking place you have a 500-m walk to the viewing points at Harholmen. There is a hide 100 m out in the reeds.

# HOVRAN AREA

60°20N 16°03E

The site comprises a series of shallow lakes that are part of the River Dalälven system. The area includes the Lakes Hovran, Flinesjön, Trollbosjön and Svinösjön. In some of the lakes (Hovran and Trollbosjön) there are extensive reedbeds but otherwise the dominant vegetation types are sedge and willow.

The decrease in grazing and haymaking during the last 50 years has caused widespread encroachment by trees and bushes. Stands of Aspen, sallows, birch and Alders are now common and some of these new deciduous forests are valuable as bird habitats.

The area is a Ramsar Site and some small parts of it are now nature reserves. More areas are to be protected and work on a detailed management plan has started. Around 200 species have been recorded and 70 are annual breeders.

TIMING
The early spring is the best season to look for woodpeckers which will be calling and drumming. In March and April, the Whooper Swans arrive, followed shortly by numerous ducks and waders. June is perhaps the best month for songbirds, after which the area is generally rather quiet until the autumn. From September to November, large flocks of swans and ducks arrive (up to 1500 Whooper Swans in October) and migrating raptors pass through.

*Whooper Swan*

SPECIES

◆ *Resident* Black, Lesser Spotted and Green Woodpeckers, tits.
◆ *Breeding season* Bittern, Mute Swan, Teal, Osprey, Corncrake, Curlew, Grasshopper, Marsh and Icterine Warblers, Thrush Nightingale, Common Rosefinch.
◆ *Passage* Whooper Swan, ducks, White-tailed and Golden Eagles, Goshawk, Sparrowhawk, Hen Harrier, waders.
◆ *Winter* Rough-legged Buzzard, Kestrel, Great Grey Shrike.

ACCESS

The site is close to the town of Hedemora in the county of Dalarna in south-east Sweden.

Visit the three observation towers. From the purifying plant and Sörbogrundet you have the best views of the main wetland. The forest stands and open scrub you pass are good for different passerines. A visit to the tower at Flinesjön could be combined with a walk through the mixed deciduous forest on the island of Rankholmen. Otherwise, travel around and stop where it looks good. Trollbosjön is easily surveyed from the road.

# TANDÖVALA-TISJÖN AREA

60°45N 13°25E

Tandövala is a nature reserve and a hilly wilderness area with mixed conifer forests, mires and tarns, covering some 4500 ha in all. The forest is dominated by Scots Pine and shows a virgin character, but with some signs of forestry activity. Some of the trees may be 500 years old. Lake Tisjön is a good site for breeding waterbirds.

TIMING

The best time for Tandövala is April to June with woodpeckers, owls and grouse as highlights. If you come during November to April you need skis and have a chance to see Pine Grosbeak. The Tisjön area is best visited in May to August.

SPECIES

◆ *Resident, Tandövala* Ural, Tengmalm's and Pygmy Owls, Siberian Jay, Willow Grouse, Black and Three-toed Woodpeckers, Capercaillie, Black Grouse, Parrot Crossbill and other forest birds.
◆ *Breeding season, Tandövala* Brambling and Redpoll, *Tisjön area* Red-necked Phalarope, Redshank, Little Gull, Ruff, Red-throated Diver and Arctic Tern.

ACCESS

The area is 13 km from Lima in the county of Dalarna. Before you visit you should buy two detailed topographic maps (14 d SV and 13 d NV); these are vital. Two ways of exploring the area are as follows:

To Tandövala: travel westwards from the village of Heden in the Lima area. Pass the chalet 'Mosätern' and after about 5 km you will come to a sign 'Gräsbrickstigen' on the right side of the road. Park the car and walk along the track into the area. The western loop to Tisjön has the oldest forest and is best for woodland birds. It is easy to get lost here.

To Tisjön area: from V. Ärnäs drive west to Tandövala, pass the chalet 'Tisjölandet' and further to the south to where the road crosses the south-east corner of the lake. At a crossroad you will find three road signs. One sign shows the direction to an observation tower at Tisjön. Follow the track for about 1 km and from the tower you will have a good view of the lake.

# KOPPÅNGEN AREA

61°15N 14°50E

Covering some 5175 ha, this is one of the largest mire complexes in the county of Dalarna. The area is dominated by open peat bogs mixed with tarns and conifer-covered islands of solid ground. The surroundings are dominated by mixed conifer forests. To avoid disturbing the nesting birds, the open mires should be avoided during the breeding season.

TIMING

Early spring, from late March to mid-April, provides the best chances of seeing or hearing woodpeckers and owls. The breeding season lasts from April to late June and, thereafter, the summer months are rather quiet except for family parties of breeding birds. Some northern visitors arrive to spend the winter in the area.

SPECIES

◆ *Resident* Capercaillie, Tengmalm's and Pygmy Owls, Black and Three-toed Woodpeckers, Crossbill, Redpoll.
◆ *Breeding season* Common Crane, Curlew, Whimbrel, Golden Plover, Greenshank, Wood and Green Sandpipers, Yellow Wagtail, Meadow Pipit.
◆ *Winter* Great Grey Shrike, Siberian Jay, Parrot Crossbill, Pine Grosbeak.

ACCESS

The area is 25-km north of Orsa in north Dalarna. Access is easiest by following road 81 between Orsa and Sveg. The road passes through the site and you should stop where you think it looks good.

# HORNSLANDET

61°37N 17°26E

This 7400-ha, forested peninsula juts out into the Baltic in the Swedish county of Hälsingland. The forest is predominantly coniferous but there are pockets of deciduous trees as well. Mires, lakes and swamps are part of the inland habitat, while bare cliffs, skerries and coastal plants feature along the extensive coastline.

Some parts are protected as nature reserves or bird sanctuaries but most of the land is subject to modern forestry. Despite this, the area offers several good spots for birding both in the forest and on the coast. Around 230 species have been recorded in the area, 115 of which are regular breeders.

TIMING

Hornslandet is worth a visit all year round, even though the numbers of each species are seldom high. In March and April, birding is possible both day and night. From late evening onwards you have a chance to hear owls and as dawn approaches, the woodpeckers start calling and drumming. In April too, large flocks of seaducks and grebes rest between Hölick and the southern cape.

Breeding migrant songbirds are best in May and June, and from August to November returning migrants from further north pass through the area.

SPECIES

◆ *Resident* Capercaillie, Ural, Tawny and Tengmalm's Owls, Black, Great Spotted, Grey-headed and Three-toed Woodpeckers.
◆ *Breeding season* Osprey, Hobby, Goshawk, Little Ringed Plover, Arctic Skua, Black Guillemot, Wood and Greenish Warblers, Red-breasted Flycatcher.
◆ *Passage* Slavonian Grebe, Eider (rare), Steller's Eider, Long-tailed Duck, Pine Grosbeak, Rustic Bunting, Red-throated Pipit, Bluethroat.

ACCESS

The area is 30-km east of Hudiksvall. The best spots include the fishing grounds at Kuggören and Hölick, and the deciduous forest areas in the eastern part of the peninsula. Kuggören and Hölick are easily reached by car, and from Hölick you can walk along the shore to the cape of Hornlandet. This route is 3-km long. Migrating waterbirds mostly pass along the west coast of Hornslandet and are best observed at Hörneudde.

The areas with deciduous trees are mostly found close to the road between Kuggören and Hölick. During late winter and early spring, bring your skis, as most of the forest roads are covered by snow.

# ÅSTHOLMEN

62°23N 17°44E

This 200-ha area is dominated by conifers. Close to the coast are bare cliffs and some copses of deciduous trees. Around Tynderö sound are some fields and meadows. 194 species have been recorded here and of those around 70 probably breed; this is also a good migration spot.

TIMING

The first migrant passerines arrive in late March and early April and by mid-April, duck numbers have started to build up. The most intensive migration period occurs, however, in May, starting with divers, ducks, raptors and gulls, and featuring terns and passerines later in the month.

From June to August, birdwatching interest is largely confined to breeding species. Return wader migration is marked in August and September and duck, gull and raptor numbers increase throughout the autumn period. Depending on the winter climate, ducks and gulls can be numerous.

SPECIES

◆ *Resident* Black Grouse.
◆ *Breeding season* Goosander, Red-breasted Merganser, Velvet Scoter, Turnstone, Black Guillemot, Marsh and Grasshopper Warblers.
◆ *Passage* Divers, Velvet Scoter, Teal, Wigeon, waders, Pomarine Skua (scarce), Arctic Skua, Common and Arctic Terns, Grey-headed and Three-toed Woodpeckers, Yellow Wagtail, Snow Bunting.
◆ *Winter* Ducks, gulls, Crossbill.

ACCESS

Take the road E4 north from Sundsvall for some 28 km. Turn right at the signs Åstön and Stångrid, drive through Söråker and further to Skeppshamn. Park at the bay at west Skeppshamn. From here there is a 2.5-km walk to the outermost cape. Good observation points are at the cape, and at the small hill behind the chapel at Skeppshamn. Stop also at Tynderö sound. Beware of the roped off area which marks a shooting range. Sign displays when shooting is planned.

# STORNÄSET

62°27N 17°30E

Stornäset is a flat coastal meadow, covering 50 ha, on a cape in Klinger-fjärden Bay in the Baltic. Away from the sea, the terrain consists of patches of woodland and scrub; the main area is a nature reserve. A resting place for migrant waterbirds, especially ducks and waders, although plenty of birds breed here too.

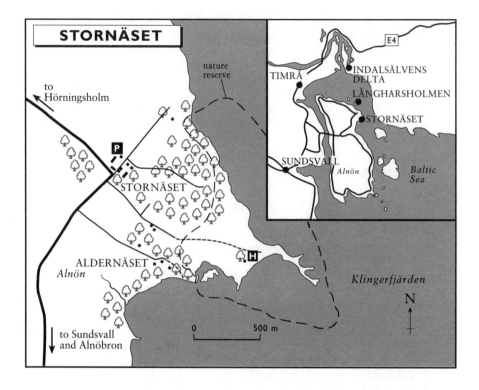

TIMING

Spring migration peaks in mid-May, at which time large flocks of ducks and waders are present. A few species remain in the area to breed. In late July and August, many Arctic waders are seen on return migration. Raptors and passerines pass through in good numbers from September to October after which time the area becomes frozen.

SPECIES

◆ *Breeding season* Oystercatcher, Little Ringed Plover, Icterine Warbler, Common Rosefinch.

◆ *Passage* Diving and dabbling ducks, Rough-legged Buzzard, Ruff, Golden Plover, Dunlin, Curlew Sandpiper, Knot, Temminck's and Little Stints, Sanderling, Wood and Green Sandpipers, Terek Sandpiper (rare), Spotted Redshank, Bar-tailed Godwit, Red-necked Phalarope, Caspian Tern, Red-throated Pipit, Bluethroat, Lapland and Snow Buntings.

ACCESS

The area is 14 km from central Sundsvall. Drive northwards for 2-km along road E4 and turn right to Alnö. Follow the road to Alnö and turn left 2 km after the bridge. Follow the road to Stornäset and the parking place.

From the parking place at the Stornäset hospital there is a 1.5-km walk to an observation tower located at the open meadows. Please do not walk through the meadows during the breeding season. There is also a new hide 300-m west of the tower. Follow the forest edge.

From the parking place, you could also follow the main road towards Eriksdal until you reach Hörningsholm.

# SKULESKOGEN

63°00N 15°60E

Covering an area of 2950 ha, Skuleskogen is an exciting mountainous and hilly area with deep valleys, rocky outcrops and old forests. The point where the mountains meet the Baltic in the east is stunning, the mountains being 300-m or so above sea level. The forest is mature with many dead and fallen trees. Norwegian Spruce is the dominant tree at lower levels with fertile soils; Scots Pine is more abundant in the rocky areas at higher altitude. The area is a National Park. Boreal Swedish birds are found in good numbers and Lynx still occur, although they are hard to see.

TIMING

The first weeks of April are best for finding woodpeckers; the birds will then be drumming and calling. Later in April and in May can be good for lekking Black Grouse and other displaying gamebirds. Songbirds are best in May and June. July and August are quiet months but raptor and passerine migration can be seen along the coast from September to November. Snow blankets the landscape during the winter months but it is possible to ski in the area.

SPECIES

◆ *Resident* Capercaillie, Black Grouse, Willow Ptarmigan, Hazel Hen, Tengmalm's, Pygmy and Eagle Owls, Black, Grey-headed and Three-toed Woodpeckers, Wren, Siberian Jay, tits, Crossbill.
◆ *Breeding season* Buzzard, Honey Buzzard, Osprey, Goshawk, Greenish, Marsh and Grasshopper Warblers, Chiffchaff, Goldcrest, Red-breasted Flycatcher, Rustic Bunting.
◆ *Winter* Pine Grosbeak.

ACCESS

The park is signposted from road E4. To reach the south entrance, turn off towards the village of Käxed where the road to the southern parking place is just north of the village of Käl. From this point there is a path that leads directly into the park.

The north entrance is reached from Bjästa on the highway. Follow the signs to Näsa and Näske bridge. South of Näske bridge is the parking place with access to the park.

There are several marked trails and cottages where you can stay overnight. The site merits at least a whole day's exploration.

# FLATRUET

62°43N 12°45E

Flatruet is a low Alpine plateau, about 1000-m above sea level, and covering an area of 50 km². The vegetation is dominated by lichens and scrub on the open moorland with a few pools and wet meadows also being found.

TIMING

The area is more or less impossible to visit from November to May due to the snow conditions. June and July are the best months for breeding birds although, from August to October, migrating thrushes can be seen.

SPECIES

◆ *Resident* Ptarmigan, Willow Ptarmigan.
◆ *Breeding season* Wigeon, Velvet Scoter, Scaup, Rough-legged Buzzard, Merlin, Whimbrel, Redshank, Ruff, Dunlin, Temminck's Stint, Golden

Plover, Dotterel (rare), Red-necked Phalarope (rare), Long-tailed Skua, Short-eared Owl, Bluethroat, Fieldfare, Lapland Bunting.

◆ *Passage* Thrushes.

ACCESS

The area is 25-km north of Funäsdalen and 15-km south of Ljungdalen. Follow the road between the two villages and stop anywhere. The best stop is south-west of the highest point (Falkvålen) close to a Reindeer fence. Here you will find some small lakes with breeding ducks and waders.

## LAKE ÅNNSJÖN

63°16N 12°33E

This 11,000-ha shallow freshwater lake is surrounded by marshland, mires, peat bogs and woodland dominated by conifers and birch. It is an oligotrophic lake influenced by two rivers, and with three deltas; the total area of the lake is 57 km². Ånnsjön is a Ramsar Site. Marked tracks, hides and observation towers allow visitors to explore the area without disturbing the birds.

TIMING

A few hardy birds are resident throughout the year but the best time to visit the site is in late May and June when wetland birds and songbirds are present. There is plenty of bird activity in July and August although the songbirds are silent.

SPECIES

◆ *Resident* Capercaillie, Willow Ptarmigan, Hazel Hen, Tengmalm's and Hawk Owls, Three-toed Woodpecker, Siberian Jay, Crossbill, Parrot Crossbill, Pine Grosbeak.

◆ *Breeding season* Black-throated and Red-throated Divers, Scaup, Tufted Duck, Scoter, Velvet Scoter, Long-tailed Duck, Pintail, Red-necked Phalarope, Golden Plover, Ruff, Temminck's Stint, Wood Sandpiper, Curlew, Whimbrel, Short-eared Owl, Great Grey Shrike.

ACCESS

Ånnsjön is located in the county of Jämtland 100-km west of Östersund in central western Sweden. The two best spots are close to the village of Ånn in the north and Handöl in the west. Start at the small cottage of Ånn. Trails start close to the railway station (point 1 on the map). From Klocka farm, a little further west, are some more marked trails. By following the system of tracks and visiting the viewing points, you will encounter both forest and wetland birds. In Handöl (2) is a wetland area, an impressive waterfall and an observation tower.

## STEKKENJOKK AREA

65°00–65°10N 14°10–14°40E

The mountain plateau 'Daimaplatån' is 1000-m above sea level and covers some 10 km$^2$; it is located close to Norway. The area has many small lakes and the vegetation is dominated by birch and willow scrub. On the way up to the plateau you will pass through conifer and birch forest. Stekkenjokk is a former mining area and derelict buildings can be seen close to the road.

TIMING

The roads are not normally open before late May or early June because of the snow. Mid-June is, therefore, an ideal time to visit the area for its breeding birds, although many are still found in July and August. In September, flocks of migrating geese can be seen but by October, snow has normally closed the road.

SPECIES

◆ *Resident* Willow Ptarmigan.
◆ *Breeding season* Long-tailed Duck, Scoter, Bean Goose, Lesser White-fronted Goose (rare), Dunlin, Temminck's Stint, Ringed Plover, Dotterel, Long-tailed Skua, Bluethroat, Lapland Bunting.

ACCESS

Coming from the south, take the road from Östersund towards Strömsund. In Gäddede turn to St Blåsjön. Once you have passed Blåsjön, the whole area is good for birding. You can see birds either from the road or by taking short walks. Appropriate shoes or wellington boots are essential.

## UMEÄLVEN DELTA

63°45N 20°20E

This 1040-ha site is a delta area where the River Umeälven enters the Gulf of Bothnia. There are sediment islands which are overgrown by willows and alders but there are also areas of shallow, open water as well as meadows dominated by sedges.

The area is a Ramsar Site and also includes a nature reserve of 170 ha. Umeälven Delta is important for migrant geese, ducks and waders. A good range of wetland species also breed in the area.

TIMING

November to March is cold and icy and there is little to see. From late April to early June, however, large flocks of geese, ducks and waders rest. Breeding birds are present in July and August and, in September and October, raptors, waders and passerines migrate in good numbers.

SPECIES

◆ *Breeding season* Scaup, Osprey, Little Gull, Caspian Tern.

◆ *Passage* Bean Goose (up to 2600), Pink-footed Goose (rare), Goosander, Teal, Wigeon (up to 3800), Pintail, Garganey, Gadwall, Smew, Greenshank, Spotted Redshank, Temminck's Stint, Broad-billed Sandpiper, Red-necked Phalarope, Black-tailed and Bar-tailed Godwits, Little Gull, Red-throated Pipit, Rustic Bunting, other passerines.

ACCESS

The area is 7-km south of Umeå in north-east Sweden. Follow the road from central Umeå towards Obbola in the south. Close to Bergö bridge is a hill from where you can watch raptors in August and September. If you follow the road south for 1 km to a road sign 'Berga' and park there, you can then walk 200-m west to the bay. Please do not trespass into private gardens.

Another good observation point is if you take road E79 from Umeå towards Holmsund. After 10 km a small yellow sign indicates 'Villanäs' to the right. Drive 800 m to a railway crossing after which the road splits into three directions. Take the middle one and stop at the parking spot after 150 m. Walk towards the bay, but avoid gardens. At low water, the area is good for waders and gulls.

# HOLMÖARNA

63°45N 20°35E

The site comprises a collection of islands and skerries, the four largest of which harbour a number of small lakes and ponds (150). The terrain is flat and conifers, are the dominant trees although birches are common and juniper scrub is also widespread. In the south, there are several small and barren skerries. Man has had comparatively little impact on the vegetation of the area as a whole. Seventy five per cent of the area is nature reserve. 250 species have been recorded of which 130 are regular breeders.

TIMING

During the winter months from November to March, ice and snow make the islands virtually impossible to reach. The timing of the spring thaw varies from year to year but the ice usually breaks up in mid-April. Peak diver migration occurs in the first two weeks of May when up to 1000 Black-throated Divers may be seen; north-easterly winds also bring good numbers of other seabirds within viewing range.

June is the month to listen for songbirds and the return migration of Arctic waders starts in late July and August. If high pressure weather conditions prevail, rarities from the south-east can turn up at this time of year. September and October are months for goose and passerine migration.

SPECIES

◆ *Resident* Black Grouse.

◆ *Breeding season* Black-throated and Red-throated Divers, Greylag Goose, Shoveler, Pintail, Scaup, Common Crane, Greenshank, Redshank, Turnstone, Arctic Skua, Arctic and Common Terns, Black Guillemot, Short-eared, Tengmalm's and Hawk Owls, Three-toed Woodpecker, Rock Pipit, Greenish Warbler (rare), Marsh Warbler, Blyth's Reed Warbler (rare) and River Warbler (rare) , Red-backed Shrike, Rustic Bunting.

◆ *Passage* Black-throated Diver, White-billed Diver (rare), Brent Goose, Eider, King and Steller's Eiders (rare), Whimbrel, Bar-tailed Godwit, Grey Plover, Knot, Pomarine Skua (scarce), Great Spotted Woodpecker (2000 in one day in an invasion year), Richard's Pipit, Nutcracker, Little (rare) and Rustic Buntings.

ACCESS

From the ferry berth at Norrfjärden, north-east Umeå you can take the boat to Holmön, a trip which takes 40 minutes. No cars are allowed, but bicycles are recommended. If you do not bring your own bike you can rent one at Holmön. Walk or cycle along Ängeön and Holmön (bridge connections). One good area is at Gebäckssundet between the main islands.

If you want to go to the isolated, but exciting island of Stora Fjäderägg, where the regional bird society has a bird observatory, you have to arrange your own transport. Johan Nyman (Tel. +46–(0)90–55142) is one of several people offering reasonably priced transport.

At Stora Fjäderägg 5–6 persons can stay overnight at the bird observatory. You must check in advance, however, if space is available so contact the SOF office for a contact name and number.

## GAMMELSTADSVIKEN

65°38N 22°00E

This 450-ha wetland and lake area was formerly a bay in the Baltic; today it has become isolated from the coast due to land elevation. The vegetation in the lake is dominated by reeds, reed-mace and water-lilies. Mixed forests with both conifers and deciduous trees surround the lake.

The area is a Ramsar Site and also a National Reserve. The main threat to the area comes from the expansion of the town of Luleå which is close to the site. A buffer zone between city and lake has been created.

TIMING

The best time to visit is in May and June when breeding waterbirds are present along with spring migrants. July and August are relatively quiet months but there is a reasonable autumn migration to be seen during September and October.

SPECIES

◆ *Breeding season* Red-necked and Slavonian Grebes, Bittern, Garganey, Pintail, Wigeon, Pochard, Smew, Osprey, Curlew, Snipe, Wood Sandpiper, Ruff, Little Gull, Yellow Wagtail.

◆ *Passage* Ducks, passerines.

ACCESS

The site is reached by car and the road between Piteå and Haparanda passes the north-west corner of the lake. East of the lake are parking places, information boards and a bird observation tower.

## HAPARANDA SANDSKÄR NATIONAL PARK

65°34N 23°45E

This site covers some 6000 ha, of which 770 ha are land. The main island, Sandskär, is 5-km long and 2.5-km across at the widest point. It comprises moraine material covered by sand: moors and dunes are the dominant habitats although forests, mires, shore lagoons and bays occur. More than 200 species have been recorded here and 70 of these are regular breeders.

TIMING
Best time for visiting is in May and June or in September and October; late July and August can also be good for migrating waders.

SPECIES

◆ *Resident* Black Grouse, Willow Ptarmigan.

◆ *Breeding season* Shoveler, Teal, Pintail, Velvet Scoter, Oystercatcher, Curlew, Ruff, Redshank, Temminck's Stint, Red-necked Phalarope, Arctic Tern, Hawk Owl, Lesser Spotted Woodpecker, Little Bunting (rare).

◆ *Passage* Waders, Red-throated Pipit, Shore Lark, other passerines.

ACCESS
The island is 33-km south-west of Haparanda archipelago and you need to rent a boat to get there. Boats can be rented in Nikkala, Båtskärsnäs and Seskarö. More information can be obtained from the tourist information service in Haparanda or Kalix. Once on the island, walk around, following the shorelines and tracks. This is an area to be explored by yourself.

# ABISKO NATIONAL PARK

68°20N 18°50E

Abisko is a large Arctic mountain area covering some 7700 ha with valleys, gorges, lakes, streams, birch forest and scrub. The scenery is stunning and the juxtaposition of so many different habitat types results in rich and varied birdlife. The National Park was established in 1909.

TIMING
The area is normally covered by snow from October to May. In the second half of May, migrants can be found where the snow has melted; many arriving at this time stay to breed. The best period for birdwatching lasts from June to August; songbirds are vocal in early June. The presence and abundance of raptors is highly dependent upon the lemming population in any given year. If rodent numbers are poor then the raptors may well have left the area by early July.

SPECIES

◆ *Resident* Ptarmigan.

◆ *Breeding season* Red-throated Diver, Slavonian Grebe, Velvet Scoter, White-tailed Eagle (rare), Golden Eagle, Rough-legged Buzzard, Merlin, Gyrfalcon (rare), Whimbrel, Wood Sandpiper, Greenshank, Dotterel, Long-tailed Skua, Hawk Owl (rare), Red-throated Pipit, Arctic Warbler (rare), Bluethroat, Ring Ouzel, Redwing, Siberian Tit (rare), Brambling, Redpoll, Arctic Redpoll (rare).

ACCESS
The area is located south of Lake Torne Träsk in the county of Norrbotten. You can travel by road or train from the city of Kiruna to the small village of Abisko.

This is wilderness territory so visit first the Abisko Naturum Information Centre for all the information you need for a safe and rewarding trip.

Ten-kilometres east of Abisko lies Stordalens Nature Reserve. It is an easily viewed wetland area with tarns and mires.

# AMMARNÄS

65°58N 16°13E

The village of Ammarnäs lies beside an inland delta where the Rivers Vindel-älven and Tjulån meet. The area offers a mixture of interesting habitats for birds: mountain plateaux, moorland, lakes, marshes, forests and open scrub areas.

Ammarnäs is part of Vindelfjällens Nature Reserve, the largest reserve in Sweden. Some areas are restricted to visitors during the breeding season, but otherwise access is very good.

TIMING

The area is largely inaccessible during the winter months. Late May and June are peak months for birdwatchers since not only will the waders be present but songbirds are at their most vocal and gamebird leks are active. The presence and abundance of raptors depends upon the numbers of lemmings, a factor that varies from year to year.

July and August are relatively quiet months although many of the breeding birds are still present, but by September and October, only the hardy, resident species remain.

SPECIES

◆ *Resident* Ptarmigan, Willow Ptarmigan, Hazel Hen, Three-toed Woodpecker, Siberian Jay, Siberian Tit.
◆ *Breeding season* Scaup, Long-tailed Duck, Scoter, Golden Eagle, Rough-legged Buzzard, Merlin, Peregrine (rare), Gyrfalcon (rare), Hen Harrier, Red-necked Phalarope, Ruff, Greenshank, Temminck's Stint, Dunlin, Broad-billed and Purple Sandpipers, Golden Plover, Dotterel, Long-tailed Skua, Short-eared Owl (rare) and Hawk Owls Shore Lark (rare), Bluethroat, Redstart, Ring Ouzel, Redwing, Fieldfare, Brambling, Lapland and Snow Buntings.

ACCESS

You can get to Sorsele by train, bus or car. From Sorsele it is 90 km to Ammarnäs. There is a daily bus service and the trip takes about two hours.

Ammarnäs is one of the most popular areas for Swedish birdwatchers when they go to the 'Swedish Alps'. Ideally, travel as a backpacker with a sleeping bag, tent and field kitchen; this enables you to spend a few days on the high plateau around Ammarfjället mountain. Also visit the delta, walk in Ammarnäs village and follow tracks through the birch forest close to the River Vindelälven.

*Ruff, male*

In order to get more detailed information and good tips on where to go, visit the Nature Information Centre.

# MUDDUS NATIONAL PARK

66°54N 20°10E

Muddus is a vast area of ancient forest of 25,000 ha of coniferous forest and 20,000 ha of bogs. Most of the wooded areas are classified as virgin forest. The area also includes rock plateaux, river valleys and scattered lakes.

In the southern part of the largest rock plateau, there are amazing erosion features with gorges and canyon formations. The largest canyon is called Måskokårså and is 2.5-km long and 50–70-m deep. The abundance of dead and decaying wood is generally high. The wetlands have peat ridges and muddy expanses and are, consequently, almost impossible to cross. The National Park was created in 1942.

TIMING

Daring visitors venture into the park in April on skis but access by more conventional means in spring varies according to the snow conditions in each particular season. The ideal time to visit is between 1 June and 25 July when displaying waders and singing passerines will be much in evidence. Later in the summer can still be good for birds but from 25 June to 31 July it is a nightmare because of mosquitoes!

SPECIES

- *Resident* Capercaillie, Tengmalm's and Ural Owls, Three-toed Woodpecker, Siberian Jay, Siberian Tit, Pine Grosbeak.
- *Breeding season* Slavonian Grebe, Whooper Swan, Golden Eagle, Goshawk, Hen Harrier, Common Crane, Red-necked Phalarope, Spotted Redshank, Wood Sandpiper, Waxwing, Rustic Bunting.

ACCESS

The area is located between Highway 97 and the River Stora Luleälv 40-km south-west of Gällivare and 20-km east of Porjus. The best way to reach the park is from Skaite in the south where it is possible to leave the car.

Two tracks start from Skaite and pass through the southern part of the park. At Muddusfallet you can find an overnight cabin. Entrance is prohibited between 15 March and 31 July around Muddusjaure and Sörstuobba.

The road to Ritsem can be good as can Tjuoltajeggi, a wetland area close to the road to Gällivare.

# SJAUNJA

67°17N 19°49E

Sjaunja is a 188,600-ha area of woodland and mire complex with shallow lakes, marshes, bogs and hilly ground. The vegetation is dominated by conifers and some parts of the landscape show glacial features such as moraine ridges and tundra polygons. This is a pure wilderness area where European Brown Bear, Lynx, Wolverine and Otter still occur.

The area is a Ramsar Site and most of it is a National Reserve. Sjaunja is also proposed as a World Heritage Site.

TIMING

The best time for birdwatching is from the end of May to 20 June. Later on in the season the mosquitoes become almost unbearable.

SPECIES
- ◆ *Resident* Capercaillie, owls, Black and Three-toed Woodpeckers, Siberian Jay, Siberian Tit, Crossbill, Pine Grosbeak.
- ◆ *Breeding season* Whooper Swan, ducks, Golden and White-tailed Eagles, Hen Harrier, Merlin, Jack Snipe, Broad-billed Sandpiper, Spotted Redshank, Brambling, Rustic Bunting.

ACCESS
The area is 50-km south-west of Kiruna in northern Sweden. From Gällivare or Porjus take the road to Vietas. From here you drive to Satisjaure where you need a boat to go across the lake. From the east you can reach it from Lina älv, Fjällåsen or Harö. You can also take the road to Ritsem and enter the area from the south.

Travelling on foot or by canoe, this is one of the most exciting areas to explore in Sweden. Large parts of the site, especially the immense mires are quite impassable. Before you decide to visit, study detailed maps and consult Tourist Information in Porjus or Gällivare. It cannot be stated too strongly that Sjaunja is not for the faint-hearted backpacker.

# VITTANGI-RIPAKAISENVUOMA
67°50N 21°37E

Vittangi is a small village from which the visitor can gain access, from the south and west, to Ripakaisenvuoma, one of the largest mire complexes in Sweden; its total area exceeds 100 km$^2$. A mixture of peat ridges, marshes, lakes, pine ridges and swamp forests encourages a rich and varied bird life.

TIMING
Mid-May until the third week in June is the best period for birding. Thereafter, there are far too many mosquitoes and too little bird activity.

SPECIES
- ◆ *Resident* Black Woodpecker, Siberian Jay, Siberian Tit, Pine Grosbeak.
- ◆ *Breeding season* Black-throated Diver, Whooper Swan, Bean Goose, Smew, Scoter, White-tailed and Golden Eagles, Hen Harrier, Spotted Redshank, Jack Snipe, Broad-billed Sandpiper, Short-eared Owl, Waxwing, Rustic Bunting.

ACCESS
The site lies 45-km east of Kiruna on road 396. It can be reached by bus from Vittangi, a village which merits a stop to explore the river bank. Sappisadsi is the name of a cottage which is locked most of the time. You can, however, camp in the adjacent fields or simply use it as an orientation point for your excursions.

The most exciting spot is the enormous mire complex, Ripakaisenvuoma, east of the road to Soppero; the area between Kokkavvara and Kulijärvi is particularly good. Or you could take the road to Nikkojärvi and follow the pine ridge at Uijajärvi. Be sure that you have a good map and a working compass.

# PADJELANTA NATIONAL PARK
67°20N 16°39E (Staloloukta)

The 198,000 ha of this site comprise bare mountains, high peaks, glaciers, valleys, lakes, watercourses and meadows; this variety produces extremely attractive scenery. The forests are restricted to about 1500 ha of mountain birch forest and the highest peak is over 1800-m above sea level. Lake Virihaure, close to Staloluokta, is called 'Lapland's most beautiful lake'.

Padjelanta links with Sareks National Park (1970 km²) to the east and Stora Sjöfallets National Park (1278 km²) to the north-east. Stora Sjöfallets NP then links with Sjaunja. This is the largest complex of protected areas in Sweden. A new protection plan will ensure that in total 7000 km² will be protected. The park is the best area in Sweden for Arctic Fox; Wolverines breed here as well.

TIMING
June is the best month for birds but even July and August can be good, especially if the scenery, plants and mammals capture your interest. There will still be quite a number of birds around, although they will be heavily outnumbered by the mosquitoes!

SPECIES
◆ *Breeding season* Black-throated Diver, Long-tailed Duck, Velvet Scoter, White-tailed Eagle, Rough-legged Buzzard, Golden and Ringed Plovers, Long-tailed Skua, Snowy Owl (only in lemming years), Arctic Warbler (rare), Bluethroat, Ring Ouzel, Redpoll, Lapland Bunting.

ACCESS
Kvikkjokk is reached by bus or car on the road from Jokkmokk. You can walk from Kvikkjokk (*see* following site) or take a flight from Vietas or Kvikkjokk to Staloluokta. Here you can stay in well-equipped cottages or camp and make daily tours. There are marked footpaths and several cottages both north and south of Staloluokta if you want to make longer tours. When going back you can follow the footpath 'Padjelantaleden' 75 km to Kvikkjokk and pass through Tarradalen and a part of Pärlälven Nature Reserve.

# KVIKKJOKK AND TARRADALEN

66°55N 17°45E (Kvikkjokk)

Kvikkjokk is a small village near Kvikkjokkdelta, a 6-km² area of mixed habitats. There are open meadows, ancient spruce forests, delta wetlands, lakes, watercourses and bare mountains; Kvikkjokk is a good entrance to Sweden's high mountain areas with three National Parks (Sareks, Padjelanta and Stora Sjöfallets) in the vicinity.

## TIMING

Late May and June is the best time for birdwatching here. The scenery is especially stunning from July to September, although the birding is comparatively poor.

## SPECIES

◆ *Resident* Hazel Hen, Three-toed Woodpecker, Siberian Jay, Pine Grosbeak.
◆ *Breeding season* Tufted Duck, Smew, Goldeneye, Pintail, Wigeon, Teal, Velvet Scoter, Scoter, Rough-legged Buzzard, Merlin, Wood Sandpiper, Ruff, Ringed Plover, Arctic Tern, Bluethroat, Robin, Redwing, Ring Ouzel, Fieldfare, Bullfinch.

## ACCESS

Kvikkjokk is easily reached by road. From the railway station 'Murjek' you can take the local bus via Jokkmokk to Kvikkjokk. In the Kvikkjokk area you can visit the rich spruce forests at Prinskullen, climb the bare mountains, or hire a canoe and take a trip into the delta.

A footpath runs through Tarradalen (Padjelantaleden, *see* map). Take a boat from Kvikkjokk to Bobäcken and then walk 2–3 km through part of the Pärlälven Nature Reserve with virgin birch forest and mixed woodland. There is a bridge over Valiebäcken and after about 10 km you come to Njunjes where there are chalets. There are also several chalets along the track to Staloluokta. The next stopping place is at Tarrekaise on Lake Tarrajaure (7 km) and after another 12 km you come to Såmmarlappa where there is a public phonebox.

Continue a further 16 km to Tarraluoppar and you are in Padjelanta National Park. The next chalet is at Tuottar after a 10-km walk. The last stage to Staloluokta is a mere 1.7 km.

# USEFUL ADDRESSES

Danish Ornithological Society
  (DOF)
Fuglenes Hus
Vesterbrogade 140
DK 1620 Copenhagen V
Tel. +45 31311404

BirdLife Finland, Head Office
PL 17
FIN-18101 Heinola
Visitors:
Heinola Water Tower
IV Floor, Heinola
Tel. +358 18 152 579
Fax +358 18 143 682
E-mail: veistola@cc.helsinki.fi

Icelandic Society for the Protection
  of Birds
BirdLife International Associate
  Partner
P.O. Box 5069
125 Reykjavík

NORWEGIAN
ORNITHOLOGICAL SOCIETY
  (NOF)
SEMINARPLASSEN 5
7060 KLÆBU
TEL. +47 72831166
FAX +47 72831255

Swedish Ornithological Society
  (SOF)
Box 142 19
S-104 40 Stockholm
Visitors:
Skeppargatan 19
Stockholm
Tel. +46-(0)8-6626434
Fax +46-(0)8-6626988

# INDEX OF BIRD NAMES